The Foreign Affairs Fudge Factory

The fact is that the [State] Department has not been run primarily as a decision-making instrument. It has been run as a fudge factory. The aim has been to make everybody happy, to conciliate interests, to avoid giving offense and rocking the boat.

—JOSEPH KRAFT

THE FOREIGN AFFAIRS FUDGE FACTORY

John Franklin Campbell

Basic Books, Inc., Publishers

NEW YORK LONDON

Library of Congress Catalog Card Number: 73–158438
SBN 465–02478–5
Manufactured in the United States of America
DESIGNED BY THE INKWELL STUDIO

For Brenda

PREFACE
HOW THIS BOOK CAME TO BE WRITTEN

These pages draw to some degree on reflection on my Foreign Service experience of the past nine years in Germany, Washington, and Ethiopia, but they are not a memoir. The book is a study of bureaucracy and an argument about the influence of organization on policy. It tests the lessons of my own short career against the experience of others, and it is written on the hopeful premise that Patrick Anderson was right when he said not long ago, "Someday, some President is going to have to undertake the long, thankless job of reorganizing and rebuilding the Department of State." I hope it contributes to serious discussion about the ways American institutions can be changed, and that it may awaken some interest among younger readers in the public service as a career.

The study is not directed, however, just to today's and tomorrow's presidents, diplomats, congressmen, and other officials. It is also written for anyone who has an interest in foreign policy and a curiosity about how it is made. I know of no book that describes the way the foreign-policy bureaucracies of Washington—the "fudge factory," if you will—really function. It is a pity that no such book exists, for much intelligent public discussion is needed before the present system can be improved. In a way, this book tries to fill the gap.

A few years ago, while serving as a staff officer in the State Department, it occurred to me that the institution was remarkably inefficient. A new Under Secretary had just arrived, and he discovered one morning that a routine diplomatic cable—the kind that Under Secretaries are not supposed to see—bore the signatures and initials of twenty-seven different officials. None of us on the staff were able to convince our boss that a routine message needed to be approved by that many people.

I began to realize that I knew very little about the bureaucracy of which I was a member, and set out to try to document some of my dissatisfactions with it. Collecting statistical information and charts of organization, even though they were needed to educate a new Under Secretary, proved difficult. The administrative segment of the department informed us that its functions were "much too complicated" to be put down on a single piece of paper—it had not had a simple table of organization for years, for only a hypothetical three-dimensional chart could adequately describe its work. After much prodding and nagging, the administrators finally prepared the missing table for the Under Secretary; I was later told that it was considered "threatening" to ask people for organizational charts. From that time forward I promised myself that one day I would try to do a thorough analysis of the administration of American foreign policy.

The opportunity came three years later after an African assignment. I received an International Affairs Fellowship for 1969–1970 to the Council on Foreign Relations, sponsored jointly by the Council and the State Department. The original topic for the year's research, "American Diplomacy: The Case for Reform," has grown into this book. Many friends and colleagues at the Council, the Department, and elsewhere helped the project along, offering advice and encouragement. It would only be an embarrassment to name them all, for that might seem to associate others too closely with some of the heresies in these pages. But I do owe special thanks to a discussion group organized by the Council, under the chairmanship of McGeorge Bundy, for helpful criticism. If I have come to learn anything during the year's work, it is that many otherwise sober and intelligent men are capable of violent disagreement over the question of how to reform the State Department, though all are agreed that something is badly wrong with the present system.

Parts of the first, second, and last chapters expand on some ideas expressed earlier in "What Is To Be Done?" an article published in the October 1970 issue of *Foreign Affairs*.

J.F.C.

CONTENTS

PART 1

Why the System Fails

PART 2

Toward a Better Structure

PART I

Why the System Fails

1

THE PROBLEM

Midnight, March 31–April 1, 1965: business as usual in the State Department's around-the-clock Operations Center. Manned by four Foreign Service officers, one colonel on loan from the Pentagon and a bleary-eyed clerk-typist, the "Op Center" staff was ready to monitor any late-hour international crisis. But no crisis occurred that night. Each hour, to be sure, one of the officers routinely tested the teletype circuit on the Washington–Moscow hotline, while his colleagues scanned five wire service ticker tapes and two diplomatic cable machines, checking for emergencies. A telephone console with flashing lights dominated one side of the room at the end of a T-shaped table. Next door a typewriter was clicking. Another edition of the Top Secret Daily Summary *was going to press.*

The editors of the Summary *(I was one of them) had for several days planned a special April Fool's Day supplement to their official document. Each morning between midnight and dawn we produced a secret news digest of the major diplomatic and intelligence reports of the U.S. government, intended only for the eyes of the President and some two dozen other Washington officials.*

Our April 1 supplement included the following implausible stories:

1. *A report captioned* Gaullefinger, *asserting that "hard intelligence" confirmed the existence of a plot by French secret agents to burglarize* Fort Knox;
2. A *"highly classified report" from* Algiers *indicating that* Dr. *Albert Schweitzer had been invited to give the keynote address at the upcoming Afro-Asian conference of nonaligned nations;*
3. A *"flash message" that* North *Vietnamese aircraft had just bombed Saigon, causing Ambassador Henry Cabot Lodge to declare, "This day will live in infamy";*
4. *Another dispatch from* Vietnam, *headed* Kurds in Hue, *alleging the discovery of a sudden and baffling influx of Middle Eastern refugees into Southeast Asia;*
5. *The purported discovery, by CIA, of an elaborate canal-building program in northern France, part of a scheme by President De Gaulle to divert water from the English Channel in order to "dry up the British fleet."*

Joining in the spirit of the prank, the Pentagon representative at the Operations Center contributed a convincing road map of North *Vietnam, complete with fictitious air force "targets" for the night's bombing raids. In deadpan officialese, the text accompanying the map declared that* F-104s *on armed reconnaissance had attacked a number of "cyclists on* Route *9," but since cloud cover obscured the results of the action, it had to be "recycled." Earlier in the evening, his report continued, another bombing mission had hit "the last outhouse north of the DMZ."*

Our satirical document reached some, but not all, of the normal recipients of the Daily Summary. *A directive to "lay off the humor" came down the next day. The reason? At least one high official had believed the information in the April*

Fool's edition, had briefed other officials on the basis of this information, and had a very red face as a result.[1]

* * *

Eighteen months later, in the last half of 1966, a newcomer to high office in the State Department stood beside me in a map room a couple of doors away from the site of the Daily Summary *spoof. A group of men, military and civilian, were examining a blown-up aerial photograph of the city of Hanoi. It was clear from the photo that bombs had hit in residential areas in the city, although the targets were supposed to be military installations in the suburbs. "I don't understand how it happened," the new official kept saying, "I just don't understand."*

* * *

In 1969 another administration came to power, inheriting the problems of its predecessors. President Nixon planned an innovation: a "State of the World" message to Congress designed to give the nation a detailed picture of his foreign policy. Word came down from the White House. Each country desk in the State Department was asked to write a few paragraphs about its area, to be used in the President's message. During late 1969 and early 1970 the draft statements traveled slowly upward and were finally collected in a bundle of more than 500 pages and sent over to the White House. "We couldn't use a word of it—not a word," recalls a presidential aide who worked on the message. "They just didn't understand what the President needed."[2]

* * *

Why the System Fails

After several years' absence in private life, an elder statesman was recalled by the President to temporary duty in the State Department. He noticed that there were twice as many assistant secretaries and "deputies" as he had remembered from his last stint in public service a decade before. "I have three people on my staff," he told me in an interview, "who spend all their time attending meetings so they can come back and 'brief' me about what was said at the meetings. The funny thing is," he added, "I don't give a damn about what's said at any of those meetings."[3]

There ought to be a moral to these stories, and there is. The State Department is in trouble. Ten years ago President Kennedy called it "a bowl of jelly."[4] Five years later columnist Joseph Kraft reported that it was being "run as a fudge factory."[5] In 1969 President Nixon was described by a newsman as "now more determined than ever to turn the place upside down."[6] In 1970 one of State's ablest younger officials asserted that the proper name for Washington's foreign policy apparatus is "The Machine That Fails,"[7] and a famous diplomat, George Kennan, declared, "I would have mixed emotions about recommending the Foreign Service as a career to any bright young person who asked me today."[8]

The critics are right, but they have not been able to change the organization they criticize. Perhaps that is because they have not fully understood the problem. It is not just a State Department problem, but a government-wide dilemma, touching each of the four dozen separate Washington bureaucracies that determine American foreign policy today. It encompasses the White House, the Pentagon, and the Central Intelligence Agency, and it will not be mastered until there is clear agreement about what has gone wrong and why it has gone wrong.

The time is ripe for reassessment. Twenty-five years after World War II American foreign policy is beginning to change. The Nixon administration launched itself on the hopeful prophecy, "After a period of confrontation, we are entering an era of negotiation." Giving more than two decades of history an official burial, the President reported to Congress on February 18, 1970, "The postwar period in international relations has ended."[9] If Mr. Nixon is right, there is every reason to reform our institutions as we restructure our policy. For the nation is not well served by the immense foreign affairs bureaucracies that have grown up in Washington over the past quarter century. They are an organizational accident whose present size and shape were largely unintended and unforeseen at the time of their founding in the late 1940s. Fashioned at the height of the cold war, the machine chugs ahead into the 1970s hauling a freight of outworn policies and ideas.

While the State Department (hereafter simply "State") is criticized for its weakness, the Defense Department and the CIA are attacked for their strength. All are assigned a share of the blame for costly American miscalculations in Southeast Asia. Another part of the foreign affairs apparatus, the Agency for International Development (AID), which dispenses foreign aid, is the target of a coalition of congressional conservatives and liberals who slash its budget every year. A smaller cog in the system, the United States Information Agency (USIA), which conducts foreign propaganda, has been described by a former official as a "Great Wind Machine"[10] that ought to be abolished. In the White House, as well as in Congress, thoughtful men worry that the bureaucracies are not really under control. In 1968, less than a year before he became President Nixon's assistant for national security affairs, Henry Kissinger remarked that there was "a sort of blindness in which bureaucracies run a competition with their own programs and measure success by the degree to which they fulfill their own norms, without being in a position to judge whether the norms made any sense to begin with."[11] He was only echoing criticisms that have been expressed by former President Truman, former Secretary of State Dean Acheson, and many other recent high officers of government.

Searching public debate is the hallmark of democratic politics and can be a healthy first step toward repairing flawed institutions. But many of the present complaints are sporadic, deriving their strength more from passing events than from any testable theory of why Washington is badly organized and how a better system could be built. The logical starting place for any serious study of the present discontents is a review of postwar history.

Most of America's foreign policy institutions are less than twenty-four years old, dating from the National Security Act of 1947. From the moment of their birth they were hasty contrivances, assembled in what seemed a time of national emergency. In the late 1940s most military men and many civilian leaders as well believed that World War III might break out at any moment.* Washington reorganized itself to meet the

* The atmosphere of that period is well summarized in a cable to Washington from General Lucius Clay, then U.S. military governor in Berlin, dated March 5, 1948: "For many months, based on logical analysis, I have felt and held that war was unlikely for at least ten years. Within the last few weeks I have felt a subtle change in Soviet attitude which I cannot define but which now gives me a feeling that it may come with dramatic suddenness. . . ." Noting that the effect on Washington of cables like this one was "cataclysmic," Walter Millis adds that, upon receiving it, "The CIA went furiously to work; not for eleven days was it to come up with an 'appreciation,' and the furthest this ventured to go was the conclusion that major war was not probable within sixty days." (Millis, *Arms and Men*, New York: Mentor, 1956, p. 285.)

threat. Most of the thinking about how to do so expressed itself in closed discussions within the executive branch of government. In public, the case for new organizational departures was simplified in terms of the perils of the hour. Extraordinary times called for extraordinary measures, which meant that diplomacy must be put on a wartime footing. As the years passed, succeeding international crises were handled short of general war, but there was no thorough review of the bureaucratic mechanisms first constructed in 1947 and the years immediately following, and no careful reconsideration of the assumptions underlying them.

Since the second Hoover Commission concluded its work in 1955, no comprehensive public report has been published on the CIA. No over-all study of the government's foreign policy apparatus has appeared since the first Hoover Commission report of 1949. Private citizens, scholars, and journalists in the meantime have investigated small parts of the complicated whole and have published their findings. Until quite recently, however, public opinion was remarkably patient with a system that cried out for searching study. Expert opinion has offered little critical leadership to a general public that is less well-informed, for a generation of American scholars, who have moved from university to government and back again, have often asserted that the bureaucracies of Washington either cannot or need not be changed. Roger Hilsman, a professor and former assistant secretary of state, spoke for many of his colleagues when he wrote, in 1965, "There is probably no quick or easy way of making improvements. Certainly tinkering with the organizational 'machinery' is not going to help very much."[12]

Faced with the complaisance of their elders, a growing number of younger Americans have come to despair of the difficulties involved in "changing the system." Working against or around it seems, to many, more realistic than trying to reform it. The young pessimists and the old cynics may be right, but their argument cuts against the grain of much of the nation's political experience to date. Many of the greatest questions of American politics, from the Constitutional Convention of 1787 down to the present, have been questions of organization. Our first decade as an independent people saw a series of debates over the structure of government. Later, in the 1820s and 1830s, the question of whether or not to charter a national bank dominated the American scene. Civil-service reform and industrial monopoly were the most burning issues of the last quarter of the nineteenth century. Franklin Roosevelt's New Deal of the 1930s concentrated heavily on reorganizing our institutions, as did Woodrow Wilson's New Freedom twenty years earlier. There is ample reason to recall these traditions today, as Americans once more give serious thought to the way their government should be organized. Already a crucial problem for cities, schools and domestic programs, organizational renewal may in time become a major theme of our national politics in the 1970s and 1980s.

Public inquiries are already beginning to spark the reexamination that is required. In the year 1970 alone there appeared the Fitzhugh Report on the Pentagon, recommending that the powers of the military chiefs be curbed; the Peterson Task Force Report on foreign aid, proposing the abolition of the Agency for International Development; a self-critical reform study from within the State Department; and a careful scholarly review of American intelligence, which concluded that "control, as it has existed through much of CIA's history, has perhaps been more a matter of form than actuality."[13]

The timing of these reports coincides with what may be a turning point in American foreign policy. The longest and least popular foreign war in our history is not yet over, but already nearly half of the troops we had in Vietnam in 1965 have come home. American military power is withdrawing rather than expanding overseas for the first time in twenty years. There is a general sense, shared by people in and out of government, that the threat of nuclear war is declining, that domestic needs in America are pressing, that U.S. commitments abroad have been overextended, and that our foreign policy is entering a new phase. It is not yet fully clear what that new phase will be like, but its rough outer edges are beginning to emerge as the recent past is reinterpreted.

An English observer, Anthony Hartley, describes what is happening as the outcome of "three periods of American world policy," which he delineates as follows:

> 1. From 1946 to 1960, during which time the present structure of overseas commitments was largely acquired on an empirical basis without any very logical principle other than a broadly conceived anticommunism dictating their shape
> 2. 1961–1963: the period of the Kennedy administration, during which a conscious intellectual effort was made to rationalize American policy and impart to it a genuinely global cohesion; and
> 3. 1964 to the present day: the years during which the Kennedy strategy gradually proved itself a failure and American opinion, under the impact of the Vietnam War, swung more and more away from the very concept of a global role.[14]

What Hartley is saying is that the "global sacrifice" theme of the Kennedy Inaugural Address ("We shall pay any price, bear any burden . . . ") is dead or dying. Vietnam has killed it as far as American opinion is concerned, while political evolution outside the United States has made it "overtaken by events." In any case, more resources must be spent and more attention paid to exploding home problems if America is to survive its own social ferments.

Why the System Fails

Nuclear weapons and an advancing technology that knits continents together make a return to prewar isolationism unlikely, although that may be what many Americans want. A 1969 public opinion poll showed that only a quarter of the U.S. public favored sending our troops abroad to defend allies under attack by communist forces.[15] The prospect for the 1970s would seem to be not isolationism, but rather a much more selective, less globalist American foreign policy. For by now the faults of active engagement on a worldwide basis, whether designed negatively to prevent "communist" gains or positively to foster "stability" and "modernization" in the Third World, seem evident. That policy has failed in several major respects. It has been: (1) too costly economically and psychologically; (2) ineffective even in accomplishing its own ambiguous purposes; (3) in contravention of international law and national sovereignty, for it has required deep "interference in the internal affairs of sovereign states"; (4) dependent on the perception of a "national emergency"—a wartime rather than a peacetime psychology—at a time when it is increasingly difficult to discern an unremitting foreign threat to the nation; (5) not credible to friend or foe, for an *absolute* commitment to all (as in the equation of Saigon with Berlin, the Elbe with the Mekong as "frontiers of freedom") undercuts a *relative* commitment to some; (6) pretentious in overstepping the limits of American wisdom and experience in world affairs, by assuming that a knowledge of local political conditions (which in any case Americans may not possess) is only marginally relevant to the solution of tough international problems; and (7) worrying to other major countries, by suggesting the absence of a sense of proportion in the highest American councils.

But the Washington bureaucracies have not yet gotten this message. Rigidities of size and structure built into the process of bureaucratic action make it hard to change foreign policy, even when the changes have been announced by the President. In the present system, national purpose can easily become mired in a swamp of "interagency coordination," while expert advice from the lower working levels of government rarely reaches the place it is most needed—the top. Organization, in other words, undercuts policy. Until policy makers change the structure of their organizations, they will have great difficulty in changing the shape of their policies.

The two main features of the American bureaucratic system are dispersal and gigantism, or, in the phrase used by Harvard political scientist Stanley Hoffmann, "elephantiasis and fragmentation."[16] Anyone starting today to build a system from scratch, Hoffmann has argued, would never dream of imitating the institutional pattern that has evolved in Washington since 1947. For Washington has not one but many foreign offices, autonomous organizations chartered in the late 1940s to wage the cold war on separate fronts. Diplomacy, military force, economic subvention, propaganda, and clandestine operations and research are pursued in the separate entities of the State and Defense departments, AID, USIA, and CIA. Four dozen other units of the executive branch, including the Treasury, Commerce, and Agriculture departments, have foreign staffs and programs. White House committees and staffs, including a National Security Council (NSC), try to coordinate the competing offices beneath. A five-man committee composed chiefly of the President, Vice-President, and Secretaries of State and Defense, advised by the Chairman of the Joint Chiefs of Staff, the CIA Director, and the assistant to the president for national security affairs,* the NSC is sup-

* A rather obscure official, the Director of the Office of Emergency Preparedness is, by historical accident, the fifth statutory member of the NSC. The present Director, Mr. George Lincoln, is responsible for coordinating fed-

ported by a staff of more than 100 employees who work in the White House basement and the Executive Office Building next door under the direction of Henry Kissinger. Another presidential office, the 550-man Bureau of the Budget (recently renamed the Office of Management and Budget) apportions money among separate agencies before their budget requests are sent to Congress.

Fragmented authority in this complex system tends to make government policies both inflexible and unstable. When delicate diplomacy is needed in the Middle East or in strategic arms talks with the Soviets, false starts and conflicting directives show the difficulty of obtaining agreement within the separate American bureaucracies. Change is another casualty of the system, for with responsibilities so divided, it is the path of least resistance to stick with inherited policies and procedures. Organized in their present pattern, the committees and bureaucracies are capable of reaction, but not initiative. Whether they are political appointees of the President or government career officers, most of the officials who operate the system hold a particular position for only a short period of time before rotating to another assignment. It was unusual in the 1960s, for example, for an assistant secretary of state to serve much longer than an average of two years, barely enough time for most such officials to begin to learn their way through the intricate structure of bureaucratic Washington. In this setting, diplomatic initiatives occur in spite of rather than because of the strength of our institutions, a situation reminiscent to some observers of the weaknesses of the Fourth French Republic.

Beyond interagency chaos is the problem of sheer size.

eral disaster relief programs for the fifty states, civil defense in event of nuclear attack, and advice on the stockpiling of strategic materials.

Twenty-three thousand Americans, only one-fifth of them employed by the State Department, man our diplomatic missions abroad (see Table 1).

Table 1
American Personnel Attached to U.S. Diplomatic Missions June 30, 1969

Department of Defense	8,264
Agency for International Development	5,324
Department of State	5,166
U.S. Information Agency	1,380
Peace Corps Administrative Staff	473
Other	2,401
TOTAL	23,008

SOURCE: Senate Hearings Before the Committee on Appropriations, 91st Congress, H.R. 12964, p. 950. These data do not include 10,500 Peace Corps volunteers. Personnel figures for the Central Intelligence Agency (CIA) are classified, and it should not be assumed that they are included in these totals.

A cross-agency census has never been taken, but within Washington alone there are at least another 50,000 workers in the foreign affairs complex.* Inside this mammoth machine it is difficult to locate authority and assign responsibility. Communication within and between departments is time-consuming and imprecise, and it is nearly impossible to change ingrained attitudes and patterns of routine. Because the system is difficult to manage and unreliable, a modern president is tempted to bypass it completely and develop his own more informal methods of decision. In time of crisis the President may turn to a closed circle of top advisers who have little knowledge of the subject being discussed but are unable to consult expert opinion lower down in the government because

* If one includes all of the military intelligence agencies, whose size is estimated in Chapter 6, the figure might more nearly approximate 100,000.

of fears of a breach of secrecy. President Johnson's major decisions about Vietnam were made in this manner. And when President Nixon was deciding on whether or not to intervene in Cambodia in April 1970, he, too, isolated himself from his State Department and depended almost entirely on military advice and White House staff work. President Nixon's decision, when announced, led several middle-level officials of the State Department to resign while some 300 others circulated public and private memoranda of protest. These evidences of internal dissent have no precedent; they indicate a growing *malaise* among insiders about the method and competence of the present decision-making apparatus.

The complaints themselves are hardly novel, however, for the failures and weaknesses of the American foreign-policy machine have been evident to a majority of Washington-watchers for at least a decade. John Kenneth Galbraith, in his *Ambassador's Journal*, has written, "In State the multitude must all make policy." In a letter to President Kennedy, reporting on a visit to the State Department, Galbraith said, "One of my assistant secretary friends attended the Secretary's staff meeting from nine-fifteen till ten. Then he had a meeting with the Under Secretary on operations until ten-thirty. Then he took until eleven-thirty to inform his staff of what went on at the earlier meetings. Whereupon they adjourned to pass on the news to their staffs. This is, I am told, communication." The effect of this elaborate system, Galbraith concluded, is that "when a deadline approaches, everyone repairs hurriedly to what was agreed several years ago. Accordingly, the sheer size of the Department freezes it to all of its antique positions."[17]

Columnist Stewart Alsop recalls what happened when the White House asked the State Department for a policy paper on British Guiana (now the nation of Guyana) in 1961. A radical change of government seemed imminent, and the President wanted a quick assessment of what the United States position should be. He was told that the paper would take a week or two to prepare, since first

it would have to be drafted, and then it would have to move up through the various levels of the office of Inter-American Affairs. Then there would be clearances and concurrences—European Affairs, International Organization Affairs, Intelligence and Research, Political Affairs. Then when it got up near the Secretary's level, there would be inter-agency clearances—the Pentagon, the Central Intelligence Agency, maybe Treasury or Commerce. And finally the paper would have to be cleared by the National Security Council. A policy in an afternoon? Good God![18]

A desk officer of State, who follows U.S. relations with one small African country, has recently calculated that while in theory he is the focal point of all Washington efforts concerning "his" country, in fact there are sixteen other people in Washington just like him, working on the same country in different chains of command. They receive information directly from the American officials in the country through up to nine different channels. No one sees all the communications in every channel. Through great effort the desk officer has come to know all of his sixteen Washington counterparts, but, he points out, they change regularly; someone is always out of town or sick; most importantly each one has his own boss, who can determine his future career; each one has his own set of priority projects and problems. "All I can do is try to stay on top of the really important problems,"[19] he says.

The "task force" phenomenon is another vote of no confidence in the normal bureaucratic mechanisms. Whenever something called a "crisis" occurs, whether it is the Arab-Israeli war of June 1967, or an abrupt change of government in an obscure foreign country, a special task force is hastily put together to "stay on top of the crisis." The existing offices, in other words, are thought to be so slow, unresponsive, and inefficient as to be incapable of bringing a sense of urgency to their daily tasks. When fast decisions are needed, one must instill a sense of crisis and institutionalize it in a special task force which bypasses the normal government structure. There is thus the temptation to glamorize even the most mundane international occurrences by calling them "crises," for this is the only sure way to generate speedy action and high-level attention.

Immense size and deeply divided authority recur at every level of official Washington. Counting all agencies, the United States probably employs from five to ten times more people in foreign-affairs work than each of its major allies—Britain, France, Germany, and Japan. No accurate figures are available for the Soviet Union, which does not make public the size of its foreign-affairs apparatus; but it is not unusual in many world capitals for the American embassy to be twice as big as the Russian.

Yet the State Department's portion of money, personnel, and control over U.S. programs abroad is only fractional; no other major government gives its foreign office less authority over other cabinet departments. By Washington standards, State is a bureaucratic pygmy. It has the smallest annual budget ($400 million) and one of the smallest staffs (7,000 Americans at home and 5,000 overseas) of all 12 executive departments. The Department of Defense, which spends $70 billion a year and employs 1.2 million civilians and 3.3 million military men, one-third of them stationed overseas, naturally looms large in foreign affairs. The CIA, too, is acknowledged by former officials to have a budget and a staff measurably greater than those of State.

While bigness in money and staffing need not automatically be translated into big influence over foreign policy, the pressure in the American system of government is certainly in that direction. Gaps in organizational planning and coordination contribute to the result. The U.S. government has no single central foreign-affairs budget. Each agency bargains for funds on its own with different officials of the President's Budget Bureau and with different committees of congressmen. Virtually no central planning and control measures have been established to determine how many American officials of how many different agencies should represent the nation in each country abroad. No single agency in Washington has ever determined or been able to enforce on others a set of global priorities in foreign policy. Recent presidents and secretaries of state have not developed central levers of decision making over the national expenditure of money and manpower in foreign affairs. In effect, these expenditures have been considered a purely technical matter to be worked out separately by each agency within broad budget guidelines.

Today's confused and fragmented system is susceptible to change, for it is within the President's power to undertake a major reform of his foreign-affairs departments. Piecemeal tinkering will not do; the nature and size of the entire structure need to be reconsidered. The best way to begin is to reassess the philosophies that underlie the organizations.

2

POWER, IDEOLOGY, AND ORGANIZATION

> The damage caused by unnecessary people is equal to the square of their number.
>
> —George Kennan

Two conflicting strands of diplomatic theory weave in and out of the fabric of postwar U.S. foreign policy. Perhaps the simplest way to distinguish these strands is to label one the "old" and the other the "new" diplomacy.

Old Diplomacy

The first, more traditional theory holds that power and interest are the main engines of international relations, and ideology is a secondary force. According to this view, it is the anarchy of competing nation-states—the lack of agreed, enforceable rules to control violence or provide an ultimate arbiter of legitimacy—that distinguishes international from domestic politics. Law accepted by the community and enforced, when necessary, by policemen sets the limits of the home environment, but no restraints except those imposed by military power, diplomacy and the occasional agreement of world bodies such as the United Nations circumscribe the actions of sovereign states. Insecurity is rare among citizens under law, but constant among nations in anarchy. States compete not because they are wicked but because they have genuinely conflicting interests that are bound to clash. Diplomacy is not only a method of communication but also a means of easing these normal tensions and competitions of an insecure world. Traditional theorists stress the differences between the home politics and the foreign policy of a democracy. Indeed, some have believed that the two things are incompatible. With the America of the 1830s freshly in mind, Alexis de Tocqueville wrote, "Foreign politics demand scarcely any of those qualities which are peculiar to a democracy; they require, on the contrary, the perfect use of almost all those in which it is deficient."[20] More recently Harold Nicolson made a similar point, arguing that it is a mistake to "imagine that a foreign policy is framed in much the same manner as a budget or an education bill . . . and that thereafter all that remains to be done is to hand it over to the Foreign Office for execution." To assume that "an ideal foreign policy . . . has only to be devised in order to be carried out," Nicolson continued, is to ignore the fact that "other countries, with equally powerful armaments, interests and prejudices, must similarly be consulted if any policy is to be effective."[21]

The main aim of the old diplomacy is the maintenance of peace among competing national units, which is generally taken as a self-evident social good. Peace is thought to depend upon negotiation that respects the sovereignty of separate states and works to maintain balances of power among them. Here is where the diplomat finds his role. He exists, in George Kennan's view, "to constitute an effective channel of communication with other governments and a perceptive observer of life in other countries."[22] Diplomacy, so defined, is something between a craft and a profession: the study of particular foreign languages and cultures, combined with residence abroad and frequent intercourse with foreign decision makers, is seen as a method to develop special skills and insights that are of use to the nation in understanding the outside world and framing policies to cope with it. Nicolson stated it more simply, calling diplomacy "the art of negotiation." A famous prewar diplomat, Jules Cambon, believed that the fundamentals of negotiation are unalterable in a world of separate states, because "human nature never changes; there exists no other method of regulating international differences; and the best instrument at the disposal of a government wishing to persuade another government is the word of an honest man."[23]

These theoretical assumptions about diplomacy were shared by many of the men who made foreign policy during the Truman administration, particularly in the State Department. Although World War II had shattered the earlier substance of international relations, these men did not think that it had killed the diplomatic method. When competition with Russia became the dominant issue, they saw it not primarily as a modern ideological aberration but as the continuance of a long tradition of conflict among rival great powers. The government, they believed, should be organized not to conduct a crusade against communism but rather to maintain a defensive balance of power with the Soviet Union. They favored simplicity and economy of structure and staffing in Washington, a primary role for the Secretary of State as the President's number-one adviser, and the centralization of foreign expertise and authority in the State Department. Some of them foresaw that creating giant new bureaucracies with divided duties would make American foreign policy less discriminating and more interventionist, for the programs of separate agencies would generate their own self-justifying momentum. They had reservations about the government reorganizations of 1947, fearing that diplomacy and political judgment would be subordinated to something called "national security policy."*

Transferring authority from the State Department to a large White House staff, in this view, would divide responsibility further, undercut a secretary of state, and isolate a president. Dean Acheson later argued that this organizational innovation is what "blighted the high promise of President Johnson's administration."[24] Acheson recalls in his memoirs that he had "the gravest forebodings" about the establishment of a Central Intelligence Agency in 1947, and warned President Truman that "neither he, the National Security Council, nor anyone else would be in a position to know what it was doing or control it."[25]

Seen from this "traditional" perspective, the State Department has become too large, too weak, and too overshadowed by other departments to do its proper job. Acheson, George Kennan, and Hans Morgenthau have separately suggested

* As an historical picture, this may oversimplify a bit. Most Washington decision makers, to judge by their memoirs, by 1947 were buoyed with the awareness that they were participating in a historic change, what Charles Bohlen has called, "The Transformation of American Foreign Policy." But many of these same men who helped draft the Truman Doctrine and Marshall Plan had deep reservations about the ideological "oversell" of the new programs, and had fought alongside the Foreign Service contingent in State against the creation of large, new, separate bureaucratic entities in foreign affairs and in favor of State Department rather than military control over occupied Germany and Japan.

that State be cut down to about half its present size, and that other foreign affairs agencies be even more severely curtailed. As Kennan states, "Excess people in the Government . . . cause a kind of damage that multiplies throughout the system. . . . the damage caused by unnecessary people is equal to the square of their number."[26]

So much for the old diplomacy. What is the usefulness, if any, of this approach in the world of the 1970s? Many would argue that this diplomatic tradition is irrelevant today, that changes in world politics and technology since 1945 require the transformation of foreign offices and embassies into some wholly new bureaucratic form, a form whose evolution is already well advanced. Other criticisms commonly leveled at the traditionalists are that they are obsessed with Europe and insensitive to the Third World, that their rational bias blinds them to emotional factors in world politics, that they are elitists, and that foreign affairs are not *that* different from domestic affairs.

Still, were there no body of traditional thought today, we would not have a State Department and a Foreign Service cut roughly from the same organizational cloth as the Foreign Offices and diplomatic services of other nations. Every postwar study of the American bureaucracy has at least paid lip service to the main traditionalist maxims: the need for foreign affairs personnel of high intellectual caliber; the desire for as economical, efficient, and simple a system as possible; the requirement for greater "responsibility" and fewer clearances and committees in decision making; and the importance of avoiding chaos, indecisiveness, and uncertainty in fashioning foreign policy.

New Diplomacy

A second, rival theory of diplomatic organization has come from those who believe that the old diplomacy died in 1945, that revolutionary changes in warfare, communications, and economics have altered the nature of international politics. Destructive war seemed for a time to extinguish nationalism in Europe, and, after Yalta, President Roosevelt declared that the new United Nations organization meant "the end of the system of unilateral action and exclusive alliances and spheres of influence and balances of power and all the other expedients which have been tried for centuries—and have failed."[27] This was much the same thing Woodrow Wilson had said after the previous war: that if *only* other nations would be "reasonable" and would adopt in international life some of the internal procedures of American democracy, peace was assured. The Wilsonian tradition, in which much of the American public and most of our modern presidents are steeped, personalizes international politics. The stage is inhabited by good and wicked actors, heroes and villains in a world morality play. Battle with the villains is necessary and righteous; conflict among the heroes is irrational and is caused only by misunderstandings or faulty communication. Objective conflicts of interest do not exist; thus any prolonged disagreement leads one to question the motives and morality of the nation doing the disagreeing. With only sufficient goodwill on all sides, world leaders at summit meetings or through their representatives at the United Nations should be able to harmonize their interests without much difficulty.

This neo-Wilsonian view was a natural one to have in 1945,

because Hitler had just provided our world with its most vivid example of the evil genius as statesman, and it required the most extensive and cooperative military alliance in history to defeat him. The breakup of that common-interest alliance was disillusioning to the American people; they had been told that its bonds went far deeper than traditional expediency. As postwar euphoria was succeeded by conflict with Stalin's Russia, the Wilsonian new-diplomacy theory interpreted the challenge as an ideological one to be met and mastered on roughly the same terms as the war against Nazism.

The more active U.S. foreign policy commenced in 1947 and the extensive reorganizations in Washington that accompanied it were deeply influenced by this newer perception of international affairs. Military staff work during World War II had given American leaders a novel organizational model of how to deploy vast resources and manpower overseas. Interagency bodies such as the State-War-Navy Coordinating Board offered a new pattern of military-political coordination. Eighteen months before the Truman Doctrine committed the United States to the defense of Greece and Turkey, Ferdinand Eberstadt of the Navy Department drafted for Secretary Forrestal his plan for a National Security Council. Federation of the three armed services in a single Defense Department and coordination of high policy among military and civilian leaders and the President within the NSC (to which the new CIA would also be attached) were necessary, Eberstadt argued, because "experience in the late war had revealed serious weaknesses in our present organizational set-up" and "integration is compelled by our present world commitments and risks, by the tremendously increased scope and tempo of modern warfare, and by the epochal scientific discoveries culminating in the atomic bomb." The Eberstadt Report went on to say, "The great need, therefore, is that we be prepared always and all along the line, not simply to defend ourselves after an attack, but through all available political, military and economic means to forestall any such attack. . . . Much has been said about the need for waging peace, as well as war. We have tried to suggest an organizational structure adapted to both purposes."[28]

As originally conceived, the NSC assigned one seat to each of the three secretaries of the armed services departments (War, Navy, and Air), one to the Secretary of State, and one to the chairman of the National Security Resources Board. The Joint Chiefs of Staff were also to be a part of, and to meet with, the Council, as was the CIA and its director. It was not initially certain whether the new body would be located in the Pentagon, the White House, the State Department, or elsewhere, but in structure and number the NSC from the start was heavily weighted toward the representation of military interests. The Eberstadt Plan was championed by military officials, who believed that the United States had entered a revolutionary new age that rendered traditional diplomatic methods obsolete, but was greeted with something less than enthusiasm by the State Department. By 1947–1948 most military men thought that World War III was imminent and would be decided by the same techniques that turned the tide in World War II. Massive mobilization of resources, weapons technology, and a "battle for men's minds" were the keys to the future of world politics.

The military-ideological theorists won most of the battles in the bureaucratic fights of 1945–1947; they have been Washington's main organizational planners ever since. In each administration men of this viewpoint have proposed new foreign policy superstaffs. An NSC Psychological Strategy Board created in 1951 was father to the Operations Coordinating Board of the Eisenhower years. Following the same tradition, a Special Group-Counterinsurgency was organized under President Kennedy, who was also urged by General Maxwell Taylor to create a "Cold War Strategy Board." Nothing came of the latter proposal, but General Taylor later, in the Johnson presidency, drafted the plan for a Senior Interdepartmental Group (SIG), which was finally established. Stressing the military and intelligence preoccupations of these high-level committees, Taylor argued in a speech in 1966 that "there are many troublemakers creating for us many trouble spots around the world," and that the main need of our foreign policy apparatus is for "watchful eyes looking constantly in all directions and giving warning before we are surprised."[29]

Many civilian leaders have embraced the Taylor view of world affairs, which is an odd mixture of Wilsonianism and military staff thinking. At the start of the 1960s, for example, the emerging Third World was widely regarded as an important ideological "battleground," although more traditional theorists discounted its place in the East-West power balance. The Herter Report of 1962, *Personnel for the New Diplomacy*, suggested that American diplomacy should bring about "rapid social, economic, and political progress" in developing countries, and that the ideal "new diplomat" must be skilled in such fields as: "intelligence; political action; technical assistance and various types of foreign economic aid; military aid programs; information and psychological programs; . . . educational exchange; cultural programs; trade development programs; . . . and . . . measures to counter insurgency movements." "Most of these," the report continued, "fall outside the older definition of diplomacy, but all of them must be considered actual or potential elements of United States programs. Together they constitute what is here called the 'new diplomacy.' "[30]

Like the men who first proposed the creation of the National Security Council, the authors of the Herter Report rested their case on the assumption that a new epoch in world politics had begun. The main feature of this epoch was "conflict between the free countries, struggling to build a world of free, independent, peaceful, and progressive peoples, and the Communist world." The report concluded, "Our interest in every part of the world is today extensive, and our commitment to the pursuit of growth and progress among the free nations is well-nigh total."[31]

Within a few short years Vietnam has made the new diplomacy of the Herter Report seem more a transient fad than a wave of the future. To many foreigners and to American critics as well, U.S. programs of "intelligence; political action; technical assistance and various types of foreign economic aid; military aid programs; information and psychological programs . . . and . . . measures to counter insurgency movements" look like manipulative interference in other people's business. The global ideological concept of an American policy to bolster noncommunist governments everywhere and to stimulate "modernization," "stability," and "progress" in the Third World appears costly, unwise, and impossible. It is also a highly ambiguous policy. (What do "progress" and "stability" really mean? Are they mutually exclusive?) More recent formulations such as the Nixon Doctrine propose the beginning of the end of "well-nigh total" commitments.

To salvage those insights of the new diplomacy advocates that are still serviceable, it may be necessary first to slough off the breathless rhetoric that tends to smother the argument. This means discarding the notion of a "long twilight struggle" against implacable foes. It means admitting that we lack the wisdom as well as the resources to do more than scratch the surface of Third World economic development problems, and that we will provoke irritation rather than modernization if we continue to see the task in diffuse global terms. It means understanding that doubling the number of sovereign states, inventing missiles and jets and television and nuclear warheads, and establishing the United Nations and the multinational corporation do not alter the fundamental framework of international politics: sovereign national units that recognize no higher legitimacy than their own, and that strive to regulate their governmental relations by the methods of negotiation and violence. "The ultimate arbiter," George Ball has written, "remains what it has been since the beginning of time, the possession of power. The power of the poor countries is definitely limited. . . . Priorities have not been changed by improved communications or even a more active social conscience; our first need is to maintain an effective balance between East and West."[32]

This is not to deny that there is often much generosity of motive in the new diplomacy world view. But that viewpoint, Wilsonian, ideological, and impressed with military power, is heavily ethnocentric and thus misperceives much of the nature and framework of conflict among states. Its central weakness is an assumption that conflict is somehow "unnatural," and that to reconcile clashes of interest by the diplomatic method is less honorable than to discover the alleged "causes" of conflict and attack them root and branch either by military means or by direct appeals to peoples over the heads of their governments. But it is not so much the theories of the new diplomacy advocates as the enthusiastic "oversell" of those theories that has done organizational damage. The new diplomacy was conceived as an adjunct rather than as a replacement of more traditional methods, but in practice it has sought to confine the older diplomacy to Europe while carving out for itself a new preserve in the developing countries. While diplomats have tried to work in terms of traditional power relationships, separate organizations for propaganda and intelligence and economic subvention have tended to focus on more ambiguous notions of "communist threat," "social change," and "reaching *people*" (a word italicized in the Herter Report, in an effort to stress that U.S. policy should no longer confine itself to governments but should also actively solicit man-in-the-street appeal).

Sheer numbers of personnel working in the new diplomacy fields have swamped the pre-existing organizational structure over a twenty-year period, but at an accelerating rate in the 1960s. In the 1970s, however, we shall have to operate programs abroad more modestly and less massively, eschewing interference in the internal affairs of other states where it is not wanted or not likely to accomplish an agreed objective. If no more convincing rationale for foreign aid can be found than the old anticommunist "national security" argument coupled with a generalized American "responsibility" to raise the living standards of poorer states, then AID appropriations will continue to decline. These arguments offer no guidelines for the apportionment of limited U.S. resources and no yardsticks of accomplishment. They are essentially ideological arguments, and they have been used not only for economic aid but also to justify U.S. military, intelligence, and propaganda programs.

Military Influence on Foreign Policy

Those who believe that American foreign policy has been "militarized" in the past three decades since Pearl Harbor are probably correct, if they mean that the organizational method of Washington decision making in foreign affairs is an imitation of the military staff system employed during World War II. Such a system may be useful and necessary in wartime, or even during prolonged international crisis, but Eberstadt's National Security Council, with its notion that "waging peace, as well as war" are simply two sides of the same coin, seems bound to distort out of all recognition the traditional kinds of diplomacy pursued by great powers in peacetime. The military and intelligence viewpoint that sees foreign events in terms of "troublemakers" for the United States clashes with the traditional diplomatic viewpoint that sees sovereign states with objectively differing interests to be reconciled by negotiation. The traditional view may underestimate the force of ideology, but the military view almost always takes the most banal expressions of ideology ("wars of national liberation," for instance) with deadly seriousness. There can be little doubt that the NSC system, and the powerful role that Franklin Roosevelt and his successors have given to military and intelligence officials in foreign policy deliberations have contributed to a much more activist, interventionist American policy than would otherwise have been the case. Priorities are reversed in the minds of policy makers when they come to regard diplomacy as the tool of "national security policy," instead of conceiving military power as the servant of foreign policy.

The distinction is important, and many of its practical implications flow from nothing more nor less than the way the governmental bureaucracies are organized.

It is time to reconsider the military and ideological approach to world politics, and the latest version of new diplomacy that it has spawned, as modest aids rather than major organizational competitors to the more settled diplomatic traditions. The verbal theme of an "era of negotiation" is one way of saying that ideological warfare is an aberrant phenomenon, diverging from the mainstream of a long tradition of more restrained interstate relations. That tradition is more valid and more useful than many Americans were prepared to admit after World War II. Indeed, in an unstable nuclear world, its rediscovery is essential. In organizational terms, this means that some of the cold-war agencies formed two decades ago may have to be disestablished or severely cut back in a program that improves the quality but diminishes the quantity of our overseas representation.

Before leaving our discussion of theory and moving on to practice, the approach taken by American scholarship to the study of bureaucracies should be considered. It is precisely from the centers of learning that one would expect to obtain critical studies of government and proposals for change. Little of this has taken place in the field of foreign affairs organization, however, although many scholars have served in government. Such service, instead of sharpening the critical faculties of academicians, has often seemed to have just the opposite effect, turning them into apologists for the system they have served. In the social sciences, during the 1960s fascination with problem solving, theories of sociological determinism, and mechanistic puzzles such as game theory have tied scholarly enquiry to the uses of those who see world affairs in military and ideological terms. The fact that government research funds have flowed most freely into these fields has also probably contributed to this result. The study of diplomacy at our major universities has languished outside of history departments, while negotiation has been studied as a form of game conflict rather than of rational accommodation. The emphasis of such studies is on forms of deception, of "winning the game" or "scoring points" against an antagonist, rather than on building confidence and rapport with him.* Hans Morgenthau is probably right in contending that the "dogmatic outlook of modern political science has greatly contributed to our failure in Vietnam," since it has "prevented us from understanding the true nature of the issues we were facing and, more particularly, their complexity and imponderable qualities."[33] Scholars have spent more time on quantitative technique than on qualitative political judgment.

The Bureaucratic-Politics Thesis

At least one group of political scientists, however, has recently begun to study the Washington decision-making apparatus. Headed by Richard Neustadt of the Kennedy Institute of Politics at Harvard University, this group has sought to follow the twists and turns of policy makers in Washington and the system in which they work by a case-study method. Instead of suggesting that the bureaucracies

* In contrast, the traditional method, according to one of its pre-1914 practitioners, Sir Edward Grey, holds that "gullibility is in diplomacy a defect infinitely preferable to distrust."

need to be changed, however, the Harvard researchers have thus far seemed to conclude that the present system is at bottom sound, or at any rate is evolving of its own accord in a self-improving direction. Writing in 1966, Neustadt claimed to see the beginnings of "a new institutional breakthrough, a pragmatic innovation in our Constitution" that would center power in Washington in a new "Administrative class" of White House staffers, " 'in-and-outers' from the law firms, banking, business, academia, foundations, or occasionally journalism," and a handful of influential senators close to President Johnson. He welcomed the new class as "a political resource to nurture," and promised that the institute he heads would try to educate "in-and-outers" as future Washington decision makers.[34]

Neustadt and his colleagues believe that foreign policy is the outcome of a complex bureaucratic-political process, in which individual bureaucrats and their organizations compete for power and influence. In a book published in 1970, Neustadt described this process as a "game of governance," and argued that not often enough have our officials had "an adequate conception of the overlapping games in which they were engaged."[35]

Proponents of the bureaucratic-politics thesis say that they are building descriptive "models" of behavior, free of policy bias. They believe that the State Department functions as an organization in much the same way that a large business firm operates, and that foreign policy is best understood as a series of "bargaining games." Their object is not to suggest which foreign policies are "better" than others but rather to show how foreign policy is made in Washington. "Rationality" and formal relationships are described as the part of the iceberg that projects above the water, whereas the deeper reality is office politics: the power drives, subjective judgments, peer-group "effectiveness" and access to the President of his appointed officials. One effect of the focus of the study, probably unintended, is to suggest (and, by inference, to legitimize) a Washington-centered universe in which foreign events play a subsidiary role to internal Washington bureaucratic considerations in the decision-making business. If there is more bloody-mindedness than disinterested professional advice to be had in Washington, that is because every action by a bureaucratic "player" carries a personal ego-investment and masks status climbing or effectiveness-building drives.

One of the most compelling attributes of the bureaucratic-political school is that some of its members have been "in-and-outers" in recent administrations, and their later reflections on government carry the authority of self-descriptions by participant-observers. Neustadt himself has been a frequent government consultant, and many of his colleagues have served in the Defense Department and the White House staffs of Presidents Kennedy and Johnson. What they have given us, in part, is a study of the behavior and motivations of "in-and-out" presidential appointees of the 1960s, men of cabinet, assistant secretary, and White House staff rank, and their personal aides. For such men, "interpersonal relations" appear to be the propeller of government. Of the career officials beneath and around them, they are ambivalent. While some career men in State and Defense are seen as coequal "players" in the bureaucratic game, most are described as having a clerkish *fonctionnaire* mentality, which renders inertia and the defense of established policy their chief contribution to government.

As a method of describing the interplay of men and events, bureaucratic political analysis at its best competes with good journalism and historical writing. As prescription rather than description, however, the bureaucratic-politics school has had little to offer to date, except to stress the need for a better understanding of how to play the government game.* One comes away from immersion in the literature of decision-making analysts with the impression that those who describe our foreign affairs system have a vested interest in the system they are describing. There is, at least, a note of fatalism if not self-satisfaction with the main lines of U.S. foreign policy in the 1960s, and an unquestioned assumption that the immense size and fragmented shape of the Washington bureaucracy are "givens" that cannot or should not be changed. To shake up institutions is made to seem a chimerical exercise, worse, a tautology; bureaucracies are the way they are because bureaucrats are the way they are.

This is not to say that bureaucratic-political studies lack descriptive power. They do focus attention on the political in-fighting that is one important facet of the foreign policy process. The outcome of their argument, however, is a shade reminiscent of Social Darwinism: the status quo, once described, is legitimized as a fundamentally "natural" and unalterable condition. Wisdom consists in comprehending the laws of bureaucracy and adjusting one's behavior accordingly, so as to be in maximum harmony with the environment. Changing the environment itself—reducing the size of the bureaucracy, for example, to a point where fewer staff meetings and clearances are required and more time is allotted for thinking—seems an impossible violation of natural law. But what if the status quo thus legitimized is an odd, accidental, unplanned, and unsatisfactory status quo? Should the De-

* An example of this viewpoint is Morton Halperin's "Why Bureaucrats Play Games," in *Foreign Policy*, 2 (Spring 1971).

fense Department of Robert McNamara and the State Department of Dean Rusk and the White House of John F. Kennedy and Lyndon Johnson be taken as "ideal types" of bureaucratic performance?

Perhaps we need not only change the players in the bureaucratic "game" but the rules as well.* The bureaucratic-political persuasion is not very helpful here. Its virtues are essentially descriptive and historical, its vices an uncritical acceptance of things-as-they-are, a set of psychological premises that pull toward cynicism, and a Washington-centered view of foreign affairs that is likely to exaggerate the ability of the United States to influence overseas events by virtue of its internal decision-making apparatus. Dean Acheson has remarked of the decision-making analysts that, like Machiavelli, they are writing advice for weak princes.[36]

These disagreements among military men, diplomats, and academics show that our foreign-policy process is looked at in different ways by different people. Not many realize how recent and how extraordinary a process of birth and growth has changed the nature of the Washington bureaucracies since World War II. The pre-Pearl Harbor State Department, located next to the White House, made do with a staff that was one-seventh the size of today's State. The 21 personnel who comprised Secretary Cordell Hull's office staff in 1938 have grown to 336 staff members serving Secretary William Rogers and his deputies. Over the same three decades the geographic and functional offices of State have expanded from 449 to 2625 personnel, whereas administrative overhead has

* Students of Washington officialese will think of alternate metaphors to express the same thought. Two possibilities that occur to the author are (1) "We need not only new bodies but also a new can of worms," and (2) "We need not only to change the policy-types, we also need to change the scenarios."

Table 2
Staffing the Department of State

CATEGORY	NUMBERS OF PERSONNEL 1938	1948	1969
Secretary's Office (including secretariat and under secretaries)	21	186	342
Geographic Political Offices	112	318	980
Functional Offices Economic, Intelligence, UN, Educational, Scientific, Legal, Protocol, etc.	387	881[a]	1645
Administrative Offices (including consular divisions)	443	2813	3307[b]
Miscellaneous (personnel seconded to other agencies, in training, on leave status)	—	—	600
TOTALS (Actual)	963	5648	6874
TOTALS (Adjusted)	963	4198	6874

° SOURCES: For 1938 and 1948: The Commission on Organization of the Executive Branch of the Government ("Hoover Commission"), *Task Force Report on Foreign Affairs* [Appendix H], Washington, Government Printing Office, January 1949, p. 76. For 1969: Department of State, *Domestic Staffing Patterns, October 31, 1969,* prepared by Office of Operations, Automated Data Processing Division. The chart *Organization of Federal Executive Departments and Agencies* (January 1, 1970), published by the U.S. Senate Committee on Government Operations gives a slightly higher figure of 7163 total State employees, broken down as follows: Secretary's Office (490); Geographic Political Offices (1036); Functional Offices (1769); Administrative and Consular Offices (3868).

[a] Actual total of 2331 adjusted downward to account for 850 personnel subsequently transferred to USIA, 300 transferred to CIA, and 300 transferred to economic agencies.

[b] A figure more accurate for purposes of comparison would be 3900, to take account of administrative staffs now "buried" in the geographic and functional offices. The "adjusted" totals for 1969 for other areas would then be: Secretary's Office, 300; Geographic Offices, 800; Functional Offices, 1325.

risen from 443 to 3307 employees (see Table 2). Overseas, the prewar U.S. representation at 323 embassies, legations, and consulates was below 2000, while today we employ 23,000 Americans at 259 diplomatic missions. The White House national security staff of Henry Kissinger now includes about four times more personnel than the staffs of McGeorge Bundy and Walt W. Rostow during the Kennedy and Johnson administrations. When new agencies that conduct intelligence, aid, propaganda, and military programs are counted, the postwar expansion in U.S. foreign-affairs personnel has been more than twenty-fold.

We have acquired our bureaucracy, like some of our foreign commitments, in a fit of absence of mind. Postwar studies of government organization have regularly criticized overstaffing and diffusion of authority, but little corrective action has been taken. The past four presidents have cursed the State Department while at the same time presiding over a twenty-year decline in its effectiveness, abetting the process by building an intermediary foreign office in the White House. While Secretaries Marshall, Acheson, and Dulles were able, by force of personality and implicit delegation to them of presidential authority, to hold the main reins of foreign policy and keep the other agencies in check, their successors at State have not been so fortunate.

Although every president requires his own staff and each impresses on the government his own personality and habits of work, it has been forgotten that any president stands to benefit from having a strong and able State Department. For State's stock-in-trade is a kind of expertise in foreign politics and international negotiating skill that has no other institutional home in Washington. The stronger and abler the department, the better the chances for wisdom in foreign policy, or, put another way, the higher the "reality input" into presidential decision making in foreign relations. Paradoxically, the way to strengthen State may be to cut back its size drastically, as Acheson and Kennan (and most of our recent Presidents, in private utterance) have proposed, while at the same time giving it new authority over the forty-odd other agencies which play partial roles in foreign affairs.

The Hoover Commission Task Force Report

The suggestion is not entirely new. A Task Force Report on foreign-affairs organization, prepared for the Hoover Commission and submitted to Congress in 1949, made proposals fully as drastic as these. Twenty-two years later the questions addressed by that Task Force continue to haunt Washington policy makers. Two of its four main recommendations have only passing historical significance today and can be mentioned briefly. "Policy," the report believed, should be centered in the State Department and separated from "operations" in such fields as propaganda and economic aid, which should be left to separate agencies. The operational agencies, it was assumed (wrongly, as time has shown), would not themselves compete for a policy role, but would function "under the observation and with the advice of the State Department."[37] A second recommendation, actually carried out six years later, was that some 2000 civil servants in State be integrated into the Foreign Service, so as to end internal feuding between the two distinct personnel groups.*

* The 1949 report noted that there was a "cancerous cleavage" causing "serious unrest" in the Department between civil-service specialists who manned the functional and administrative offices and Foreign Service officers who controlled the geographic political offices. One symptom of the cleavage, noted by the Task Force, was that FSOs were said not to be reading the intelligence reports prepared by their civil-service brethren, because these reports were "duplicative" and "unreadable." The Task Force concluded: "Whether the fault lies with the geographic units for not reading or the research division

The two main recommendations of the Task Force that read most interestingly today concern the role of the President and the internal organization of State. The report agonized over the perils of presidential decision making. "The personal participation of the President in the conduct of foreign affairs," it noted, "particularly in the role of policy initiator and formulator, is marked with many pitfalls. History, as well as the present, bears witness to the validity of the principle that the President should consult his foreign policy advisers in the executive branch before committing the United States to a course of action."[38]

Normally, the report assumed, a president would consult his secretary of state, whose department "is cast in the role of the specialist in foreign affairs." In nominating ambassadors, the President was expected routinely to select professional diplomats, and whenever making an exception to this rule "should by tradition explain his special reasons."[39]

Below the President, the report continued, the "departments and agencies other than the State Department . . . show an increasing tendency to establish policies or make policy recommendations in the foreign affairs area which are not coordinated with the foreign policies or interpretations of the State Department." Complicating coordination further was a legal and conceptual problem: "The powers granted by the Congress to the Department of State are intrinsically different in character from those granted to the other departments and agencies," since "the State Department's organic statute gives it power over the *means* of conducting foreign relations"

for producing unreadable material, the fact remains that maintenance of the research activity . . . is an expensive luxury, if, as appears, they do not use the material produced."

[emphasis added] whereas other departments have more specific, substantive powers.[40]

What to do? The National Security Council, then less than two years old, seemed to the Task Force to have terms of reference "so broad that in the name of security it can and does get into numerous matters of foreign affairs which are strictly not its business." The Task Force lamented the fact that the military departments were heavily over-represented on the NSC, thus allowing them more influence in nonmilitary areas than had been customary before the war. In fact, there was "real danger" that the NSC "can easily slip into a highly improper role," although in 1948 this was more a future than an immediate concern, since the Council had "only 11 full-time staff personnel—3 officers and 8 clerical."[41]

The answer, the Task Force decided, was to "recommend that the President should establish cabinet-level committees to advise him on both the domestic and foreign aspects of matters affecting foreign affairs and involving more than one department or agency of the executive branch. They should be on a regular or ad hoc basis as the occasion demands." The staffing should be limited to "an executive secretary with purely procedural and no substantive powers" who "should not build up a large secretariat but should meet the bulk of his personnel needs by calling upon the various departments and agencies."[42]

But the main burden of the Hoover Task Force's recommendation was to strengthen State by cutting down its size. A radical restructuring would be needed to do this, centering authority in four geographic divisions, each responsible for one of the main areas of the world. Outside this regional scheme there would be left within State only one other key official, an "Assistant Secretary for Multilateral Affairs," who was to handle U.S. diplomacy in international organizations, supervise small groups of economic specialists, and attend to several "matters transcending the spheres of the regional assistant secretaries" as well as interdepartmental coordinating chores. State's large economic, intelligence, and public-affairs offices were to be disbanded. To prevent diffusion of authority through a committee system that would compromise issues at the bottom rather than forward them up to the top, the Task Force insisted that action "should be assigned in each case to a single officer . . . who must consult (but never be required to secure concurrence of)" the other offices affected, "and then report their consultation and comment with his recommendation."[43]

It is a pity that Harvey H. Bundy and James Grafton Rogers, who, with the advice of Henry L. Stimson and the assistance of a staff of twelve aides labored for as many months to produce the Hoover Task Force Report, "deemed it neither desirable nor practicable to undertake a management engineering survey of the State Department nor of the many other Government departments and agencies operating in the field of foreign affairs" in an effort to clear up what they described in the preface to their study as "this confused and complicated picture."[44] Despite this failure, a failure to be repeated by every succeeding report on the subject, the 1949 Task Force study remains the most wide ranging of the many analyses of the ills of U.S. foreign affairs organization that have since appeared. Its recommendations were never effectively carried out, but they are still the beginning of wisdom. Only part of the wisdom, to be sure: for the symptoms first detected in 1949 have gone untreated for two decades and the illness has spread.

3

HAMILTON, JEFFERSON, AND THE KENNEDY ADMINISTRATION

> There was . . . a divorce between the people who daily or minute by minute had access to information . . . and the people who were making plans and policy decisions.
>
> —Robert Hurwitch (Cuba desk officer during the Bay of Pigs Invasion, 1961)

A Washington lawyer who advised Presidents Roosevelt, Truman, and Johnson said to me not long ago, "We called people like Chip Bohlen Fascists in the Thirties and Commies in the Forties." That statement suggests the enormous misunderstanding many Americans have about their career diplomatic service.

My lawyer friend went on to explain that Bohlen, a career ambassador who served seven presidents over the past forty years, was "too cosmopolitan" to commend himself to most Washington politicians. The knowledge, detachment, and even the loyalty of the successful career man made some of his fellow-citizens regard him as a rather cold fish, and a conceited one at that. When, in time of public excitement, a professional diplomat dares to say that power and national interest are more permanent factors of international life than ideology, he risks being thought of as an uncommitted man of dubious morals, a "Fascist in the Thirties and a Commie in the Forties." If he honestly reports from his embassy in Germany that Nazism is gaining ground, or from his consulate in China that communist revolution will succeed, he may, like the bearer of bad tidings in folklore, be disbelieved and even dishonored at home, for it is not always easy for domestic opinion to accept unpleasant foreign realities. John F. Kennedy, a president who knew and liked Bohlen, once asked, "What's wrong with that goddamned Department of yours, Chip?"

"You are," Bohlen replied.[45]

Differences of philosophy over the proper relationship of elected and appointed officials to career public servants have made it hard for recent presidents to understand why their State Department behaves the way it does. Presidents Kennedy and Johnson both hoped to reform and revitalize their foreign affairs bureaucracies, and failed. As we consider the problem anew in the 1970s, we should be able to learn something from these failures of the 1960s.

Two Opposing Views—Hamiltonian and Jeffersonian

At heart, two historic and conflicting perceptions of public service are involved, the Hamiltonian and the Jeffersonian views. Almost from the beginning of George Washington's presidency, his brash, thirty-three-year-old Secretary of the Treasury, Alexander Hamilton, clashed with the first Secretary of State, Thomas Jefferson, who then presided over a total staff of five clerks, one custodian, and one part-time translator of French. In a letter to the President on September 9, 1792, Jefferson complained of his colleague's "cabals with members of the legislature" and his habit of communicating directly with the American diplomatic ministers in Europe and with French and British representatives in New York.[46] The fledgling federal government experienced its first "breakdown in coordination."

More than mere personal rivalry was at stake. Hamilton believed in a strong national administration with five indispensable qualities: "energy, unity, responsibility, power, and duration." Jefferson favored rotation in office and thought it "a wise and necessary precaution against the degeneracy of the public servants" to offer them "drudgery and subsistence only."[47] Each citizen, in Jefferson's view, should take part in the administration of public affairs; federal jobs should be reapportioned with every election lest a permanent administrative caste develop in the executive branch of government.

The Jeffersonian approach has prevailed throughout most of the past two centuries, for it responded to the needs of congressional and party politics. But there have also been periods of "Hamiltonian backlash," as when a U.S. Military Academy was established in 1802, civil-service reform brought the beginnings of a permanent federal bureaucracy in the 1870s and 1880s, and the Rogers Act, creating a career Foreign Service of professional diplomats, was passed by Congress in 1924. Politicians live and work for the most part within the constraints of the Jeffersonian tradition. Career diplomats, on the other hand, are one of the few groups of civilian

Americans whose existence comes close to being a pure form of Hamiltonianism.

Selected by a rigorous competitive examination, which only 5 percent of all applicants pass, America's 3,200 Foreign Service officers, the elite of the State Department, are chosen and trained to serve the nation's foreign interests without regard to partisanship. Existing in a disciplined organization that is protected from the changing winds of home politics, they conceive their job as one of representing the United States abroad, carrying out the policies of whatever president happens to be in office, and giving him expert advice. Although they work side by side with the political appointees of each incumbent president, they bring, by definition, a different kind of perspective to their work than that of the elected politician and his appointed cabinet and staff officers.

Lack of sensitivity to this fundamental difference in outlook, which has deep roots in American history, may cause immense misunderstandings between the State Department's career officials on the one hand and congressmen, presidents, and cabinet officers on the other. Such misunderstandings—amounting sometimes to a total breakdown in communication—have occurred in every recent presidency. Thus Franklin Roosevelt thought his Foreign Service of the 1930s was reactionary, John Foster Dulles believed his of the 1950s was full of left-wing New Dealers who must be required to swear "positive loyalty" to the Eisenhower administration, John F. Kennedy suspected his of the 1960s to be ideologically unfriendly to the New Frontier, and now, coming full cycle, Richard Nixon is said to think *his* Foreign Service of the 1970s is tainted with liberalism. A man who has served in both the Kennedy and Nixon administrations puts it this way: "Kennedy was angry because he thought the Foreign Service was too conservative; Nixon thinks they are too liberal. They are both wrong. The Foreign Service is just the Foreign Service."[48]

George Kennan has described the way the Hamiltonian in the State Department looks at his Jeffersonian boss in the White House. Although speaking of President Roosevelt, Kennan could easily have been speaking of any other modern president: "He had little or no understanding for a disciplined, hierarchical organization. He had a highly personal view of diplomacy, imported from his domestic political triumphs. His approach to foreign policy was basically histrionic, with the American political public as his audience. Foreign Service officers were of little use to him in this respect."[49]

It is not surprising that intelligent men in the President's office frequently do not understand or even trust intelligent men in the career Foreign Service. Each set of officials operates in a different world. What is reasonable to the Jeffersonian may be incomprehensible to the Hamiltonian. In the Kennedy administration in 1961 this divergence became especially apparent.

The new president had come to office determined to strengthen his State Department. On February 20, 1961, Secretary Rusk addressed State's career officers, telling them of the President's "active expectation" that "this Department will in fact *take charge* of foreign policy."* Overriding objections from the Defense Department and the CIA, three months later Kennedy sent a circular letter to all ambassadors abroad giving them authority to "oversee and coordinate all the activities of the U.S. government" in their countries. His assistant, McGeorge Bundy, informed Senator Jackson by letter that the President wanted to emphasize "the clear author-

* Emphasis added.

ity and responsibility of the Secretary of State, not only in his own Department, . . . but also as the agent of coordination in all our major policies towards other nations." Kennedy, according to White House aide Arthur Schlesinger, Jr., "earnestly hoped that the State Department would really serve as his agent of coordination. He wanted to end the faceless system of indecision and inaction which diffused foreign policy among the three great bureaucracies of State, Defense and the CIA."[50]

Why then did State and the Foreign Service fail to "take charge" as the President had requested in 1961? Why did the Kennedy administration, whose initial gestures were welcomed by the State Department, soon develop a distaste for the career service? What made the President so disillusioned with State that he began to talk about "establishing a secret office of thirty people or so to run foreign policy while maintaining the State Department as a facade in which people might contentedly carry papers from bureau to bureau"?[51] What caused White House staffers to speak later of "the intellectual exhaustion of the Foreign Service," and to conclude that "the definition of a Foreign Service officer was a man for whom the risks always outweighed the opportunities"?[52]

Schlesinger, in his memoir, *A Thousand Days*, suggests two reasons for this abrupt change in attitude. State's "vast increase in size" during the 1950s, he feels, combined with "the trauma of the Dulles-McCarthy period" sapped its vigor and made it unable to respond to Kennedy's needs. "As it grew in size," he argues, "the Department diminished in usefulness. This was in part the consequence of bureaucratization . . . [and] a system of 'concurrences,' which required every proposal to run a hopelessly intricate obstacle course before it could become policy."[53]

Kennedy's Interventionist Policy—The Bay of Pigs

What Schlesinger says is true enough, but there were additional reasons as well, and added complexities to the question. It was the President himself, his political appointees and military and intelligence officers, who, with little or no advice from career diplomats, ordered the disastrous Bay of Pigs invasion of April 1961 and took the first steps toward U.S. military intervention in Vietnam. Another former White House aide, James Thomson, Jr., has accurately described some of the President's advisers as "a new breed of military strategists and academic social scientists . . . who had developed theories of counter-guerrilla warfare and were eager to see them put to the test."[54] These doctrines seemed to many career men what John Davies called at the time: "crusading activism touched with naïveté."[55] It was, again, the President himself and his closest partisans, acting without and even against the advice of State's skeptical career men, who popularized the word "counterinsurgency," established an Interagency Youth Committee to instruct U.S. embassies abroad to agitate among potential young leaders in developing countries, and generally stressed the importance of U.S. engagement and direct or indirect intervention in the complicated internal political and economic struggles of the Third World. State's slowness to respond to these directives may have looked like either incompetence or sabotage, possibly both. To older men schooled in the diplomatic method, however, some of the New Frontier programs seemed a repudiation of the most honorable and compelling lessons of a long tradition.

Naturally the career men were less than enthusiastic, and

just as naturally the White House felt frustrated. Ten years later, however, it seems clear to many that the interventionist thrust of the Kennedy foreign policy was unwise. But it seems equally clear that that policy *was* carried out, however grudgingly, as much by the faithful work of career men as by the president's own advisers and partisans, although Foreign Service officers had no part at all in formulating it. By its own lights, the Service exists to bring prudence and professionalism to bear on foreign policy through the advice it gives the men who have the ultimate responsibility of decision. In most cases, however, the career men lacked even *that* restraining influence in the 1960s. The call for State to "take charge," especially after the Bay of Pigs, seemed empty of meaning.

The curious thing about reminiscences of the Kennedy administration like those of Schlesinger and Roger Hilsman is the conclusions they draw. Both authors think that the State Department somehow "failed" Kennedy at the time of the Bay of Pigs decision. Hilsman writes that the Bay of Pigs "revealed to the President just how far the State Department had fallen short of taking up the role of leadership he had assigned to it."[56] At the time Hilsman was Director of Intelligence and Research at State, yet he knew nothing of the planned Cuban invasion. When he heard a chance remark by CIA Director Allen Dulles that made him "realize something was up," Hilsman reports, he went to Secretary Rusk to ask about it. Rusk told him not to inquire further into the matter because "this is being too tightly held."[57]

State's Cuba desk officer, Robert Hurwitch, was equally in the dark. "There was, in my judgment," Hurwitch says, "a divorce between the people who daily or minute by minute had access to information, to what was going on, and the people who were making plans and policy decisions."[58]

The lesson that might have been learned in April 1961 was that it is dangerous for a president to fail to inform and consult expert opinion in State before making a major foreign-policy decision. But, according to most accounts, exactly the opposite lesson was drawn. The failure of the Cuban invasion was said to have made Kennedy "distrust the experts." What "experts" had he consulted? CIA and Pentagon officials, and his own White House staff, who insisted that the matter be "tightly held." The only State Department officials involved, by Schlesinger's account, were Secretary Rusk (who seems to have expressed no strong opinion pro or con), Under Secretary Chester Bowles (who strongly opposed the invasion) and Assistant Secretary Thomas Mann (the one career FSO eventually consulted, who, at the final April 4 meeting said that he "would have opposed it at the start, but, now that it had gone so far, it should be carried through").[59]

The full story has not yet been told, and even when it is it will probably be subject to several interpretations. But however interpreted, the episode casts doubt on the President's seriousness in asking State to "take charge" of foreign policy. Kennedy had appointed as his Secretary of State a man who would not use the expertise of his department at critical moments.*

The pattern of the Bay of Pigs was repeated in later crises until it has become a bureaucratic law, described by one former official as follows: "The more sensitive the issue, and

* Rusk's passion for "security" was such, according to ex-White House staffers, that, unlike McNamara, he refused to discuss classified information with the President over the phone. The Secretary's aloofness, combined with the heavy reliance of Presidents Kennedy and Johnson on their respective White House staffs, put both Presidents in an Isolation Booth. Whether this is what the two chief executives consciously intended, or instead, something unplanned and accidental, is an argument for future memoirists and historians to debate.

the higher it rises in the bureaucracy, the more completely the experts are excluded while the harassed senior generalists take over (that is, the Secretaries, Under Secretaries and Presidential Assistants)." The same ex-official, who has Vietnam decisions in mind, adds that another cause of what he calls "the banishment of expertise" is a desire of top policy makers for "the replacement of the experts, who were generally and increasingly pessimistic, by men described as 'can-do guys,' loyal and energetic fixers unsoured by expertise."[60]

Kennedy and his aides may have actually meant something rather different than the normal sense of the words when they declared that State had failed to "take charge." It seems likely that what troubled the President was not so much State's failure to assert itself as his unhappiness with the tendency of the few department officials whom he consulted to be so "negative" about the active thrust of his foreign policy. In the Hilsman and the Schlesinger view, this lack of energy and activism indicated either bureaucratic incompetence or political conservatism. It is just as possible that some of the diplomatic professionals, true to their tradition, were advising prudence and suggesting, with deference, that the President might be misreading the situation.

Apertura a Sinistra

The Bay of Pigs was followed by other crises—in Laos and Berlin—and other policies—the Alliance for Progress in Latin America and the *apertura a sinistra* in Italy—which made the Kennedy White House unhappy with the State Department and Foreign Service. In every case the President's staff accused the diplomats of insufficient imagination, foot-dragging delays, and reactionary hostility to the aims of the New Frontier. Foreign Service officers, for their part, complained of "interference by amateurs and dilettantes," "excessive zeal," and "press-agentry." Such differences of outlook are built into a government that includes political appointees and careerists. It seems incredible that sophisticated men on both sides should be unaware of the distinction and able only to interpret each others' behavior in simplistic clichés.

The two-year White House battle for more active U.S. support for an "opening to the left" in Italy makes a fascinating case study of this problem. As with Bay of Pigs and, possibly, the 1961 Laos and Berlin crises as well, it seems likely that the White House drew the wrong conclusions about State for the wrong reasons. Schlesinger and another aide, Robert Komer, who later headed the pacification program in Vietnam, championed American support for the idea of a coalition government in Rome composed of two old enemies in Italian politics, the Catholic Christian Democratic party and the left-wing Socialists. Schlesinger believed that such a coalition "might offer a model for other nations—for Germany after Adenauer, for France after De Gaulle, even for Spain after Franco," and President Kennedy is said to have thought that this model would also "be helpful in forming more democratic governments in Latin America." During a meeting in June 1961, the president told Italian Prime Minister Fanfani, who favored the coalition, that Washington would "watch developments with sympathy."[61]

Schlesinger interpreted this as a presidential decision that implied active U.S. encouragement of a change of government in Rome in line with Fanfani's plans. But the State Department and the American embassy in Rome, he has alleged, sabotaged this policy with "stratagems of obstruction and delay" caused partly by State's "chronic difficulty of changing established policies; partly the patriotic conviction on the part of certain Foreign Service officers that they . . . knew better than the White House; partly an innate Foreign Service preference for conservatives over progressives along with a traditional weakness for the Roman aristocracy." One argument used by State against active U.S. espousal of the center-left experiment was that "it was coming anyway and therefore did not require our blessing." Until the first center-left government was finally formed in December 1963, Schlesinger reports, he battled constantly on the President's behalf against the entrenched conservatism of State. "It was an endless struggle. Meetings would be called, decisions reached, cables sent; then the next meeting would begin with the same old arguments. One felt entrapped as in a Kafka novel."[62]

The ambassador to Rome at the time was a career diplomat, Frederick Reinhardt. In an interview, published in 1970, Reinhardt took issue with the Schlesinger account. "What he fails to point out," the Ambassador alleged, "is that this did not really correspond to the official policy of the United States Government, nor does he at any time give any evidence that he had a mandate from the President to be so active in this sector. It was quite apparent that there was a cabal, so to speak, trying to move American policy in this field in a more aggressive and active stance."[63]

One senses that this was a jurisdictional dispute, with two men—Schlesinger and Reinhardt—challenging each other's credentials. The interpretation of motives on each side is probably oversimplified. It seems likely that most of the diplomats, aware of the considerable multiparty and multipersonality complexities of Italian politics, were professionally disinclined to interfere in the internal affairs of a NATO ally. The White House staffers, anxious to promote change in foreign policy consistent with the activist, progressive claims of the New Frontier, chafed at the caution of the professionals. "Why," one imagines them saying to themselves, "doesn't the embassy in Rome *do* something?"

Who was right? The center-left coalition finally came about in December 1963 and it was hardly the millennium. Italy has since had nearly a dozen governments, with mild instability and frequent cabinet paralysis. The Christian Democrats and Socialists have both lost votes in each successive election. Theirs is not a "model" that the rest of Europe has yet adopted, and no such coalition is in power today in Latin America. Center-left coalitions may still have a future on both continents, but they are more likely to occur, if at all, in response to local conditions rather than from any inspiration derived from the Italian example.

To date, the *apertura a sinistra* has been neither a bold success nor a ghastly failure. It probably made little difference whether the United States supported or opposed the move in 1961. Too active support would have provoked cries of outrage from the other Italian political parties and a nationalistic backlash against U.S. "pressure." Too active opposition might have stirred an "equal but opposite" response in Italian politics, which, perversely, could even possibly have increased the chances for an early center-left coalition. A sensible diplomacy would have worked between the margins "too much" and "too little" influence, avoiding interference in the internal politics of an ally, but giving a discreet hint here and there, when it might help, of where the sympathies of the United States lay. Public statements, either from Washington or from the embassy, could have supplemented diplomatic legwork by making known the more general sense of the American position. For all the in-fighting within the U.S. government, there is evidence that this is exactly what occurred.*

The main reason for studying the episode is *not* for its effect on Italian-American relations, which seems slight, but for its effect on the balance of confidence between the Kennedy White House and the State Department. Diplomats confronted presidential aides, Hamiltonians faced Jeffersonians, actors in foreign politics were pitted against men who defined themselves in relation to domestic politics. Of course there was more to it than that; there were at least some policy differences at stake, however minor they may appear in his-

* Ambassador Reinhardt, in a letter to the author on October 19, 1970, confirmed this interpretation and added additional background. According to Reinhardt,

> I was present when President Kennedy made the statement regarding Italy that he would "watch developments with sympathy" and took the words at face value, namely to mean "watch with sympathy" and did not read into them a call to step out and actively agitate on the Italian scene. In a later private conversation the President confirmed to me this interpretation of his intentions.
>
> There was one respect, however, in which we were diplomatically active throughout this period. That was in repeatedly making clear to Nenni and his associates in the leadership of the Socialist Party that the United States could not view with sympathy an Italian coalition in which a major partner pursued an actively anti-NATO policy. The alliance of the Socialists with the Communists had lasted from World War II until the Hungarian events of 1956. Thereafter Nenni gradually pulled his followers away from their intimate relationship with the CPI in the political arena, although no effort was made to effect a parallel separation on the labor front where the Socialists remained linked to the Communists in the CGIL as they do to this day. Nenni succeeded, however, during the last months before the first centro-sinistra government in moving his party away from its traditional anti-NATO and anti-European stand to a more or less neutral stand in these matters.

The Ambassador added,

> Off in Rome I was not aware of the intensity of meetings and debate as described by Schlesinger in his book. Certainly they did not produce many instructions to the Embassy and none which would have called for the kind of action he apparently sought.

toric retrospect. But the main difference, the only way to explain the vehemence of Schlesinger and Reinhardt, was one of White House against State Department perception.

There were other reasons for the failure of the Kennedy effort to strengthen State and the consequent disillusion of the President's advisers with the Foreign Service, reasons that in practical terms may be more important than any others. Even if one could have assumed greater goodwill and understanding all around among men steeped in two quite different traditions of governance, and even had there been no divergence in policy outlooks, much more than a presidential speech and a letter to the ambassadors was needed to revitalize the State Department. Schlesinger is right in asserting that State was unusually weak in 1961. Senator Joseph McCarthy's attacks in the early 1950s had forced a number of the ablest career men to resign. The purge was aided after 1953 by Security Chief Scott McLeod, who took as his personal motto the Elbert Hubbard homily: "An ounce of loyalty is worth more than a pound of brains." And while recruitment from the bottom stopped temporarily, a personnel reform program tripled the size of the Foreign Service by "integrating" 2,500 Civil Service and other-agency newcomers in 1954–1957. If anything, Schlesinger understates the case when he remarks that this "had a disturbing impact" on the Service.

On the heels of these changes, any further tampering with the basic structure of the foreign affairs bureaucracies seemed untimely in 1961. But without a program of structured reform, without cutting State back to a more manageable size, and by deed as well as word transferring to it control over the foreign activities of the military and intelligence agencies, it was not honestly possible for State to "take charge." CIA station chiefs, AID mission directors, and military assistance commanders in the field were able to treat the President's letter to ambassadors as a "scrap of paper." For they retained their independent budgets, having much more money at their disposal than the ambassadors whom they served, who had no right to control how they spent it. And they held on to their independent channels of communication to Washington, which the ambassadors could not monitor. After President Kennedy's famous letter, subsequent "clarifying" messages, most of them classified, went out on the letterheads of the separate agencies addressed to *their* field representatives, listing "exceptions" and revoking much of the purpose of the White House directive. In Washington, more by behavior than by words, the White House, Defense, CIA, Treasury, and all the others soon made clear that they were not about to let a weakened State Department "take charge." The President had spoken, but he had neglected to give State the power and the practical means to carry out his mandate, which left his first words open to the cynical interpretation that they were not really meant to be taken seriously.

Four years after his brother's assassination, and shortly before his own tragic death, Senator Robert Kennedy wrote words that lend themselves to this interpretation. Noting with approval the relative weakness of American ambassadors, he observed, "In some countries of the world, the most powerful single voice is that of the AID administrator, with the ambassador . . . having relatively little power. In some countries that I visited, the dominant U.S. figure was the representative of the CIA; in several of the Latin American countries, it was the head of our military mission."[64] Here, to most career diplomats, is the real failure of organizational insight in the Kennedy period. Through mutual misunderstanding on both sides, this failure has left an unfortunately bitter taste in the mouths of two groups of intelligent and dedicated men—the careerists and the presidential aides. Nearly a decade later this feeling still runs high. Several former Kennedy aides and several career diplomats attended a recent seminar on the subject of diplomatic reform. One of the ablest of the former White House assistants took me aside during a recess in our discussions and gestured toward one of the other participants, a retired career ambassador with a distinguished record, who is known for his caustic criticism of U.S. economic and military intervention in the Third World. "Whatever made you invite that stupid old so-and-so?" my questioner asked.

Mutual disillusion between the Kennedy White House and State Department has had long-term effects, although it did not prevent President Johnson from attempting several somewhat more technical reforms in foreign-affairs structure. It caused many of the natural allies of diplomatic reform to lose faith in the possibilities of the career service. It made the Service turn further inward and the State Department lose more ground in bureaucratic Washington. By 1968 an FSO reform committee concluded that although State remained "eager and willing to take charge of America's foreign affairs," it had now become "not so much a question of grasping a nettle as of trying to mold a marshmallow."[65]

The Hamilton-Jefferson debate is really a never-ending confrontation in American politics. The logic of Jefferson's position should be closely studied, for it continues to have great impact. Is there a case to be made for doing away with a structured professional diplomacy altogether? Or is there a desirable "medium position" like that of Robert Kennedy, who thought it useful to have at least some CIA and AID and military chiefs in the field who were more powerful in their countries than the American ambassador? After all, that is the situation today, so why change it?

Hamilton's response would be that that is a very irresponsible way to manage our national affairs. It gives foreign governments the impression that the United States has not one but many conflicting foreign policies and it allows tools and techniques to predominate over purpose and policy. It promotes uncertainty, incoherence, and unwisdom. A large, fragmented system, a "plurality of the Executive," in Hamilton's phrase, "tends to deprive the people of [their] two greatest securities . . . *first*, the restraints of public opinion, which lose their efficacy . . . on account of the uncertainty on whom it ought to fall; and, *secondly*, the opportunity of discovering with facility and clearness the misconduct of the persons they trust."[66] To weaken the role of the ambassador and the Secretary of State is, in Hamilton's terms, "to trust the great interests of the nation to hands which are disabled from managing them with vigor and success."[67] Considering the question of whether executive departments ought to be headed by one man or by a committee or "board" of men, Hamilton argued convincingly that "a single man in each department . . . would be greatly preferable. It would give us a chance of more knowledge, more activity, more responsibility, and, of course, more zeal and attention. Boards' . . . decisions are slower, their energy less, their responsibility more diffused."[68]

Jefferson would reply that this is all beside the point. A free system with maximum citizen participation requires changes in leadership every four or eight years not only in the presidency but also in every lower office of the executive branch. A permanent bureaucracy loses touch with the popular source of its authority, tends to become a closed administrative caste, and prevents a number of citizens from taking their periodic turn at government service. If this harms our foreign relations and precludes the development of long-range expertise in diplomacy, so be it. Inefficiency is an acceptable price to pay for greater democracy.

Most American bureaucracies are organized along lines of compromise between the Hamiltonian and Jeffersonian principles. Of the 2,800 senior nonclerical positions in the State Department today, approximately 13 percent are held by presidential appointees or by men who owe their appointments to congressional patronage, another 27 percent by specialists of the civil service and short-time temporary appointees, and the final 60 percent by career Foreign Service officers. The political appointees generally hold four of the top five jobs in the department, and about half of the next-echelon positions, assistant secretaryships. With each change of administration, a new Secretary of State and his deputies normally bring in a total of 50 to 100 politically appointed staff members from outside, while congressional patronage accounts for about 250 more jobholders in State. By way of comparison, AID has a much higher ratio of presidential and patronage positions to permanent jobs, whereas CIA is almost exclusively staffed by career men.

At the 117 U.S. embassies abroad, about two-thirds of the ambassadorships are held by career diplomats and one-third by political appointees, but the latter group generally has most of the major embassies. At the beginning of 1970, for example, fifteen noncareer and two career officials filled the seventeen ambassadorships in Western Europe. These ratios have been reasonably constant for the last fifteen years and seem likely to continue, a pragmatic accommodation between the need for skilled permanent officials *à la* Hamilton and the pressure for rotation in office *à la* Jefferson.

The Populist Tradition of Distrust—Jackson to McCarthy

A more extreme form of Jeffersonianism, which Jefferson the Virginia gentleman farmer and believer in a "natural aristocracy of talents" would personally disavow, could tilt the balance. Elements on the right and left fringes of our domestic politics are equally unhappy with bureaucracy in any form, and have a particular animus toward the Department of State. Permanent Washington officials seem wicked enough to the followers of George Wallace as well as to the Weathermen faction of Students for a Democratic Society, but they are doubly wicked when they have dealings with foreigners. Many Americans closer to the political center have similar latent suspicions that occasionally come to the surface, as occurred at the height of Senator Joseph McCarthy's popularity from 1950–1953 and earlier in our history during the presidency of Andrew Jackson and the campaigns of the People's (Populist) party in the 1890s. Taking Jefferson literally and applying his concept of rotation in office to the population at large rather than to a small, talented, and landed minority, the Jacksonians developed a spoils system bureaucracy that in its theory is nearly identical to the administrative format recommended by Lenin in *State and Revolution*. Lenin argued that the tasks of government consist mainly of "simple procedures of accounting and control" that are well within the capacities of the average citizen to perform.[69] In pure Jacksonian, as in pure Leninist theory, service in the bureaucracy becomes a sort of jury duty that all take turns performing.

This, of course, is an idealized version of the two theories. Nothing like "pure" Leninism was ever tried in organizing the

Soviet government. In practice, the Jacksonian spoils system produced such corruption and incompetence that it provoked a mass movement for civil-service reform later in the century. By 1906, during the administration of Theodore Roosevelt, the beginnings of the present career system finally came to the Department of State, which at that time had less than 100 employees. For 130 years, however, the Republic had gotten by—and, some would argue, gotten by very well indeed—without a professional diplomatic service.

Jacksonian and Populist suspiciousness of foreign affairs and of federal officeholders converge on the person of the diplomat, an ideal target. These two traditions are alive and well today, exerting influence on both major parties as well as on public opinion. Just as there is a little bit of Hamilton and a lot of Jefferson in the thinking of most Americans, so too there is a touch of Populist xenophobia and resentment of East Coast "snobs." A gentleman from Jackson, Mississippi, wrote to *Newsweek* during the 1968 election campaign as follows: "We Wallace supporters . . . believe that correcting the faults in this country is not the complicated problem the educators and press would have us believe, but is a simple matter of doing three things: (1) balance the budget; (2) clean up the State Department, which is both Red and homosexually infested, and which influences the starting of Vietnam-type involvements and the policy of fighting with only one hand; (3) give states' rights back to the states."[70]

With a program no more complicated than that, Joseph McCarthy attacked and partly destroyed the State Department twenty years ago, and another demagogue could undoubtedly do it again. When McCarthy called Foreign Service officers "un-American" and falsely accused State of harboring "205 card-carrying Communists," he was in a deeper sense attacking that institution for being a Hamiltonian island in a Jeffersonian sea.

McCarthy was also demonstrating that neither by history nor tradition is America prepared to play a world-power role, and that the frustrations caused by this novel experience can be blamed on the men who represent us overseas. In 1947, three years before McCarthy became a household word, Senator Taft had declared, "Keep America solvent and sensible, and she has nothing to fear from any foreign country."[71] Taft's isolationism was the opposite pole to Woodrow Wilson's universalism, his belief that "American" principles are "not the principles of a province or of a single continent. We have known and boasted all along that they were the principles of a liberated mankind."[72]

But both views are a challenge to the outlook of the professional diplomat, who is bound to see things differently. It is the tendency of his profession to regard the United States as a nation among nations, not as a unique and exemplary "way of life" that exists to transcend vicious and irrelevant foreign traditions. In this sense McCarthy was right in calling diplomats "un-American," for their experience leads them to question the traditional self-image of American politics—the notion that ours is a unique society that the rest of the world should regard as the model for its own aspiring development. Instead, the insights of diplomacy suggest that other states also have a sense of self-esteem and mission, that the self-evident truths of Americans are not always so evident to everyone else, and that diversity rather than uniformity may be the best of all possible worlds. Diplomats, if they are any good at their business, bring a sense of reality about the outside world to the Washington dialogue that challenges the assumptions of much of our domestic rhetoric, and may therefore be considered threatening. "I must confess," writes George Kennan, "that the professional diplomatist is often possessed by a congenital aversion to . . . domestic-political competition." He has "little tolerance for its egotism, its ambition, its thirst for popularity. . . ." He sees relations between governments "as largely the product of the follies and brutalities of that minority of the human race which is always attracted by the possibility of exercising power over the remainder of it," and knows that even with respect to his own government, "the truth about external reality will never be wholly compatible with those internal ideological fictions which the national state engenders and by which it lives."[73]

A persistent criticism of the State Department is that it is not sufficiently attuned to trends in domestic politics. The "weary skepticism," which Kennan believes is the temperamental characteristic of most experienced diplomats, may explain why. In the 1960s congressmen and journalists were fond of pointing out that our diplomacy was out of touch with home opinion. Some of the critics said that State should forge alliances with domestic interest groups and engage more consciously in the rough and tumble of congressional politics in order to be an effective presidential agent in foreign affairs. In partial response, the Foreign Service, beginning in the Kennedy years, has tried to project a more folksy image. Career officers have been exhorted in exactly these words, to "discover grass-roots America." FSOs at every level are encouraged to speak on behalf of administration policy around the country, and families returning from overseas are importuned to spend their home leave on travels through the hinterlands in department-supplied housetrailers. This is mostly public-relations posturing, but it does not really touch the more serious question: What is the proper role of a foreign office in home politics?

There is no simple answer. Until recently, however, it has

been the prevailing view that the President and his appointees should "take the heat" from the domestic front, and that it is improper for their permanent, nonpartisan staffs to do so. President Truman went so far as to tell his diplomats not to give him assessments based on domestic political factors, a subject on which *he*, not *they*, was the expert. Kennan, an exponent of this classically nonpartisan view of the diplomatic career, was reproached in January 1948 by a Washington journalist for failing to lobby with Congress for the Marshall Plan legislation. Kennan replied:

> I pointed out that personally I had entered a profession which I thought had to do with the representation of U.S. interests vis-à-vis foreign governments; that this was what I had been trained for and what I was prepared to do to the best of my ability; and that I had never understood that part of my profession was to represent the U.S. government vis-à-vis Congress; that my specialty was the defense of U.S. interests against others, not against our own representatives; that I resented the State Department being put in the position of lobbyists before Congress in favor of the U.S. people; that I felt that Congress had a responsibility no less than that of ourselves toward the people; that we were not their keepers or their mentors; that it was up to them to inform themselves just as it is up to us to inform ourselves. . . .[74]

This is not to say that the nonpartisan public servant need or can be blind to domestic politics. He is, after all, a taxpayer and elector himself, and his work at home and abroad requires dealings with countless fellow-citizens having interests in foreign affairs. But for FSOs to become "front men" for the President before Congress and the American public, or to solicit private citizen group participation in the government's work, may compromise their most crucial functions: to be effective government-to-government intermediaries, perceptive observers of foreign politics, and unbiased advisers to the Secretary of State and the President.

The kind of expertise accumulated by diplomats tends to make them more sensitive than any other institutional group to the complexity and diversity of foreign relations, and more inclined to be "anti-evangelist" in their approach to meeting foreign problems. This kind of skepticism can be a valuable thing to have around; kill it, and you kill an intellectual restraint on rash action abroad that may be lacking in other parts of the executive branch. The costs of keeping and nurturing this kind of professional diplomacy may be politically high; they may even, at times, seem "un-American." Before directing the permanent part of his State Department to play more of a domestic political game, however, a president must recognize that this would require fundamental redefinition of the role of the institution. The debate, once more, pits Hamilton against Jefferson. It will never be resolved to the complete satisfaction of either.

4

THE JOHNSON YEARS

> I don't care what the Russians think about *Hello, Dolly!* And neither should you.
> —Dean Acheson to Lyndon Baines Johnson

Dean Acheson was called to the White House a short time after President Kennedy's death for his first foreign policy consultation with the new commander in chief. As Acheson tells the story,* he found Lyndon Johnson furious, pacing up and down behind his desk. What angered the President was that the Soviet government had just cancelled permission for an American theatrical troupe to perform *Hello, Dolly!* in Moscow. The show's leading lady was a close friend of the Johnsons.

As the President explained these facts to the former Secretary of State, an aide dashed into the office with a late bulletin on the "crisis": the "damn State Department," he reported, advised against any retaliation to the Russian affront. Johnson turned to his guest and asked what to do. Acheson replied that such a minor issue was not worth the time and attention

* This account, related to the author during a private interview in May 1970, appears with Mr. Acheson's permission.

of the President of the United States. Surely the President had serious questions to discuss with him. The cancellation of a Broadway stage show was not such a question. "I don't care what the Russians think about *Hello, Dolly!*," Acheson recalls saying: "And neither should you."

Acheson does not say how the meeting ended, but there is a sequel remembered by many others. President Johnson redirected the stranded players to Saigon, where they duly performed for American troops in Vietnam. That way he "showed the Russians."

The LBJ style had little in common with the traditional methods of an effective diplomacy. Like FDR, Johnson personalized foreign policy, distrusted professional advice, and seemed honestly to believe that high-flown rhetoric was a decent substitute for cool-headed calculation of the nation's interests. In Washington in 1965–1966, one felt that the President had come close to developing an emotional ailment about alleged "leaks" to the press. When the *Wall Street Journal* published speculation that the United States might bomb oil depots near Hanoi, Johnson, who had already ordered such an attack, cancelled it and launched an investigation of the bureaucracy to determine the source of the "leak." In a pattern that had been repeated before and would be repeated again, FBI agents descended on the State Department to interview all officials who were privy to the secret information.

Although the investigators never reached a conclusion, they did succeed in demoralizing the bureaucracy, making honest dissent within the system seem that much more dangerous. The President never understood that whatever "leaks" occurred were more the result of probing by an intelligent Washington press corps, able to put two and two together, than from deliberate sabotage within the government. It was not the career men at State, but the President himself and his own political appointees who in "off-the-record" conversations with newsmen provided most of the information that later distressed LBJ when he saw it in print.

Johnson's Vietnam public relations extravaganzas often seemed more designed to impress domestic opinion than to accomplish foreign policy results. The President himself may not have been aware of the difference. His Christmas "Peace Offensive" of 1965–1966 sent high-level American envoys circling the globe during a thirty-seven-day bombing halt of North Vietnam. It was typical Johnson razzle-dazzle, high on visibility and short on substance. Averell Harriman went to Warsaw, Belgrade, Karachi, and New Delhi; Arthur Goldberg met with the Pope in Rome; Mennen Williams was sent to Africa and Thomas Mann to Latin America; Vice-President Humphrey and McGeorge Bundy covered points between. Every American ambassador at each of more than 100 countries was instructed to have an "urgent" meeting with the highest foreign official available. Called "Operation PINTA" (after the caravel in Columbus' fleet that first sighted land in the New World), the effort produced reams of newspaper copy and diplomatic cables but no negotiations with Hanoi. Peking's New China News Agency summed up the U.S. diplomatic spectacle in a dispatch that began: "Certain monsters and freaks are scurrying hither and thither. . . ." Those who sat in the State Department reading the cables and plotting the progress of the special envoys wondered if Peking was far wrong.

There were other hastily contrived "spectaculars," most of them with more of an image-building than a problem-solving purpose. Johnson's Honolulu meeting with Prime Minister Ky and President Thieu, in February 1966, his Manila conference with Asian allies seven months later (just before the congressional elections), and his globe-trotting visit to Cam-Ranh Bay in December 1967 capped with a surprise, last-minute stopoff in Rome to see Pope Paul on Christmas Eve were all arranged more to disarm domestic critics than to solve the problems of Southeast Asia. In the fading, lame-duck days of December 1968, it took massive argumentation from every presidential adviser to dissuade Johnson from pushing for a pointless summit meeting with the Russians.

Foreign relations were continually cheapened for what might bring a short-term domestic gain. Allies in Europe and Asia and even Latin America were constantly dunned for "contributions" to the American effort in Vietnam. The arm-twisting had little effect, other than to strain relationships with friends. The White House released lists alleging that more than forty nations were "aiding" South Vietnam. The "aid" included humanitarian Red Cross relief, routine commercial credits for exports, and a German hospital ship wrung out of Chancellor Erhard, who was also asked to pay lip service to the concept of a global Great Society while visiting the President. Ambassadors and their career staff officers winced at each new request for a worldwide *démarche* to solicit ungettable support from friendly and neutral leaders, but faithfully carried out the President's instructions. Meanwhile, the foreign-aid program was celebrated as a global war on poverty that in a short time could be expected to eradicate disease, illiteracy, and the other age-old problems of mankind. It was all so unbelievable that it seemed to suggest hypocrisy on the part of the U.S. government. Greater cynicism about American aims was the logical outcome.

It was possible at the time to think that President Johnson was perfectly sincere, that he really believed he was playing the role of heroic war leader in the mold of FDR. He played the role badly and was finally hissed from the stage. But his problem was more than one of image. The FDR and even the Kennedy conception of world affairs was not adequate to the time. The organization of the government machine, instead of helping Johnson overcome his own limitations of outlook, fed them further. His deep suspiciousness about the motives of the men beneath him would have made it difficult, at best, for honest advice and disagreement to get to him through the bureaucracy. Some did, but his personality and the structure he inherited did not make it easy. As Acheson later wrote, "The administrative tasks of the great departments of government are beyond the capacity of even the president's large personal staff to assume. To attempt to do so impairs both the broad direction of national affairs and the specific administration of particular parts of the whole."[75]

A journalist who knew him described LBJ near the end of his power as "this strange, proud, cruel, sentimental, insecure, naïve, and bitterly driven man."[76] Whatever his idiosyncrasies, Johnson did sponsor several technical reforms in the structure of government. Picking up where Kennedy had left off in 1961, these unsuccessful efforts bore more the imprint of Johnson's advisers than of the President himself. Still, they deserve attention. For something can be learned from their mistakes, and if it is not learned clearly, misunderstandings will get in the way of enlightenment in the 1970s.

Program Budgeting

The first of the Johnson reforms was program budgeting, which derived from the management methods brought to Washington in 1961 by Robert McNamara. With the use of systems analysis and the installation of a Planning-Programming-Budgeting-System (PPBS), McNamara and his civilian assistants in the Defense Department, Charles Hitch and Alain Enthoven, were able to choose more efficiently, they believed, among competing weapons systems. Quantifying and comparing all data, and then analyzing them more systematically than before, gave the decision maker more objective information about the relative costs and benefits of different kinds of military technology. This helped him to make a more "cost-effective" choice among many alternatives. The same techniques that had worked in choosing weapons and allocating defense funds more rationally might have wider application in other fields as well, such as urban planning and economic development programs, and even foreign policy. The fact that the defense budget nearly doubled during McNamara's seven years, going from $44 billion up to about $80 billion, that political crises such as the 1962 Skybolt affair with Britain were a high cost to pay for cost effectiveness, and that the evolution of the Vietnam war and false predictions about its progress have been blamed on faulty Pentagon quantifications have not deterred the optimists.

If program budgeting really worked that well, if all the variables could be quantified, and if the human judgments of relative value involved were accurate, then in its ideal application to foreign affairs such a system would tell at a glance whether you got more for your money in Malaysia with a military-aid program, a USIA propaganda effort, CIA "penetration" of the local labor unions, or some combination of all. Applied more broadly (again in pure theory), it might suggest whether to spend less on peace talks in Paris and more on B-52 raids in the central Highlands, or the reverse, and what the proper "mix" of these disparate "programs" should be on the basis of estimated costs and benefits. At heart this is a utilitarian calculus in the tradition of Jeremy Bentham's attempt 150 years earlier to determine "the greatest good of the greatest number."

In practice as opposed to theory, program budgeting may be a Frankenstein monster. For in dealings with the outside world, many elements of a foreign policy—and perhaps its most important ones—cannot be quantified at all. To pretend that they can be, or to quantify only some of them and dismiss the rest as "subjective and therefore not useful," is to produce the grossest distortion in the name of science. There seems a built-in bias toward action, intervention, and expenditure of money and resources in PPBS approaches to foreign affairs. To talk about program budgeting presupposes that one wishes to pursue costly physical "programs" on the territories of other nations rather than, for example, just leaving other nations alone, that is, having no "programs" at all. Admiral Hyman Rickover, a crusty critic of the systems approach, has gone so far as to charge that it is an excuse for inefficiency, a tool to routinize decision making when organization has become so large and unwieldy and staff so mediocre, that able leadership is stretched thin and simpler ways of doing things have been forgotten.

Yet there are still those who believe the State Department needs a "McNamara Revolution." The Foreign Service in the early 1970s is just beginning to see in its middle ranks officials who as younger men were indoctrinated in the new activism of the Kennedy foreign policy and the new diplomacy of the Herter Report of 1962. Counterinsurgency programs, frowned on by State as a strange innovation in 1961, are beginning to win bureaucratic popularity ten years later, just at the time when experience has discredited them. Bureaucratic time lag expresses itself in other ways as well. When President Nixon wants negotiators (whom nobody thought of training ten years ago when the fashion was all for fighting wars of national liberation), he is getting instead a surplus supply of propagandists, agronomists, and returned Peace Corps volunteers.

In fairness, one important idea has come from the program budgeters, a simple idea whose virtue appeals to good sense unaided by systems analysis. It is the notion that Washington should have a single budget for foreign affairs, combining money now scattered among fifty different departments and agencies into one pot. Although the Defense Department controls a single military budget, there is no equivalent unified foreign-policy budget in the executive branch. Budget Director Charles Schultze estimated in 1967 that an annual budget including the costs of all U.S. overseas programs, but excluding the CIA and the cost of maintaining 1.2 million U.S. troops abroad, would come to about $5.6 billion, a figure 15 times greater than the State Department budget taken alone.[77] Schultze suggested that if a single budget for foreign affairs is ever developed, it should be divided into 120 "country budgets" as the basic constituent units, each unit representing the cost of all U.S. activities in the 120 countries of the world.

It would take a bloody political fight involving major power shifts in Washington to achieve such a budget. As another budgeteer, Thomas Schelling, has observed, "What would be revolutionary is that somebody or some agency has to do this, and it has to be decided who or which agency would do it."[78] No agency likes to have its money controlled by others. Despite periodic bromides about "strengthening" the Department of State, clearly no President and no Congress is yet prepared to let it control or even review the foreign affairs appropriations requests of Defense, AID, Agriculture, Commerce, Labor, CIA, and USIA. Conversely, *until* State obtains some control over the money spent abroad by the entire executive branch, it is hardly reasonable to expect a Secretary of State to "take charge" of foreign policy, for he lacks the means to do so. Meanwhile Washington drifts along with no one central authority to manage the expenditure of foreign-affairs funds, and hence with no comparison, for example, of how what CIA spends in Mauritania compares with what USIA spends in the same country for some common (or conflicting) purpose.

The advocates of PPBS have argued that their techniques can solve this problem. Professional diplomats are not so sure, for the very words "program budgeting" have never been carefully defined, and in practice they have earned the reputation of being tools of American intervention, especially in Vietnam. One student of PPBS, Aaron Wildavsky, has noted that "there is no agreement on what the words mean" and that PPBS in practice can be "tremendously inefficient," since "it resembles nothing so much as a Rube Goldberg apparatus in which the operations performed bear little relation to the output achieved."[79]

President Johnson announced the goal of a government-wide PPBS in August 1965. Henceforth the new technique being used in the Pentagon was to be extended to the other executive departments. In drawing up its annual budget, each agency was to present "program memoranda" to the Budget Bureau showing, in quantitative terms wherever possible, the required "inputs" and expected "outputs" of its programs and policies, and using comparative analysis to prove why each recommended program was more efficient than the possible alternative courses. The State Department, and most domestic agencies as well, were simply unable to accomplish this goal, and by 1968 PPBS was for most practical purposes dead and forgotten. Some remnants lived on, but the enthusiasm of the mid-1960s had been lost.

The program budgeting enthusiasts blamed incompetence and conservatism by Foreign Service officers for the failure of PPBS to "revolutionize" State, using the same arguments that Kennedy White House staffers had earlier found to explain the failure of their own reforms of the earlier 1960s. This missed the point, but it had the satisfying simplicity of making PPBS advocates the heroes and FSOs the villains in a modern melodrama. John Harr and Frederick Mosher, two of the program budgeting reformers, have written a book about their blighted effort, complaining that it "had all the elements of a Greek tragedy."[80]

Mosher and Harr were staff members of the 1962 Herter Committee, devoutly devoted to the concept of a "new diplomacy." Their main supporters in an effort to reorganize State were management specialists and academic social scientists. Walt W. Rostow and General Maxwell Taylor held high places in their pantheon as men who sought to change the traditional State Department system. Their chief bureaucratic ally was William Crockett, a man who was brought laterally into the Foreign Service during the Wriston program of the 1950s and, according to Harr, "moved to the top on the strength of a charismatic personality, native political acumen, strong commitment to improving the State Department, and a reputation as a positive, innovative administrator" as well as "because of his ability to get along well with the two most important men on Capitol Hill as far as the Department of State is concerned,"[81] Congressmen Wayne Hayes of Ohio and John Rooney of New York. Crockett was deputy under secretary for Administration—the number-five job in State—from 1963 to 1967, when he resigned to take a job in private industry. Other top officers of State did not have a high regard for Crockett's abilities, but thought him a maneuverer who owed his sudden rise more to the assiduous cultivation of

Congressman Rooney than to any personal strength of character or intellect.

The failure of the program budgeters was more a result of the weakness of their own concepts than of the temperamental opposition of FSOs. Men such as Harr and Mosher, who had a number of useful ideas to offer but no broad familiarity with foreign policy or the diplomatic traditions they sought to change, made the mistake of tying themselves to a military-ideological conception of world affairs. They were essentially technocrats. Modern management, social science, and military technology, the perceptions of a McNamara, a Rostow, and a Taylor were to be applied wholesale to an "anachronistic" tradition of interstate relations. Instead of slimming down an inefficient bureaucracy, their goal was to expand its size, make its structure more complex, and make its functions more mechanistic.

Mosher and Harr, working with Crockett, helped direct the first experiments to apply program budgeting to foreign policy in 1963 and 1964. Thirty U.S. embassies were visited by management teams who attempted to develop a "Comprehensive-Country-Programming-System" (CCPS). Their approach was to examine and compare the budgets of the various elements of the embassies (CIA, of course, always excluded) and to perform the equivalent of time and motion studies on embassy personnel. In Bonn, for example, in 1964, the researchers interviewed Foreign Service officers, asking them: "How much time do you spend writing reports? Attending debates in the *Bundestag*? Taking German politicians out to lunch? Thinking?"

What hampered and will always hamper research of this kind is that *no one knows* how to measure the most important thing in diplomacy: good political judgment. There are no right answers about how to divide up the time representing one's nation, and the processes of political influence and negotiation vary from country to country, from culture to culture, and from diplomat to diplomat. Since things such as these cannot be measured, the researcher either assigns them an arbitrary value or forgets about them. This is not hard to do, since expenditure of funds for traditional diplomatic work at any embassy is a small fraction of the total cost of running the embassy. Thus CCPS investigators found that most of the money and most of the time spent at our diplomatic missions is in nondiplomatic work, for only 7 or 8 percent of the total American staff at embassies are Foreign Service officers. The bulk of the budget is allotted for administration and staff support, military programs, cultural and commercial exhibits, intelligence, and economic aid. These physical operations lend themselves much more readily to a calculation of cost (although not of worth) in dollars and cents than do the less tangible tasks of foreign policy that the physical programs only exist to support. The main "product" of diplomacy is written and oral communication designed to build confidence and rapport with foreign governments and to advise one's own government; and, stated simply, the only major outlays for this are the salaries of diplomats, the maintenance of their offices, and the monthly cable and telephone bills.

The CCPS analysts hoped that their studies would reveal ways for a more rational allocation of diplomatic resources. They expected to work wonders for the State Department in the same way that McNamara's systems analysts were thought to have worked wonders for the Defense Department's weapons-development program. Since the researchers were management specialists, not students of politics, they were inclined to discount the fuzzy, indeterminate diplomatic side of embassy work and focus on the more "meaningful" and costly and measurable physical programs. Being "program-oriented" in this case meant believing that that which can be measured is of much greater importance than that which cannot be measured. Millions of dollars spent for defense and intelligence and propaganda and foreign aid were significant "inputs," whereas the piddling thousands spent for diplomacy were necessarily small potatoes.

As applied to foreign policy, the program-budgeting approach seemed to contain unexamined biases that were both conservative and activist at the same time. They were conservative in the sense that their frame of reference tied them to an accidental, irrational bureaucratic status quo that they were not able to see as accidental and irrational. They were activist in that it was in the nature of their technique to be impressed with large numbers of personnel and amounts of money, which are the hallmarks of active programs pursued by Defense, AID, and CIA. Negotiation, judgment, modesty, and insight into foreign cultures, these and the other staples of a peacetime foreign policy have little to do with large outlays of resources. They do not impinge on the world of the PPBS technician, or if they do, they are likely to be dismissed as unscientifically "intuitive," useless, and old-fashioned.

Several other tendencies of the programming technique seem to pull in an interventionist direction and away from any sense of critical detachment toward existing policy. Programmers believe in a controlled environment; indeed it is the purpose of their craft to enhance such control. But there may be many foreign environments that the United States has no business, capacity, or interest in controlling. The programmer may, if anything, increase the American bureaucrat's inability to tolerate deterioration in control over situations abroad, even where U.S. interests in such control are clearly small. Even central budgeting within the U.S. government, which makes good sense, may have curiously distorting effects on the policy process unless the job is done with political sophistication. Consider the possibilities: 120 country budgets, supported by 120 statements of policy might be annually written (and then cleared with some 10 major and 40 minor agencies of the executive branch) for each of 120 nations; if what is involved is just an endless series of committee meetings, each agency haggling on the basis of an increase from last year's budget, one has wasted the time of countless people without really changing a thing—the present system, for all its faults, would accomplish as much. The result could easily be a tidy elaboration of the absurd: 120 compartmentalized foreign policies, multiplied by 10 and multiplied again by 40. The frozen assumptions of yesteryear and last year's budget have thus been uncritically accepted and even sanctified by the use of an impressive new technique, while bureaucratic focus is narrowed further.

This is a fair description of most of the "programming" efforts in the State Department to date. When Walt W. Rostow became the chairman of State's Policy Planning Council in 1962, he attempted to codify foreign policy by writing a series of "National Policy Papers." These were, in Harr's words, to "include a study in depth of a given foreign country's situation, and the situation of the United States vis-à-vis the country, in all of the key sectors—political, economic, social-cultural, security and so on." The papers "would conclude with long-range objectives, short-range objectives, and specific courses of action."[82] These were to be updated from time to time, like military contingency plans, and under the later PPBS concept they would be the basic, secret data to support specific budget requests. If the Rostow effort had been taken seriously (which it was not), the time of the bureaucracy would have been devoted in large part to the continual writing, negotiating, and rewriting of these "plans." To practitioners of diplomacy and to congressional politicians who debate it in public, nothing could seem more ridiculous. Although State should be expected to have a number of plans and much information at its fingertips, and the President from time to time should lay out in as much detail as possible the guidelines of his foreign policy, to spend most of the government's time on planning is to escape reality.

Compiling lists for the sake of compiling lists increases the already sufficiently sluggish, change-resistant character of the bureaucracy. Throughout the programming process, as it was conceived in the 1960s, there was an unstated assumption favoring quantity over quality, a faith that every problem would yield if attacked with sufficient energy, and a belief that there could and should be an American position and an American solution for each intractable foreign problem that was catalogued. As so many well-programmed activities in Vietnam have shown, this bred a false and dangerous optimism. In the real world as opposed to the programming world, conflict exists and will continue to exist. Most problems are not solved or soluble by Washington, and the best position for the United States on at least some issues is to have no position at all. In theory program budgeting made a certain sense, but in practice it was either unworkable or, where it "worked," contributed to disaster.

Johnson's Senior Interdepartmental Group (SIG)

A second Johnson reform was related to this first one. It was, on the surface, a structural change consistent with PPBS, and also an attempt to put in the State Department some of the large (though weak) coordinating and planning committees that existed in the 1950s as adjuncts to the Eisenhower National Security Council, but had been abolished in 1961. On March 4, 1966, President Johnson created a Senior Interdepartmental Group (SIG), which, less than three years later, was abolished in the first days of the Nixon presidency. Despite the fact that the SIG was announced with fanfare as a major innovation in Washington decision making, it was never taken seriously. Today, most of its functions are supposedly performed within the White House, if they are performed at all.

When creating the SIG, President Johnson directed Secretary Rusk "to assume responsibility to the full extent permitted by law for the over-all direction, coordination and supervision of interdepartmental activities of the U.S. government overseas (less exempted military activities)." It was announced that "up to now, the Secretary of State . . . has performed a coordinating function in interdepartmental matters abroad. Now he has received formal and specific over-all directive authority from the President." In a significant aside, the announcement went on to say that "the term 'interdepartmental matters' has not been specifically defined." (It never was.) To assist the Secretary in this "new role," his Under Secretary was made executive chairman of the SIG, which had six other regular members: the deputy secretary of defense, the administrator of AID, the director of CIA, the Chairman of the Joint Chiefs of Staff, the director of USIA, and the national security assistant to the President. Other agencies could be represented on particular matters affecting them. In practice, this meant that the Under Secretaries of Treasury and Agriculture and, sometimes, Commerce, were extra members of the SIG. At the same time, the regional assistant secretaries of state were asked to chair "Interdepartmental Regional Groups" ("IRGs") having a similar representation at a lower level. The new position of "country director" was created in State to replace and upgrade the country "desk officer" who had previously been the lowest working-level official of the department. A country director was to "serve as the single focus of responsibility for leadership and coordination [for] . . . activities concerning his country or countries" and assure "that the Ambassador's needs are served both within the Department and government-wide."[83]

General Maxwell Taylor, who authored the SIG concept, explained its historical genesis in a speech on March 31, 1966, entitled "New System For Coping With Our Overseas Problems."[84] It had been the Bay of Pigs, Taylor noted, that revealed "organizational deficiencies in Washington" that were now, five years later, being corrected. The SIG was an outgrowth of the Special Group—Counterinsurgency, an interagency body formed in January 1962 to "assure the unity of effort and use of all resources required to prevent and resist subversive insurgency" and to "assure recognition through the entire Federal government that subversive insurgency or the 'War of Liberation' is a major form of political-military conflict equal in importance to conventional warfare." After four years of counterinsurgency, General Taylor had concluded that "any organization adequate to meet the requirements of anticipating subversive insurgency must observe and evaluate continuously the conditions in some 90 countries of the world."

Thus, by a circuitous route, Taylor arrived at the idea of the SIG, for, he remarked, "At this point, one begins to question the wisdom of setting up a special organization study of two-thirds of the population of the world and of ignoring the remainder. Should we not recognize that the basic organizational requirement is really crisis anticipation and crisis management wherever found?"

At President Johnson's request in August 1965, when Taylor returned from a two-year stint as ambassador to Saigon, he began to consider the options. He was "surprised," he said, "when I started inquiring into the overseas authority of the Secretary of State to find how little specific authority he had for the management of interdepartmental business." Next he looked at the National Security Council and found that it "has not adequately fulfilled the original intent," had "the inherent weakness of being too big" and was not worth an overhaul. Taylor then considered "the creation of some new organization under the White House reaching out into all the countries where we have missions abroad," but concluded that such a new entity was neither desirable nor practical. (That, at least, was Taylor's *public* conclusion. Privately, former associates say, Taylor argued for putting the SIG in the White House—and lost the argument.) In the end, he decided that the only place left to look for foreign affairs leadership was the Secretary of State and his department.

Hence, the SIG idea. All of the agencies participating in the Senior Group and the five Regional Groups below would consider together overseas problems that were "interdepartmental in nature" and then reach a decision, with the executive chairman, State's number-two man, having ultimate power to outvote them all. If other members objected to the State Department's decision, then the executive chairman could tell them, in Taylor's words, " 'Boys, this is the way it is going to be unless you utilize your right of appeal.' In the latter case, any member can appeal the issue to the next higher authority," namely to the Secretary of State and then to the President.

Toward the end of his speech explaining the SIG, Taylor assessed the significance of the new body as follows: "Uncle Sam can no longer afford to be a one-eyed Cyclops able to focus attention in only one direction but must have an Argus-eyed capacity to survey the entire international scene. I believe that this organization we have discussed will contribute to that capacity for vigilance."

Considering the counterinsurgency background of the SIG, the curious thing is that it never dealt with Vietnam or any other policy issue of the first order at all. During its brief three-year history it deliberated upon such third-order problems as the size of the U.S. military-aid program to the Congo, the question of Export-Import Bank credits for a harbor improvement project on the island of Antigua, and the feasibility of an American proposal to the North Atlantic Council concerning a reorganization of NATO headquarters military staffs. Even on these lesser issues, it was unusual for a firm decision to be reached, transmitted to the Secretary of State and the President, and acted upon. Some SIG decisions were overturned by the simple expedient of a phone call from Secretary McNamara to Secretary Rusk. A year after SIG was created, two Washington reporters, Edward Weintal and Charles Bartlett, examined the new system and found it useless. It had not "dealt with world-shaking events," they noted, and decisions reached on low-level matters would have been "the same if SIG had not existed." If good relations exist between the

State and Defense Departments, Weintal and Bartlett concluded, "there is really no significant need for SIG or any other organization to arbitrate their views." On the other hand, "when there are high-level antagonisms, . . . no coordinating machinery short of the President himself is likely to resolve the dispute."[85]

If the SIG had any merit, it may have consisted in what one participant has called "getting better exposure to the other fellow's point of view," although one would think there were less formal, time-consuming ways of doing that at the top levels of government. At any rate, the SIG's lack of success may be one reason among many why the Nixon administration ended the façade and centered its own interdepartmental committee network within the White House. Two further facts contributed to the SIG's demise:

1. Making the Under Secretary rather than the Secretary of State the SIG Chairman automatically communicated to the rest of Washington that this was not *really* a major decision-making body. No Secretary of State would normally delegate major policy decisions any more than a President would delegate parts of his constitutional authority to his Vice-President; to do so would be an inconceivable abdication of his own responsibility. Once it became clear that most SIG decisions could be effectively appealed over the head of the executive chairman, the group lost much of its stated *raison d'être.*

2. The SIG was a kind of window-dressing designed to obscure the President's wish for no major changes in policy. President Johnson and his chief advisers were spending most of their time on Vietnam when the SIG was created, and it seems to have been their partial intention to assure by means of the new body that non-Southeast Asian problems be at-

tended to in a more systematic way at a high level. Indeed, the White House announcement of March 4, 1966, promised that the SIG would "assure that no sector of the foreign front is neglected at a time of preoccupation with some overriding problem."

One senses that the President expected from the SIG an effort to reduce the heat on him from other parts of the world, while at the same time *not* wanting the new body to complicate matters by proposing significant policy changes. As has been true before and since of well-publicized changes in the machinery of foreign policy, the announcement of the SIG was designed to give the public a reassuring impression of change, movement, and novelty while masking an intention that there be no change in policy and no rocking of the presidential boat. Coordination by the SIG involved no shift in the power relationships of competing bureaucracies and no structural changes in control over money and manpower in the executive branch, although the public announcements at the time stressed that the Secretary of State somehow was being strengthened and given a "new role." What Kennedy claimed to be doing in 1961, Johnson repeated in 1966, and the reasons for both failures were basically the same.

Growth of the White House Staff

Two related developments of the 1960s were the growth and institutional elaboration of a presidential White House staff for foreign affairs and the emergence of arguments for more specialized "super staffs" to surround key policy makers and, in a sense, protect them from their own bureaucracies. One reason for the first development is that a weak State Department had been slow to respond to presidential direction and unable to control or give coherence to the action of the many "little State Departments" in separate agencies. Kennedy and Johnson were both either unable to strengthen State or unwilling to do so, depending upon one's interpretation. Both moved in the end to build more competent and numerous personal White House staffs to fill the vacuum. The logical outcome is the Nixon national security staff in today's White House, which in 1970 included about twenty Foreign-Service officers on loan from the State Department and another eighty to ninety clerical workers, presidential aides, and personnel from the military and intelligence agencies.

The ten-year trend from McGeorge Bundy to Walt W. Rostow to Henry Kissinger may eventually lead to a new foreign ministry in the Executive Office Building and the White House basement. An institutional President's Office of National Security Affairs, which might employ hundreds and eventually thousands of men, could in the future emerge as a surrogate State Department designed to provide that centralizing force now lacking in a fragmented Washington. It is too early to know whether this will happen, although it seems to be the current trend.

Most informed opinion up to now has not been in favor of creating yet another layer of super bureaucracy. Men as different as Robert Lovett and Richard Neustadt at the Jackson Subcommittee hearings nearly a decade ago warned that a full-blown foreign ministry attached to the President's staff would isolate the chief executive from dialogue with the great departments of government, cause him to waste his time and engage his prestige in the nuts and bolts of foreign policy, and increase the slow and slothful elaboration of work with a concomitant lowering of responsibility throughout the system by the added layer of a new agency and even more coordinating committees. Dean Acheson has written more recently that the White House staff system of the 1960s "diluted and weakened" the Johnson presidency, and that such an apparatus "limits, by narrowing, the President's attention to a few subjects that he allows to absorb him."[86] White House staffers, unlike cabinet heads, are immune from questioning by Congress and their appointments are not subject to Senate confirmation, as is true of the Secretary of State, his assistants, and ambassadors.

These facts offer no guarantee, however, against the further growth of a more institutional White House staff. Countervailing reasons may seem more compelling to a president. If the existing departments are not competent to carry out his policies, or are giving him bad counsel, his defensive instinct may well be to insulate himself from such incompetence by building new protective devices. If the idea of a White House Office of National Security Affairs commends itself, it does so essentially for negative reasons. It may seem easier to add a layer next to the President than to take on the awesome task of shaking down the entire inherited bureaucracy. The paradox is that a new, centralized foreign office in the White House might easily prove to be of diminishing usefulness to the President, for the whole point of having a personal staff up to now has been its compact size and informal character, permitting a degree of access, flexibility, speed, and responsiveness to the chief executive that is less possible in the remote and swollen cabinet departments. There is also the chance of increased rigidity, a more Washington-centered view of the world, and greater political misjudgment or misinformation about foreign events implicit in isolating a President even more than he is already isolated from diplomatic expertise.

As the White House staff grew in the 1960s, administrative theorists offered new arguments for protecting key policy makers by giving each of them larger and more multicompetent personal staffs. A study by the Institute for Defense Analyses, completed in 1968 and published in 1969, recommended that the Secretary of State and each of his regional assistant secretaries have a "strengthened functional tier" of staff support. Two or three new deputies would appear at the top levels of State, while lower down there would be new staffs for "program review and coordination."[87] The study stressed the need of the President and his chief advisers for more checks and balances on information and analysis they receive on foreign problems. Consistent with this view, White House staffers throughout the decade have sought means of prying loose more "uncleared" papers and recommendations from the bureaucracy, for the words "interagency clearance" have become a badge of incompetence and irrelevance.

This fact is itself a comment on how the bureaucracy has failed to perform in the 1960s. There is the danger, however, that dissatisfaction may breed cynicism. What could be more cynical than to assume that the policy maker must accept his institutions as a "given" that he cannot fundamentally change, but must somehow manage to evade? Precisely that assumption is made by many students of government today. Accepting the postwar process of bureaucratic growth as irreversible, although it is only fifteen to twenty years old, this view suggests that modern executives must build up larger personal secretariats to give them extra eyes and ears to monitor squabbling subordinates, enforce decisions down the line, and offer alternative insights not otherwise available from the lower working level.

Behavioral social science carries this reasoning a step further, suggesting that modern bureaucracy inculcates in its members certain fixed behavior patterns that are nonrational and liable to undercut the public purposes of government. The best that a Yale social psychologist who studied the State Department in 1965 could suggest was that its employees strive to alter their "living system" by engaging in frequent, confessional group therapy sessions to "change their behavior and attitudes" and "shed the social, normal, everyday defenses and masks."[88] The psychologist, Chris Argyris, was hired by Willim Crockett to study "motivation, inter-personal communications and attitude change" in the Foreign Service. He concluded, not surprisingly, that there was considerable conformism and "minimal interpersonal openness" in the Service. Argyris and other students describe the diplomatic subordinate as anxious to "play it safe" with his boss and to defend particularized rather than general interests. The typical bureaucrat, like any organization man, is said to be more concerned with the kind of rug that adorns the floor of his office, the proximity of his next promotion, and emulation of his peers than with giving honest advice or suggesting rational or especially "innovative" lines of action. One possible conclusion: upgraded personal staffs would avoid these pitfalls out of a sense of contradictory selflessness and self-interest—loyalty and proximity to high policy makers, breadth of perspective, greater commitment to "rationality," and freedom from lower level bureaucratic pressures. This "super-staff" idea rests on psychological premises about the nature of modern bureaucracies. The problem, it seems to say, is one of incompetence or excessive narrowness at the working level, and the cure is to filter out these qualities with the help of expert staffs at the top, lest the policy maker become a prisoner of his department.

The idea of creating such super-staffs raises a number of problems. First, the proposal points to an even larger, more layered State Department. If the 336 staff members and office help serving State's top four men, and that 10 percent of each lower bureau's manpower that serves the office of every assistant secretary is not large enough or skilled enough to do the job, what can be expected of yet more specialist staff? Second, if the working-level offices are indeed as unreliable and incompetent as the argument suggests, why not tackle the problem right there by replacing unsatisfactory personnel, cutting down on overstaffing, and reposing more authority in leaner, fitter offices manned by more carefully selected subordinates. Third, as General Marshall remarked of his military experience, a large, institutionalized personal staff tends to become a protective buffer that shields the decision maker from reality and from a more normal and creative relationship with line subordinates. In other words, new staffs will probably slow rather than streamline action, while lowering the sense of responsibility down the line. They add a step to the policy process and interpose an extra barrier between the man who must decide and the men who have expertise to advise him. In some ways this is just what happened in the Johnson White House: the President insisted on surrounding himself with military, economic, and "pacification" experts, while keeping diplomatic line officers with Southeast Asian experience at greater distance. When one considers the 1960s, perhaps there was greater incompetence and less political sophistication at the *top* rather than at the lower levels of government. It is easy for Kennedy and Johnson White House staffers to blame the shortcomings of their bosses' policies on bureaucratic incompetence and opposition, but that lets the two Presidents and their staffs off much too lightly. It can at least be argued that the main errors of judgment in foreign policy in the past decade emanated from the White House itself.

This observation, whether or not one accepts it, raises a question of continuing importance in the 1970s: what conclusions for the machinery of foreign affairs will be drawn from the experience of Vietnam? There may be no simple answer, but the question is implicit in most proposals for organizational change. Certainly those who argue for more checks and balances in the form of better high-level technical staffing have at the back of their minds the impression that recent presidents were not getting a full enough range of information and analysis. This is probably fallacious. There was no "fact gap" about Vietnam. "Facts" such as the "weapons-loss-ratio," the body count, the rate of infiltration, the progress of pacification—military and intelligence numbers games—were, if anything, overemphasized. The failures were failures of political insight. Presidents Kennedy and Johnson received much conflicting analysis and advice from their subordinates, although Johnson did not often solicit dissenting opinions. Both were exposed to more rather than less raw information and technical planning data than were necessary for them to frame their decisions.

If the idea of institutionalizing more checks and balances in the President's and Secretary of State's staffs is a reaction to what are perceived as mistakes about Vietnam, then what is really involved is a contradiction in terms, an attempt to institutionalize dissent or at least to assure that a diversity of views is heard. Such an approach seems beside the point, for a diversity of views *was* available and *was* heard by anyone who cared to listen. The Under Secretary of State, George Ball, opposed intervention in Vietnam with vigor and with more than a dozen private memoranda to Presidents Kennedy and Johnson spanning the years 1961 to 1966. Other advisers finally convinced Johnson to order the bombing halt of March 31, 1968. A more valid complaint about Johnson's method of decision is that he did not encourage dissenters in his administration for fear of damage to his position in domestic politics, and that he insisted on limiting discussion of each new step to a small, closed circle of confidants. All too often Johnson and his aides excluded from their circle those few men beneath them in the government who had a solid background of experience in Asian politics (though, in fairness, such men were few and far between; the "China Hands" had nearly all been purged in the 1950s). It is hard to see how a different machinery consisting of bigger, more competitive staffs would have altered the significant presidential decisions of the last decade.

What might have made a difference—although the question is hypothetical—is a much stronger, more self-confident Foreign Service. But Kennedy in 1961 did not inherit such a service. He inherited instead, in the wake of the demoralizing shakeups of the 1950s, a "bowl of jelly," a relatively confused and disorganized diplomatic arm, schooled in caution and shorn of expertise, particularly in the East Asia field. Whatever the outcome of the Indochina conflict, the crucial issues would seem to depend more on a knowledge of the history and psychology of Vietnamese nationalism than on unilateral American "problem-solving" exercises in economic and military technology. This is another way of asserting the primacy of politics and the relevance of history in foreign affairs decision making, two modes of thought that normally find their strongest institutional expression in a country's permanent foreign office. If the foreign office is weak, as weak as the American State Department of the 1960s, then this perspective will tend to be lost.

FDR's Influence

No comment on Washington decision making in the 1960s would be complete without mentioning Richard Neustadt's influential interpretation of the presidency. *Presidential Power,* published in 1960, was a tract for the times, an argument for a return to the virtues of FDR's strong presidency and a criticism of the weaker leadership of the Eisenhower administration. The book influenced Kennedy, Johnson, and most of their advisers. It popularized the notion that a strong President will always "keep his options open," and, like Roosevelt (Lyndon Johnson's model and hero), "keep his organizations overlapping and divide authority among them," putting "men of clashing temperaments, outlooks, ideas in charge of them."[89] Neustadt's advice was simple and Machiavellian: distrust your subordinates, keep them guessing, foster competition among them. He quoted Arthur Schlesinger's study of FDR with approval:

> Roosevelt's persistent effort . . . was to check and balance information acquired through official channels. . . . His favorite technique was to keep grants of authority incomplete, jurisdictions uncertain, charters overlapping. The result of this competitive theory of administration was often confusion and exasperation on the operating level; but no other method could so reliably insure that in a large bureaucracy filled with ambitious men eager for power, the decisions, and the power to make them, would remain with the President.[90]

Against this model of the "good" FDR presidency, Neustadt contrasted the Eisenhower White House system, with its "superficial symmetry," "straight lines and boxes on the organizational charts," and "inter-agency committees and paperflows."

The FDR "divide and rule" method of controlling the bureaucracy may be in need of reinterpretation, especially as it affects foreign policy. Roosevelt created big government as we know it today, raising the Federal budget over twelve years of the New Deal and World War II from $4.6 billion to $96 billion, increasing government civilian employment more than tenfold, creating the foundations of our defense and foreign affairs complex, and spawning for the emergency of war our first economic aid, propaganda, and intelligence agencies. Much of America's political establishment in the postwar years had gone to school with Roosevelt, learning what they knew of managing government from the techniques and examples of the FDR presidency. But elevating Roosevelt's leadership techniques into a general theory of "the Good Presidency" makes little sense, for FDR bequeathed an ambiguous legacy in foreign relations. He concentrated on military strategy to the detriment of political decisions about the future shape of Europe in World War II, went to Casablanca, Teheran, and Yalta without senior diplomatic advisers, and ignored his foreign office in making wartime policy decisions. The Truman administration was forced to pick up the pieces in an unforesighted vacuum. Dean Acheson has written:

> President Roosevelt has been praised for a supposedly deliberate secrecy in consultation and vagueness in decision that left policy fluid, relationships uncertain, and great freedom of maneuver for the President. In the currently fashionable phrase, his constant

purpose was "to keep his options open." Flexibility in maneuver may be highly desirable in certain circumstances, but when it leaves one's own and friendly forces and commanders uncertain of the nature and purpose of the operation or of who has responsibility for what, it can be a handicap.[91]

In light of subsequent history, the Roosevelt presidency falls short of the ideal model for foreign affairs administration. Certainly the variant practiced by Lyndon Johnson was not a happy one. There is no inherent reason why one must fragment authority, confuse jurisdictional lines, and keep one's options open vis-à-vis subordinates to be a strong and wise ruler. Neither is it necessary for a president to accept the size and shape of the bureaucracy he inherits as irreversible. Beyond a certain point it may get too big and too dispersed for any President to manage, whatever the vagaries of personality and staff methods. A series of new and more competitive super staffs, call them secretariats or what you will, would institutionalize more bigness and dispersal without attacking the root problem. At its simplest, such an approach tells a president: "Accept the bureaucracy as a mess. It is too damnably difficult to cut it down, so one must try to control and get around it somehow."

As Acheson has suggested, that is neither the only nor the best solution. Reducing size and simplifying structure may make it easier to manage a bureaucracy. Taking the opposite road is in the end to pursue irrationality, to embrace what might be called the Franz Kafka Model of Self-Sustaining Government.

Reducing Personnel—BALPA and OPRED

Another line of attack was suggested by the Jackson Senate Subcommittee on National Policy Machinery, which reached this conclusion in 1961: "*There is serious over-staffing in the national security departments and agencies* . . . our government faces the problem that people are engaged in work that does not really need doing. The size of the national security departments and agencies has swelled out of proportion even to the increased number and complexity of our problems. . . . Unnecessary people make for unnecessary layering, unnecessary clearances and concurrences, and unnecessary intrusions on the time of officials working on problems of real importance."[92]

The Senate investigators saw that rising American involvements since World War II had made the bureaucracy grow on an expanding curve. The growth had been taken for granted, though most of it was never rationally planned. One way to make institutions more responsible and comprehensible, the Jackson Committee seemed to say, was to make them *smaller*, and one way to change policies was to redefine functions.

Nothing like this occurred in the 1960s, but at the end of the decade there were several modest personnel reduction programs in foreign affairs. During the last two years of the Johnson administration, the President, in a program called BALPA, ordered a 10 percent reduction in overseas civilian employment (exempting Vietnam and the Peace Corps) to obtain small balance-of-payments savings. In 1967 and 1968, 452 American State Department employees were brought home, and 567 foreign workers at our embassies were fired, for a net estimated savings of $7.8 million. A Nixon administration overseas reduction program, entitled OPRED (for Operations Reduction) eliminated 5,100 overseas civilian jobs, including 540 State Department positions, 530 in AID, 140 in USIA, and about 3,600 in Defense in 1969 and 1970.

These two programs revealed new difficulties in the bureaucracy, showing just how tenuous are the powers of a President and his Secretary of State. For in the final analysis, State and the White House had no pruning weapon other than the crude and arbitrary across-the-board percentage cut. To decide where the personnel cuts were made and how they were carried out, in the end they had to rely on the "voluntary self-regulation" of each affected department of government.

The BALPA cuts of 1967–1968, phased over a two-year period, required a lengthy process of "consultations" among all foreign affairs agencies, ambassadors, and field directors. State's fifth-ranking official, with a special working group under him, asked each ambassador to recommend which jobs at his embassy should be eliminated. Ambassadors called in their subordinates and tried to apportion cuts of 10 percent among all the separate agencies—State, USIA, AID, and so forth. Many an ambassador pleaded for "exceptions," arguing that a cut of staff at his particular post would endanger necessary work and operations, and was hence intolerable. The same complaint was heard from nearly every agency—which led to continued negotiations among CIA, Commerce, Defense, and all the other departments to try to exempt *their* staff from the cuts.

At the same time Washington's pressure for field reductions had an educational effect. It was learned that there were a good many discrepancies in the personnel records—that the figures available in Washington failed to tally with the actual numbers of employees abroad, or even with Washington's functional descriptions of their jobs. Some ambassadors, presented for the first time with the need to know how many intelligence officers were attached to their embassies, were surprised at the magnitude.

After painstaking work, with continual consultations, debates, "appeals," and complaints throughout the executive branch—and lengthy cables from ambassadors (and their AID mission directors, CIA station chiefs, military attachés, and USIA directors), along with visits to and from Washington, the modest cuts were made over a staggered two-year period. The next step was to bring home those personnel whose positions had been cut and fit them into vacant "slots" in Washington or elsewhere. That, too, was accomplished, further swelling the size of official Washington.

To the participants in the work of BALPA, the modest results hardly seemed worth the intensive effort expended and the unceasing debates and attempts to find loopholes. The results also showed what normally happens with "across-the-board" percentage reductions, namely that rank and seniority have their privileges, and that low-ranking personnel are generally the most vulnerable to having their jobs abolished.

The OPRED reductions attempted to learn something from BALPA, although a good many of the same agency antagonisms were again aroused by cutting up the pie once more. This time the cuts were supervised by an Under Secretaries' Committee of the National Security Council. Within each agency, task forces prepared recommendations for their Under Secretaries. Instead of asking ambassadors to suggest what cuts to make, Washington "recommended" its own cuts to the field, based on its own data. Then the haggling among agencies and between the field and Washington began. Several lessons have been learned from the complications of the effort. They may be summarized as follows:

1. Washington's capacity for administrative analysis of what we do abroad and how we do it is very weak; the expansion in size of bureaucracies and the fragmentation of tasks among different agencies in the last twenty-five years have left in their wake vast intellectual confusion about what takes precedence over what; this has led to the administrative presumption that "all programs are equal" and the practical conclusion that he who shouts loudest and longest gets what he wants.

2. Faced with the threat of staff cuts, each separate agency and some ambassadors, AID directors, and CIA station chiefs, will fight tenaciously to retain as many subordinates as possible.

3. As administered in the 1967–1969 period, job cuts assure —other things being equal—not the survival of the fittest, but the survival of the most senior.

4. The President, the Secretary of State, and the National Security Council are not equipped and do not have time to enforce the practical details of job reduction; but below them there is no central authority to carry this out and monitor the results over the long term; they must rely on the voluntary self-regulation of all agencies concerned.

5. When the cuts are only in overseas jobs, then the incumbents whose positions are eliminated will have to be accommodated in Washington; the effect of this will be to make the Washington staffs of foreign affairs agencies even more overcrowded.

6. Cuts in foreign programs make it increasingly apparent that the larger problem is in Washington itself, not abroad;

if there is no central administrative machinery in Washington, then there is finally no way of enforcing and policing reductions over time; since the Secretary of State is not in fact what he is in law—the officer, under the President "responsible for the over-all direction, coordination and supervision of U.S. activities overseas," he cannot as a practical matter confer full authority on ambassadors to control the non-State agencies in the field; endless appeals and evasions are inevitable; field cuts logically point toward even greater cuts in Washington, and a clarification of foreign affairs authority within the executive branch.

7. When every agency takes the same percentage cut, this only perpetuates existent patterns in the name of interagency harmony, turning a blind eye to the fact that some agencies are notoriously more overstaffed than others; the fact that the President and Secretary of State must fall back on this device is tacit recognition on their part of the difficulty of the process and of their relative impotence vis-à-vis the entrenched positions of the separate foreign affairs bureaucracies.

At the end of the Johnson years, as at the beginning, one conclusion was inescapable: there was not yet any central locus of authority in the fragmented executive branch competent to propose and carry out large-scale personnel reductions in the interest of greater efficiency at home and improved relations with foreign states abroad. While the war in Vietnam raged, technical reforms such as program budgeting and the Senior Interdepartmental Group dealt with side issues in foreign policy. Poorly conceived and imperfectly administered, the Johnson changes were not lasting. They continued the unbroken tradition of 1947, focusing on military and ideological aspects of world affairs to the detriment of politics and diplomacy.

5

THE DISORGANIZATION OF STATE

> I don't feel I have an action group at my command as they do in other departments. . . .
> —Secretary of State William P. Rogers

Secretary of State William Rogers, several months into his new job in 1969, confessed to newsmen: "I don't feel I have an action group at my command as they do in other departments. Sometimes I have a feeling things aren't going to get done."[93] His complaint was hardly new. What is remarkable is that recent Secretaries of State have not realized that the size of their staffs, the confusing structure of their department, and inattention on their own part are the heart of the difficulty.

Perhaps this charge is less than fair to the present Secretary, for he is presiding over a reform program of sorts. On July 21, 1970, the *New York Times* reported that officials of State, "concerned by what they consider to be its declining role in foreign affairs," had made "468 recommendations to strengthen the department." Five months later, on December 8,

1970, the list had grown to 508 and was published in a compendious 600-page document entitled *Diplomacy for the '70s.* This document was drawn up by 13 Task Forces employing 250 personnel, who had been ordered to study flaws in the system. One of the Task Forces devoted itself to "openness in the foreign affairs community," another to "the role and function of diplomatic missions," and yet another to "stimulation of creativity."

In a way, the present reform movement is an attempt to pick up where President Kennedy left off in 1961 and President Johnson gave up in 1966. Yet the recommendations—whether there be 468 or 508 of them—seem to offer little more promise than the blighted efforts of the Kennedy and Johnson administrations. None of the new reforms deal with the size of the machine (except to promise "modest additions to existing staff") or change its fundamental structure. Most of them concern the personnel system of the State Department, without touching on the powerful influence of the military and intelligence bureaucracies. Task Force proposals for a "systematic definition of what U.S. interests are in various areas of the world" seem to involve nothing more than a rededication to the ill-starred program-budgeting techniques of the Johnson years.

Task Force Reform Proposals

The motive behind this latest reform wave is decent enough. It all started with a Young Turk movement of Foreign Service officers, which was formed in 1967 to agitate within the system. The dissidents were bureaucrats in their thirties and forties, later joined by men in their fifties (which shows how "youth" is defined in the State Department lexicon). The Turks, young and old, won control of their company union, the American Foreign Service Association (AFSA), in the fading days of the Johnson administration. They published articles and manifestoes suggesting that General Maxwell Taylor's Senior Interdepartmental Group be strengthened, that a career man be appointed to the new permanent position of "Executive Under Secretary of State," and that younger men be given more interesting and responsible jobs. But the timing, even for such small changes, was premature. Overwhelmed with Vietnam fatigue and seven consecutive years in office, Secretary Dean Rusk was bored with organizational questions. "Change" had a subversive sound in the Washington of 1967 and 1968, for it automatically brought to mind the loud, dissenting voices of the administration's political opponents.

A new presidency in 1969 responded more readily to the reformers. The Nixon administration, after careful study, came to accept much of the Young Turk program as its own, and the dissident minority is now a bureaucratic majority. The champion of the newest reform effort is William Macomber, Secretary Rogers' fourth-ranking deputy, who gave a speech on January 14, 1970, proposing "not . . . revolution, but the acceleration of an evolution which has already begun." Macomber acknowledged that State has begun to "lose control of the action" to "new instrumentalities such as USIA, Foreign Aid, and CIA." It should, he felt, "gear up to meet the requirements of a modern diplomacy" by starting to "manage and orchestrate the over-all spectrum of our nation's activities abroad." To do this, it would need to generate reform from within, overcoming "the instinct of the traditional foreign policy establishment . . . to protect its exclusiveness and high standards."[94]

Macomber offered a few proposals of his own and then appointed the thirteen Task Forces to study the matter further. His "Program for the Seventies" is essentially designed to do for State what Robert McNamara did for the Pentagon ten years before, bringing business management techniques to bear on foreign policy. More specialists and "a pool of managers for program direction positions" will be recruited to replace diplomatic generalists, and a new entrance examination will "emphasize aptitude over specific academic knowledge." In other words, the selection test for new officers will be made a good deal easier to pass.

True to their mandate, the thirteen Task Force reports have proposed changes in accord with the Macomber speech. Although they are short on original prescription, several of the reports are eloquent in describing what is wrong with the present system. Consider these indictments (from the "Task Force on Creativity," the most lucidly written of the bureaucratic studies):

1. [During the past twenty years] most of the Department's time was devoted to applying the principles of the late '40s in an increasingly rigid way to international conditions that were constantly changing. The intellectual atrophy of the Department during the '50s was a compound of presidential dissatisfaction, political reaction, Departmental conservatism, bureaucratic proliferation, and the inability or unwillingness of individual Secretaries of State to lead and stimulate the organization. Its creative arteries hardening, the Department as an institution was unable to meet adequately and in some cases even to recognize the innovative demands of the early '60s.

2. The Task Force was forced to the conclusion that conformity

is prized in the Foreign Service above all other qualities. . . . [There are] pressures to avoid rocking the boat, to avoid dress and behavior which depart from the norms of the group, to avoid the expression of controversial views . . .

3. It is extremely doubtful that the Department and the Foreign Service will be able to go on attracting or holding the best young people if they do not succeed in establishing a climate more conducive to creative thinking.

4. . . . we found disturbing evidence that the expression of controversial views can still lead to investigation by the security service and that awareness of this can inhibit freedom of expression.

Another Task Force concluded: "Our first and most basic recommendation is that the Department take the lead in developing an explicit and comprehensive list of the interests the United States seeks to preserve or advance." To do this, "Country plans are the starting point; these should be expanded into regional plans, and finally into a global plan. . . . The same kind of systematic attention . . . should apply to the formulation of strategies for dealing with the Congress and the Public."

The planning mania of the 1960s, with all of its "papers" and "strategies," seems likely to be repeated again, and the cynical notion that nonpartisan State Department officers need to concoct special "strategies for dealing with Congress and the Public" has apparently taken root. Still, some of the recommendations make good sense, and it is impressive that this is a reform-from-within movement, something very nearly unique in bureaucratic history if one excludes Peking's self-critical Cultural Revolution.

Shorn of trivia (and there is much of it in the reform report: recommendations for the inclusion of pet animals in the baggage weight-allowance of diplomatic travelers, and for "legislation to give kindergarten educational allowances" to diplomats' children), the 600 pages of *Diplomacy for the '70s* consist of a series of hortatory appeals for "a new spirit" in American diplomacy. It is time, the authors say, "to shake off old habits, old ways of doing things, old ways of dealing with each other. What we are proposing is a change of outlook and method." This is all very elevating, and no doubt even useful; the trouble is, the new outlook and method are described in only the vaguest way. What do recommendations for "a more dynamic and aggressive style" and for "increasingly close and effective coordination" really mean? One is not sure that the would-be reformers have any idea.

One is even less sure when, all too rarely, *Diplomacy for the '70s* gets down to specifics. The goal, it declares, is to build "a corps of diplomat-managers" who will apply "modern management principles" to their craft, downplay "the traditional mode of reflection and detachment cultivated by diplomats" and turn the State Department into a series of "Strategic Management Centers." How will this new corps of management specialists be recruited? By "more extensive use of lateral-entry, . . . a greatly increased level of temporary exchange of personnel with other government agencies and with the business, professional and academic communities," and by less of a search for young "generalist" college-graduates and more room for "somewhat older recruits in their late twenties and thirties" who would not be subjected to the "academic hurdle" of a tough entrance exam but would instead be tested for "aptitude." The new diplomats would receive "semiautomatic promotions" up to the senior ranks of diplomacy without having to face "the present highly competitive promotion system."

What would the diplomat-managers do? They would work

within a "policy analysis and resource allocation system" which "would permit systematic country-by-country and function-by-function analysis of U.S. interests and the way in which these interests might be affected by events over a period two to four years ahead." How does one go about arriving at this systematic definition of U.S. interests? Consult authoritative documents, say the reformers:

"For most of the American people, an accurate characterization of their interests could probably be encompassed by the phrase: 'life, liberty, and the pursuit of happiness'. . . . . Internationally, they could be summed up in the subtitle of the President's recent report to the Congress: 'A New Strategy for Peace.' "

The prose gets muddier and muddier as one reads along. What the reformers clearly want to stress is change and novelty, a new style for themselves and a new effectiveness for their organization. How to change the system they are unhappy with, however, escapes them. All they can come up with are high-sounding, but mostly meaningless or self-contradictory slogans, a rhetorical rehash of the Kennedy and Johnson reform programs.

They do not get to the bottom of the problem, or even close to it, because they do not touch structure and size. They fail to redefine State's relationship to the White House, the Pentagon, and the CIA. They speak broadly of "management," without ever defining the word, but not at all of diplomacy. Ten years too late they praise counterinsurgency and program budgeting.

The reformers might have done a better job if they had paid more attention to a speech given in the State Department by John Kenneth Galbraith on October 24, 1969.[95] Galbraith urged that reform begin with an awareness of changes in foreign policy. Few Americans, he noted, still retain the "illusion" that their country has "a massive capacity to affect the destinies of other countries and a desperately urgent need to do so." To cherish that illusion means to carry on in the 1970s outworn bureaucratic functions born in the 1940s:

> If it is supposed that we have a powerful influence over events in Burma or Brazil or Sumatra, then it follows that we must be meticulously informed on all that goes on in these countries. And we must have the necessary numbers of men who are prepared to act on that information. We must know of the latest developments in the Shan states, and the subversive influences operating among the tribal Indians on the upper Amazon, and the designs of saboteurs against the oil pipelines in Indonesia. And we must have men who can defend against these disasters.

Surely by now, Galbraith continued, we have "discovered that the need to influence these countries is far less than we imagined." We now know that the economic development of the poor countries will be "very slow," that most of the CIA's "detection and prevention of communism, in countries where we can do nothing about it—and where it wouldn't greatly matter if we could—may well be the greatest make-work activity since WPA." We must bring our foreign operations "back into accord with the modern reality," lest much of our diplomatic establishment become "a bloated, unnecessary, and redundant bureaucracy," which "employs itself only in the wrong things."

Like so many intelligent critics before him, Galbraith was arguing for changes in structure and cutbacks in size and function for the whole machine, with particular attention to military and intelligence operations. The trouble with most of the critics, and with State's own reformers-from-within, is that they have not bothered to look closely at the institutions they would change, to learn where and why the cuts must come. Above all, they have not paid attention to the history of the problem, to the twenty-year story of how the bureaucracies have strayed from their original purposes.

Postwar Decline of the State Department

Three men have contributed heavily to the postwar decline of the State Department: Franklin Roosevelt, Senator Joseph McCarthy, and Henry Wriston. FDR, like many politicians and much of the American public, regarded the diplomatic service as a playground for dilettantes and socialites. He distrusted Foreign Service officers, referring to them sarcastically as the profession of perfection. In a memorandum to Cordell Hull he remarked of career men, "You can get to be a Minister if (a) you are loyal to the service, (b) you do nothing to offend people, (c) if you are not intoxicated at public functions."[96] During World War II Roosevelt turned almost entirely to his military commanders and a few close political advisers for diplomatic advice, virtually ignoring the State Department. FSOs were drafted into the armed services, and there was no new recruitment of diplomats in the years 1940–1945.

Still, the career service had a brief flowering during the Truman years of 1947–1950. Men who had entered the new profession in the 1920s, many of them Russian specialists such as George Kennan and Charles Bohlen, were used by two strong Secretaries of State, George Marshall and Dean Acheson. They shaped and carried out the 1947 revolution in foreign policy, when America broke with 150 years of isolation to rebuild a shattered Europe and to check expanding Russian power. Other members of the Rogers Act generation of the 1920s—Llewellyn Thompson, Robert Murphy, Foy Kohler—served alongside Bohlen and Kennan as skillful negotiators and advisers to every postwar president well into the 1960s. Diplomats do not make good culture heroes, and none of the five names mentioned above are exactly household words. But each of them has made a contribution to the solution of tough international problems and to a wiser understanding by our Presidents of the nature of power and the imperatives of peace. Except for Murphy, who nearly resigned at the time of the Berlin Blockade of 1948 because he favored sending a tank column up the *Autobahn* rather than the less risky airlift, most of these men have usually been a restraining influence on their bosses. That, after all, is the diplomatic tradition.

Kennan, a drafter of the Marshall Plan, insisted that its benefits be offered equally to Eastern as well as Western Europe and argued that the "sweeping nature" of the Truman Doctrine offered much too open-ended a commitment. Favoring a political settlement rather than a division of Europe into blocs, Kennan later argued unsuccessfully against the rearmament of Germany and the conclusion of a tight NATO military alliance. The containment of Soviet power that he forcefully advocated as wartime chargé d'affaires in Moscow and later in Washington was to be accomplished by political means, for, as Kennan wrote, ". . . ugly as was the problem of Soviet power, war was not inevitable, nor was it a suitable answer . . . there was a middle ground of political resistance on which we could stand with reasonable prospect of success."[97] Thompson, today an adviser at the strategic arms talks with the Soviets, helped negotiate the Russian withdrawal from Austria in 1955 after having guided, along with his senior, Robert Murphy, the Italian-Yugoslav settlement over Trieste in 1952–1954. Kohler, Thompson, Bohlen, and Kennan each served as ambassador to Moscow in the 1950s and 1960s and as high officers of the State Department while on home assignment. Most of these men, and many of their peers in the career service, had deep reservations about the wisdom of the Southeast Asian commitments of the Kennedy and Johnson administrations, but few of them were consulted about Vietnam by American policy makers of the 1960s and none of them were part of the inner circle of presidential decision making.

The McCarthy Era

Attacked in 1953 by Senator Joseph McCarthy, Bohlen survived a close Senate confirmation vote and stayed in the Foreign Service when a number of his colleagues under greater pressure, including Bohlen's brother-in-law, Charles Thayer, were resigning. Kennan, who had incurred the displeasure of John Foster Dulles, was "retired" from the Service in the same year at the height of his career at age forty-eight. Although McCarthy could not substantiate his public charges, made first in 1950, that the State Department was "thoroughly infested with Communists," he succeeded in ruining professional careers, destroying public confidence in State, and killing Foreign Service morale. He offered a simple theory to explain the "loss" of China and the frustrations of the Korean War, and millions believed him. As late as January 1954, the Gallup Poll reported a 50 percent "favorable" response to McCarthy, while 21 percent had "no opinion."[98]

The Truman administration, McCarthy said, was guilty of "stupidity at the top—treason just below." The State Department was full of "the bright young men who are born with silver spoons in their mouths" who were trying to "diminish the United States in world affairs, to weaken us militarily, to confuse our spirit with talk of surrender in the Far East and to impair our will to resist evil."[99] Former Secretary of State George Marshall, McCarthy alleged, was "A man steeped in falsehood . . . always and invariably serving the world policy of the Kremlin."[100] Democratic presidential candidate Adlai Stevenson was "an out-and-out pro-Communist." During the 1952 campaign McCarthy promised, "If you will get me a slippery elm club and put me aboard Adlai Stevenson's campaign train, I will use it on some of his advisers, and perhaps I can make a good American of him."[101] The domestic hysteria was spread in the columns of major newspapers as well. The *Chicago Tribune* called Secretary of State Acheson "another striped-pants snob" who "ignores the people of Asia and betrays true Americanism to serve as a lackey of Wall Street bankers, British lords, and Communistic radicals from New York."[102] Senator Butler of Nebraska declaimed against Acheson, "I look at that fellow, I watch his smart-aleck manner and his British clothes and that New Dealism . . . and I want to shout, Get out, Get out. You stand for everything that has been wrong with the United States for years."[103] After the Republicans came to power in 1953, Vice-President Richard Nixon announced, "We're kicking the Communists and fellow travelers and security risks out of the government . . . by the thousands." The new security chief of the State Department, Scott McLeod, cautioned, "Not *all* New Dealers are necessarily security risks."[104] Richard Rovere has reported that "when it came to appointing ambassadors and hiring and firing Department officers," Secretary Dulles first "cleared everything with McLeod, who cleared everything with McCarthy."[105]

John Paton Davies, Jr., one of the Foreign Service's foremost Asian experts who was fired after being attacked by McCarthy, wrote of the effects ten years later, "The violence and subtlety of the purge and intimidation left the Foreign Service demoralized and intellectually cowed. With some doughty exceptions, it became a body of conformists. . . . and many cautious mediocrities rose to the top of the Service."[106] The China specialists were particularly hard hit, with the result that by 1961, when Vietnam came to a boil, the State Department lacked a cadre of senior men having East Asian experience. The few left behind had no desire to share the fate of their discredited brethren: McCarthyism had made honesty and brilliance akin to bureaucratic recklessness. A White House staffer of the 1960s has written that "the American government was sorely *lacking in real Vietnam or Indochina expertise*" in the Kennedy years, and that "career officers in the Department, and especially those in the field, had not forgotten the fate of their World War II colleagues who wrote in frankness from China and were later pilloried by Senate committees for critical comments on the Chinese Nationalists. Candid reporting on the strengths of the Viet Cong and the weaknesses of the Diem government was inhibited by the memory."[107]

The McCarthy purge cut down some of the ablest men of the Rogers Act generation, America's first generation of career Foreign Service officers. It occurred at a time when newer

Washington agencies in the foreign affairs field, including the integrated Defense Department and CIA, unscathed by McCarthy, were just three to five years old and beginning to flex their independent muscles. Just as damaging as the dismissals and resignations of experienced officers, the purge spread fear throughout the bureaucracy. Recruitment into the Foreign Service stopped from 1951 to 1954, and special "security teams" were sent from Washington to overseas diplomatic posts to review the records of all personnel. A bad word from a neighbor or colleague, a record of political activism in college, a former teacher, friend, or acquaintance of "left-wing" views, even a well-stocked library of political philosophy were enough to make a man a potential "security risk." FSOs waited in Washington for months, sometimes for more than a year, to learn the outcome of their security clearance investigations before they were permitted to travel to assignments abroad. A new generation of diplomats was taught the virtue of caution and conformity.

The Wriston Committee

On the heels of the McCarthy purge came the Wriston flood. Henry Wriston, the president of Brown University, headed a reform panel in 1954 to recommend ways to reorganize State and restore its flagging morale. Without mentioning McCarthy by name, the Wriston report noted wryly, "For a variety of reasons, which need no elaboration, public confidence in the State Department was shaken in recent years."[108] Given just two months to propose sweeping changes, the Wriston Committee took a meat-axe to the personnel system of the

Foreign Service. Its intentions were benign, but its effects unsettling. To "democratize" the Service and end rank distinctions between Washington civil servants and overseas employees, the Wriston Committee believed that a "direct infusion of needed talents from outside, especially in the middle and upper officer grades,"[109] was required, and that the two distinct groups should be integrated into a single, larger Foreign Service. The "single service" had been proposed five years before by the Hoover Commission, but had not yet been acted upon. Now action occurred with a vengeance, with new employees from the State Department's civil service and other government agencies brought into the Foreign Service at middle grades without competitive examination at the bottom. By 1957, when the program ended, the Service had tripled in size.

Like FDR before him, Wriston believed that the Foreign Service needed to be "Americanized" lest it become an out-of-touch expatriate elite. The Committee thought it "unfortunate" that "the Foreign Service is in effect in a condition of exile abroad," and concluded, "it has been a serious mistake to keep so much of the Foreign Service orbiting overseas so long."[110] There were also complaints about an overly narrow geographic spread among FSO candidates. In the 1920s about half of all new recruits to the Service came from Ivy League colleges, in the forties and fifties the figure was closer to one third, and since Wriston's reforms it has fallen to below one quarter.* Measured by place of birth and educa-

* Prior to 1925, 64 percent of all American diplomats had attended Harvard, Yale, or Princeton. By 1936–1939, these three schools were providing 26 percent of new recruits into the Foreign Service, a figure which fell to 15 percent for the years 1957–1962 and 9 percent in 1969–1970. Of the 103 new Foreign Service officers in 1969–1970, 24 of them attended Ivy League schools as undergraduates.

tion, the Foreign Service continues to be heavily overrepresented by East and West coasters, who in 1964 made up 75 percent of the FSO corps, and to be underrepresented by Midwesterners and Southerners.[111]

Broadening the base of national recruitment was a reasonable reform, but the Wriston influx of 2500 outside bureaucrats at middle ranks over a two-year period, coming shortly after the havoc of McCarthyism, spread chaos and uncertainty. It also destroyed one of State's most useful assets—a permanent, Washington-based staff of civil servants. Civil-service employees were importuned to "integrate" and take foreign posts lest they lose the better salaries, ranks, and pension rights that could be obtained only in the Foreign Service. It is not hard to see why Dean Acheson, a man who doesn't mince words, thought the Wriston reforms "contemptible."[112]

In addition to favoring much greater "lateral entry" into the Foreign Service by men and women from other government agencies and occupations, the Wriston Committee recommended the annual recruitment of 500 new officers at the bottom. The former policy was pursued in the late 1950s and the early 1960s, but the latter was not. Today only 100 to 150 new men and women come in annually at the bottom, and the highest annual intake—in 1965—was only about 250. Over Wriston's strenuous personal objection, State Department administrators further lowered entrance standards in 1956 by dropping the requirement that all new recruits have a speaking knowledge of at least one foreign language before being hired.

The long-term effects of "Wristonization" have created a curious generation gap in our professional diplomacy. In 1954, only about 400 officers out of a total Foreign Service of 1200 had entered the profession prior to 1945. In the Wriston service of 3600 officers, the few prewar first-generation American diplomats were thoroughly swamped by newcomers. Since most recruitment in the 1950s was via lateral entry of middle-aged men, and since promotions were many and retirements few in the 1960s, today's Foreign Service is seriously "overage." There are many more men over forty-five than under thirty-five in the Service today, and two times *more* officers in the top four than in the bottom four ranks, rather like an army with more colonels than captains. (See Figure 1, Tables 3 and 4.)

Responding to the inverted pyramid, most State Department and embassy jobs have had to be reclassified an average

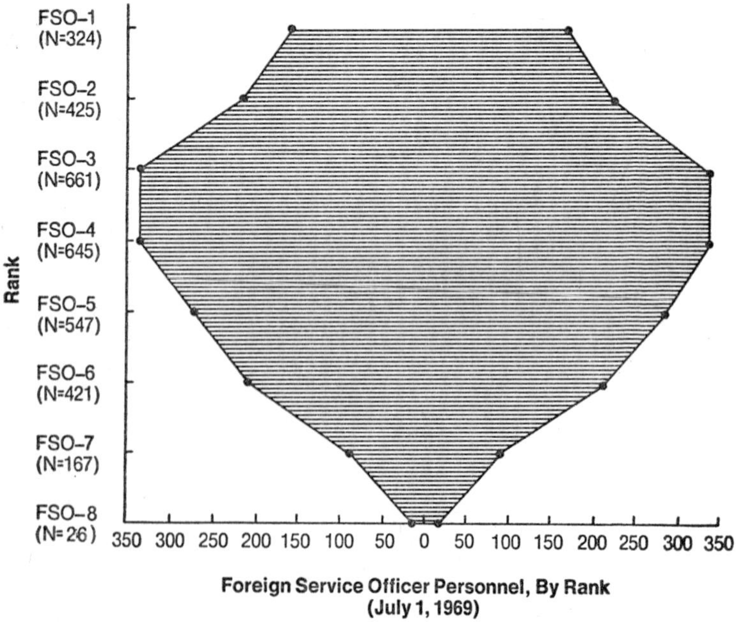

Figure 1
The "Inverse-Pyramid" Hierarchy of the Foreign Service

Table 3
*Foreign Service Officer Personnel, by Rank, July 1, 1969**

GRADE	NUMBER OF PERSONNEL	AVERAGE AGE
Honorific "Super Grades"		
Career Ambassador	3	61.0
Career Minister	55	57.5
Normal Grades		
FSO–1	324	52.1
FSO–2	425	49.7
FSO–3	661	46.8
FSO–4	645	41.1
FSO–5	547	34.2
FSO–6	421	29.4
FSO–7	167	27.2
FSO–8	26	25.1
TOTAL FSOS:	3274	

SOURCE: Personnel Chart, Department of State, July 1969. As of August 31, 1970, the figures were: Career Ambassador (7); Career Minister (56); FSO-1 (286); FSO-2 (411); FSO-3 (613); FSO-4 (633); FSO-5 (543); FSO-6 (340); FSO-7 (156); FSO-8 (39).

* A Foreign Service officer who enters the profession at the bottom begins as an "FSO-8" and progresses up the ladder, by promotion, to FSO-7, 6, 5, and so on. A very rough comparison of FSO ranks to military ranks is given on the next page. Men who reach the high rank of FSO-1 provide the bulk of our professional ambassadors overseas, and their deputies are normally FSO-2s. In the State Department, most Country Directors are FSO-2s and FSO-3s. The very highest ranks of "Career Minister" and "Career Ambassador" are, in theory, reserved for the very ablest career men at the apex of their professions, equivalent to a four or five star generalship or admiralship in the Army or Navy.

of two grades upward over the past fifteen years, creating more positions for chiefs but fewer and fewer responsible posts for Indians. (In late 1966, when I called this anomaly to the attention of Under Secretary Katzenbach, he raised the matter with Secretary Rusk. Rusk rationalized the accidental imbalance as follows: "We're a policy business. We *need* more Chiefs than Indians.") Another incalculable result of the Wriston "direct infusion" of 2500 new officers was a low-

Table 4
U.S. Military Officers on Active Duty, December 31, 1969

TITLE ARMY-AIR FORCE-MARINES	NAVY	NUMBER	ROUGH FSO EQUIVALENT
General	Admiral	40	(Career Ambassador)
Lt. General	Vice-Admiral	142	(Career Minister)
Maj. General Brig. General	Rear-Admiral	1,156	(FSO–1,2)
Colonel	Captain	18,181	(FSO–2,3)
Lt. Colonel	Commander	43,993	(FSO–3,4)
Major	Lt. Commander	69,987	(FSO–4,5)
Captain	Lieutenant	116,859	(FSO–5,6)
1st and 2nd Lieutenant	Lieutenant (jg) and Ensign	126,810	(FSO–6,7,8)
TOTAL COMMISSIONED OFFICERS:		377,168	

SOURCE: *Report to the President and the Secretary of Defense,* by The Blue-Ribbon Defense Panel (Fitzhugh Report), 1 July, 1970, page 139.

NOTE: One reason for the maintenance of a balanced pyramid of military rank is that Congress, by statute, fixes numerical limits on all promotions to the rank of Captain (Army) and above. A similar rank ordering was fixed by Congress for the Foreign Service under the Rogers Act of 1924, but was abandoned in the Foreign Service Act of 1946.

ering of training standards and a loss in the continuity of professional traditions, for relatively few senior men were left who had served in the prewar era and could educate young men coming in at the bottom. Although some of the Wriston lateral entrants brought useful "new blood" to diplomacy, the majority of them had a lower level of competence than the entrance standards of the career service would normally allow. By 1962, the Herter Report noted: ". . . present leadership in the State Department, both at home and overseas, includes only a minority of officers who entered and progressed in the Foreign Service by the orthodox examination route. . . . in Washington, fewer than one-fifth of the executive positions . . . are now held by examination officers. About 36 percent are held by officers who entered laterally and the remainder are filled by Reserve Officers, civil servants and political appointees."[113] In 1962, lateral-entry officers held about one-third of all U.S. ambassadorships and two-thirds of the number two "deputy chief of mission" posts in embassies. By 1970, even fewer men who came in at the bottom by competitive examination were reaching the top: 67 percent of all FSO-1s and 65 percent of all FSO-2s today are men who have entered the Service laterally.

However one judges the Wriston program of 1954–1957, it profoundly changed the character of the Foreign Service and of State Department officialdom. The 1924 Rogers Act had enforced by statute a fixed balance between the upper and lower ranks of the Service, assuring that there would always be many more men on the bottom than on the top rungs of the ladder. The Wriston program, and subsequent personnel policy in State, totally reversed that balance, creating an inverse pyramid and overcrowding at the top. The combined shocks of McCarthy and Wriston seemed designed to produce a surplus of cautious organization men and a shortage of trained diplomats. Today, nearly two decades later, most senior Foreign Service officers are either the survivors or the beneficiaries of McCarthyism and Wristonization.

Organization of the State Department

Structural flaws in the system encourage the tendency to duck responsibility. At the top of the State Department there are five principal officers: the Secretary of State, the Under Secretary, the under secretary for political affairs, the deputy under secretary for economic affairs, and the deputy under secretary for administration. The four top men and their staffs and the officers attached to them, who all reside on the seventh floor of the State Department Building, had a total population in late 1969 of 342 persons. These included the office of the Secretary of State and attached staffs (89 personnel), the executive secretariat (120), the policy and coordination staff (32), the office of the Under Secretary (33), the under secretary for political affairs (17), the deputy under secretary for economic affairs (11), and the inspector-general for foreign assistance (40).

Next in the chain of command (leaving aside the administrative area, which amounts to half of the department's personnel) are fifteen geographic and functional bureaus, all headed by assistant secretaries (each of whom has between three and seven deputy assistant secretaries as well as a personal office staff of ten to twenty people and, typically, technical advisers on Public Affairs, Labor, and other specialized subjects). In the five geographic bureaus, fifty "country directors" form the next level, each responsible, on the average, for a staff of ten (five officers and five clerical workers). Presently the bureaus headed by assistant secretaries or their equivalents are double the number that existed at the end of World War II, and employ the following staffs, shown in Table 5.

Within these policy bureaus of State there is a "buried administrative factor," since between 20 and 25 percent of the personnel of each bureau are, in effect, liaison officers from the administrative half of the department. Another 10 to 15 percent of the bureau staffs comprise the deputies and office help and special and technical staffs of the assistant secretaries. In all, administrative and staff overhead of each of the policy bureaus thus accounts for about 30 to 40 percent of total bureau personnel. This figure is doubly high when one considers that nearly half of the department (2580 personnel) is

Table 5
Staffing of State Department Policy Bureaus

	# OF PERSONNEL	
I. Geographic Bureaus	(OCTOBER 31, 1969)	(JANUARY 1, 1970)
African Affairs	146	174
Inter-American Affairs	166	269
East Asian and Pacific Affairs	247	188
European Affairs	171	268
Near Eastern and South Asian Affairs	250	137
II. Functional Bureaus		
Congressional Relations	27	Not Given
Public Affairs	130	116
Legal Adviser	110	Not Given
Economic Affairs	242	226
Educational and Cultural Affairs	339	292
Intelligence and Research	361	372
International Organization Affairs	198	175
International Scientific and Technological Affairs	43	45
Consular Affairs	727	663
Politico-Military Affairs (created in June 1969)	90	95

SOURCES: For October 31, 1969: Department of State, *Domestic Staffing Pattern, October 31, 1969*. Prepared by Office of Operations, Automated Data Processing Division; for January 1, 1970: U.S. Senate Committee on Government Operations, *Organization of Federal Executive Departments and Agencies* (January 1, 1970).

already compartmentalized into Administration, and that on State's seventh floor there is an Executive Secretariat of 120 persons that exists, along with the other top-level staffs, to coordinate the work of the various bureaus as a channel between them and the four highest officers of the department.

Below the assistant secretaries is the "working level." This consists, in the geographic bureaus, of country directors and, in the functional bureaus, of office directors who are generally FSO-2 Foreign Service officers (or the equivalent of GS-15 civil servants). An example in the African Bureau would be the country director for Algeria, Libya, Morocco, Spanish Sahara, and Tunisia, who is State's responsible officer for those countries and has four or five lower-ranking FSOs working for him.

The normal flow of work and chain of responsibility would seem to go from the top level (the Secretary or Under Secretary) to an intermediate level (15 assistant secretaries) to a working level (about 150 country or office directors) to an expert level (roughly 500 "desk officers" for specific countries and functions) as well as back and forth between all levels and ambassadors in the field. In fact it is not that simple.

At every level staffs get in the way, and at every level a custom has evolved of "coordinating" or "clearing" horizontally with other bureaus and offices before going *up* the chain of command. To send a cable to our embassy at Lisbon concerning the U.S. naval bases in the Azores, the country director for Spain and Portugal must first "clear" his draft message with several other offices—perhaps with the African and International Organization Bureaus because of colonial and UN ramifications, perhaps with the NATO office of the European Bureau since Portugal is a NATO member, perhaps with the Bureau of Politico-Military Affairs (and through it with the Defense Department) since this is a military matter. After these "lateral clearances" are obtained, the story is not over. The drafter may then try to consult his assistant secretary (going through one of several deputy assistant secretaries and a bureau staff). If the matter is of sufficient importance, the assistant secretary may pass the draft up through the Executive Secretariat to the Under Secretaries or the Secretary of State on the seventh floor, who may want the opinion of other assistant secretaries. The White House and other agencies such as the CIA and the Treasury may be consulted. A time-consuming process such as this requires telephone calls, committee and staff meetings, and continual rewriting or amendment of the original draft message by however many colleagues are consulted about its contents. The horizontal clearance system is a most cautious way of doing business. It reflects an institutionalized desire to diffuse responsibility among many different offices and colleagues rather than to accept responsibility oneself.

State's 10 functional bureaus had a combined staff in late 1969 of 2,267 personnel, more than double the population of the five main "action" geographic bureaus, which employed 980 people. As previously noted, the purely administrative bureaus of State employed another 2,580 people.

In the African Bureau, 44 of its 166 personnel, or 27 percent, were administrative staff dealing with such matters as budget, personnel assignments, selection of supplies for our African posts, processing of official travel between Washington and Africa, and the like. But separate and much larger department-wide administrative offices already existed for all of these functions under the deputy under secretary for administration. Thus, much of the work was duplicated and "coordinated" between two distinct offices, adding an extra layer. Another 22 positions, or 14 percent of this bureau's personnel, accounted for the 3 deputies of the assistant secretary for Africa, their office staffs, assistants, and liaison officers from other bureaus as well as specialists in labor and cultural affairs.

This pattern existed and exists in every policy bureau of State. Its practical effects should be obvious. It contributes to slowing down work, to requiring extensive and elaborate "permanent staff meetings" to keep everyone informed of what his neighbor is doing, to introducing extra buffers between different bureaus that may have a common interest in a single problem, and to delaying the process of up-and-down communication and work flow between the seventh floor, the assistant secretary, and his country directors. It results, too, in wasteful and frustrating attempts to "coordinate" and compromise disputed questions of policy at the lowest possible level, rather than transmitting a clear-cut choice of alternatives to a higher level, reflecting honest disagreement among different lower-level officers or bureaus. It contributes to excessive preoccupation with daily operational detail that leaves expert- and working-level officers no time for reflection on the wider implications of a policy.

This says nothing of the difficulties and misunderstandings caused by the distance and number of layers through which information must travel. From the Secretary of State to his country directors and desk officers is a long way. The route from the bottom to one of the top policy makers may include the alternate or "deputy" country director, the country director, a deputy assistant secretary, an assistant secretary (via his staff), the executive secretariat (and possibly the policy and coordination staff), and finally one or all of four top officials (through their personal staffs.) *And*, on the way up, any policy recommendation must normally receive clearance from all concerned horizontal layers.

Stalemate is a clear and present danger in this kind of system, as is an easy acceptance of the status quo as the best of all possible worlds. Altogether, a more cautious way of doing business could not have been invented. And it is important to recall that this one is no man's invention; it has just "happened" in a way that no President or Secretary of State consciously intended during the fast-paced postwar years.

Proposals to create more coordinating committees and superstaffs to assist harried policy makers are temporary palliatives that ignore the larger structural problem or assume it to be insoluble; yet substantial reductions could plausibly be made in the size of the entire foreign affairs machine. Rather than resulting in any loss of effectiveness, a reduction should result in improved performance. Until size and structure are recognized as *problems*, the central issue will continue to be evaded and more trouble, or at least more foul-ups, are built for the future. Above all, the system weds itself to policy assumptions of the past, with little scope or time for questioning the rightness or necessity for continuing policies in the 1970s first devised during the "national emergency" atmosphere of the 1940s and 1950s.

In pure structural terms, as one student of government has stated, the present framework "violates all the basic rules of bureaucratic organization: duties are not clearly assigned, the diffusion of authority slackens responsibility, the same job is done by different people, the proportion of staff services to the rest of personnel is unsound . . . top officials have too many subordinates reporting to them, and comparable activities are dispersed among various agencies."[114]

The McCamy Proposals

James McCamy of the University of Wisconsin, in a classic study of foreign affairs organization completed in 1964, pinpointed many of these problems. McCamy offered six rules of efficient organization, none of which, he argued, were being followed within State:[115]

1. Tell each executive what his responsibility is.
2. When an executive is made responsible for some activity, give him the authority he needs to carry out the responsibility.

3. Don't put any person under more than one boss for the same job.

4. Provide staff services, such as budget, personnel, planning and housekeeping, for each executive as he needs them.

5. Give each executive only as many subordinates as he can supervise.

6. Put together in one unit all activities that are alike.

McCamy showed that State was infected with a "virus of overadministration, of excessive growth." He reported that 45.3 percent of all State personnel were engaged in administrative staff services, a figure four to ten times greater than that of most other government agencies with the exception of the even more cumbersomely managed Agency for International Development, which had 58.6 percent of its personnel engaged in administrative tasks. State, AID, and USIA as well "use much more of their personnel for management than other departments, and more than most organizations, whether public or private. . . . The more people assigned to management services," McCamy continued, "the more work they will find to do. Soon work that was never thought necessary before gets established as a routine and begins to grow within itself, demanding more people to do it." The McCamy study also showed that by the early 1960s the Secretary of State had twenty-four subordinates who reported directly to him, not including ambassadors. This figure was markedly higher than the number in any other federal department or agency (including even the Pentagon), with one exception: again, AID. Only by "drastic change," McCamy concluded, "will we ever get a Department of State that can surely do its job."[116]

McCamy's revelations are bound to prick the curiosity of most outsiders. Aside from its structural deformations on the policy side, why is State so heavily overadministered? What do all the administrators do, and just how many of them are there?

It is difficult to arrive at an exact figure, partly because of the differing ways in which State Department personnel statistics, collected and analyzed by a number of separate offices, are categorized, and partly because of the complex nature of the State Department budget. Although the federal budget for 1970 listed 24,600 personnel on State's payroll, the figure given in the 1970 House Appropriations Committee hearings was 13,257, more than 11,000 fewer. The reason for this discrepancy is that the "missing 11,000" employees were funded *not* out of the annual congressional appropriation but from reimbursements (called "shared administrative support costs") paid to State out of the budgets of *other* executive branch agencies having overseas programs. These fund transfers ran to about $120 million in 1970, accounting for more than one-third of State's entire outlay for salaries and expenses. Here is one inhibiting factor that helps symbolize State's weakness vis-à-vis other agencies abroad. It is hardly in a strong position to curtail the foreign staffs of other departments as long as it risks losing money in the process, important money that it cannot get from Congress.

The part of State's funds received by congressional appropriation ran to an estimated $408,381,000 for fiscal 1970. The main budgetary categories are listed in Table 6 on the next page.

Administration of the State Department

Traditionally, "administration" as defined in State and the Foreign Service has had a very limited and special meaning. It concerns itself narrowly with "housekeeping" and physical

Table 6
Estimated Budget of the Department of State, Fiscal 1970

Salaries and Expenses	$207,422,000
Contributions to International Organizations (UN, etc.)	130,187,000
Educational and Cultural Exchange	40,660,000
Acquisition, Operation, and Maintenance of Buildings Abroad	15,286,000
International Commissions (U.S.–Mexico Boundary and Water Commission, International Fisheries Commission, etc.)	6,388,000
U. S. Missions to International Conferences and Organizations	5,845,000
Emergencies	1,600,000
Representation Allowances	993,000
TOTAL:	$408,381,000

SOURCE: Department of State, *The Budget in Brief, Fiscal Year 1970.*

support of the efforts of diplomats and officials to form and carry out foreign policy. Unlike any other cabinet department, State's main budget outlay is simply for the salaries of its employees and not for physical plant or programs. Administration hence has a rather lowly place in the State hierarchy, for it exists only to support the intangible, intellectual effort of diplomats and policy makers to ply their craft of political communication. The demands on the time of the Secretary of State, other senior State officials, and ambassadors have been such that administrative tasks have been delegated to a specialized class of "administrators" remote from the policy process. The Secretary of State probably pays less attention and has less of a personal role in formulating his own department's annual budget than does any other cabinet officer. He devotes his time to "policy" and leaves the "administrative details" to distant underlings. His budget, compared with that of the Secretary of Defense, or of Health, Education, and Welfare, varies little from year to year and is not a crucial consideration. It is also one of Washington's smallest budgets.

Before World War II, however, it was much smaller, only 3 or 4 percent of today's total, and its administration was much more informal. But the vast expansion of the foreign affairs bureaucracy in the postwar years posed new administrative requirements. A new machinery evolved to meet the need.

It is headed in Washington today by a deputy under secretary for administration, currently the number-five man in State's hierarchy, and run in the field by counselors of embassy for administration, who are generally the fourth- or fifth-ranking men in our embassies. Within the Foreign Service, administrative specialists are generally expected to remain in their narrow field and are considered out of the running for more prestigious "policy" jobs. Administration has become a compartmentalized and esoteric skill.

The tasks of administration are varied but they include some of the following: preparation of the annual budget, assuring organizational efficiency, paying 25,000 U.S. and foreign employees, determining all foreign and domestic assignments and promotions of personnel, arranging for shipment of supplies and of the personal effects of employees between Washington and foreign posts, providing housing and medical services, and in some cases running schools and food and clothing stores abroad for employees and their dependents, providing secure cryptographic telegram facilities connecting Washington with our foreign missions and a secure courier system for transmitting mail, running and staffing a training institute in Washington to teach languages and other job skills to Foreign Service personnel, protecting the security of embassy buildings overseas, arranging evacuation of U.S. officials and families from foreign trouble-spots in times of crisis, building embassies and leasing foreign properties for official use abroad, and keeping U.S. missions supplied with all of their needs from paper clips to motor vehicles to electricity and typewriters. In Germany during the mid-1960s, one administrative officer and his staff of local helpers were responsible, among other things, for stocking, storing, and shipping a regular supply of American toilet paper to our missions in Eastern Europe.

These are complicated jobs, partly because of their nature and partly because of the extremely large number of U.S. officials (especially of Defense and AID) stationed abroad, for State's administrators in the field provide services not only for State personnel but also on a "shared-cost" basis to representatives of many other government agencies. Nonetheless, State's elaborate administrative practices are in many cases indirectly harmful to the *policies* State attempts to carry out abroad. By segregating administration from policy, the department has failed to filter out those aspects of administration that require attention at high policy levels from those other aspects that require only low-level "housekeeping."

To reduce the State Department's present high overhead and inefficient administration would reverse trends that were initially set in motion by the expansion of our foreign affairs agencies after World War II. It also means beginning to pay some attention to the ways other countries organize their diplomacy. None of the European Foreign Services provide the kind of massive, prepackaged services to their embassy staffs that American administrators offer. They find it necessary to assign specialized "administrative officers" only to their very largest overseas missions. In an American embassy, on the other hand, the administrative section is typically larger than the diplomatic and consular sections combined. Most field administrative work done at German, French, and British embassies is handled by low-level clerical personnel, under the supervision of the number-two or -three diplomatic officer of the mission.

To adopt this course in U.S. embassies of necessity would require other major changes. It would presuppose major cuts in the total staff, particularly the personnel of agencies other than the State Department. It would mean putting an end to what has been called "the PX Culture." Instead of having U.S. supermarkets, schools, and housing compounds supervised by administrative officers, we should have to cut back these direct services and compensate our diplomats, the same as every other major nation does, with allowances to cover their expenses. A small clerical staff would still be needed to handle routine "housekeeping" functions, but U.S. diplomats would have to become more self-reliant in housing and feeding their families.

The idea of large military post exchanges and food commissaries and housing projects for Americans abroad originated with the U.S. armed forces in Europe and Japan after World War II. When Germany was occupied in 1945, the economics of scarcity and of conquest made it necessary to import U.S. products and construct American housing colonies for our military families and civil administrators. A shattered local economy was hardly able to support the local population, let alone handle the needs of a vast influx of foreigners with a much higher standard of living.

That era is long since past in Europe and Japan, yet the

PX-Culture remains. It has been extended throughout the world, not only to U.S. military bases but also wherever a sizeable American diplomatic mission exists. Its effects are pernicious both to American officials and their families and to their foreign hosts, for the system encourages isolated ghetto living that deepens American provincialism based on what foreigners see as "special privilege." In parliamentary debates in Rome, Italian legislators have pointed with mock disbelief to wives of U.S. officials in their country who may purchase American-made spaghetti in American military supermarkets. When the staff lives together in a housing compound, U.S. officials inevitably find themselves spending more time entertaining each other than mixing with the people to whom they are accredited. By making the American officials stationed abroad more self-reliant, we could help make them better representatives at the same time. As long as U.S. military personnel outnumber State Department personnel at our overseas missions, however, military administrative requirements will set the pattern of life at a majority of our embassies.

Another difficulty in employing and looking after large official staffs in foreign countries is that the very size of their presence can become provocative, breeding frictions locally that undercut the purposes of our foreign policy. Having much larger diplomatic missions than any other country, the United States strains the reciprocal basis of international law and the credulity and hospitality of other governments and peoples. An immense diplomatic presence implies, often falsely, a high degree of political influence with the host government while willy-nilly generating an impression of American interference in domestic matters that is not always intended. In some cases, of course, American interference *is* intended, but even then an ostentatious staff is rarely the best way to achieve influence. Forbearance would suggest not sending large, unskilled official staffs to areas about which Americans have little knowledge, experience, or political insight, which means most of the less-developed world. It is the limit of American wisdom as well as the limit of our power that should teach us the folly of too large or conspicuous a diplomatic representation.

In Washington the outstanding fact about the administrative structure is that it has become so confusing that few people within State are able to grasp the intricacy of its design. Although there are uniform administrative regulations, they are not uniformly applied. Whim and intrigue replace certainty and responsibility. The "operator" who is able to navigate through a tangled paper underbrush, or slice through it with random personal contacts, is the rare and bureaucratically admired individual.

Instead of routine personnel decisions being made in one place, they are now made in six or seven, for the personnel offices under the Deputy Under Secretary for administration must deal in turn with their liaison staffs under the assistant secretaries for Europe, Africa, the Near East, Latin America, the Far East, and International Organizations. This duplication is multiplied many times over when one considers all of the executive and liaison offices scattered around State, each lobbying for funds, "warm bodies" (the bureaucrat's ghoulish slang word for "personnel"), and supplies, each seeking new "clearances" and each enmeshed in its own committee syndrome.

Personnel policy—the method of recruiting new officers, training them, and determining their assignments and promotions—has always received special attention in State. "Let me control personnel," George Kennan has said, "and I will ultimately control policy. For the part of the machine that recruits and hires and fires and promotes people can soon control the entire shape of the institution, and of our foreign policy. That is why it is a curious blindness of Secretaries of State . . . when they delegate administrative parts of their responsibility to outside 'specialists.' "[117] What Kennan complains of has long been a fact of life. The daily "nuts and bolts" of personnel policy are attended to with care in the lower reaches of the bureaucracy but there is practically no long-range planning and no attention at the top.

Few organizations devote so much time to their promotion and job assignment systems as does the Foreign Service. Indeed, one has the impression that the next promotion and the next assignment are things constantly on the minds of most FSOs. The five-to-ten page "efficiency report" each officer receives annually from his boss is a document of real and ritual significance. It is a report card on every facet of the man's personality, competence, and "potential for development," and it is also likely to explore such extraneous matters as his wife's ability in the kitchen, his hobbies, and his "attitude toward the Foreign Service." By contrast, French diplomats use a single sheet of paper to rate their subordinates each year, wisely confining themselves to the more demonstrable question of job-performance.

The elaborate mechanics of State personnel administration in the 1950s and 1960s may have contributed to the molding of a conformist career mentality. Constant preoccupation with one's next promotion can easily breed sycophancy toward superiors and a patronizing attitude toward subordinates. In any case these things are a diversion from the main job of getting on with the public business. Short-term pressures toward "getting ahead" gear the system to a one-year rather than a ten- or twenty-year cycle: thus, the unplanned, unwanted bulge of underemployed senior officers today grouped around ranks FSO-1, 2, and 3.

"Selection out"—the process envisioned in the 1946 Foreign Service Act whereby the lowest performers of each rank of Foreign Service officers would be forcibly retired each year—has not been rigidly enforced. The Wriston Report in 1954 noted that selection-out was nearly a joke—only an average of sixteen men had been annually released in the first eight years of the program. Ten years later a larger Foreign Service was just as lenient. It seemed that the concept of selection-out was too ruthless a method to be practically administered by bureaucrats. Personnel boards with the power to use it charitably refrained from doing so. Indeed they did just the opposite, giving gift promotions to men approaching the selection-out line in order to protect their jobs. Thus the selection-out provision of the law has had a perverse rather than a constructive effect. Instead of keeping the Service lean and fit, it has strengthened seniority and featherbedding.

It is little wonder that by the late 1960s the Foreign Service began to have trouble maintaining its traditional appeal to able graduates of American universities. In part, this reflected the wider unpopularity of recent foreign policies in the under-thirty age group, and the youth attack on Establishment institutions. Bureaucratization and State's declining reputation, however, may have been just as much of a factor. The heavy preponderance of senior officers in a reverse-pyramid Foreign Service, leaving little room for responsible work by younger men, and the public image of State as a place of excessive paperwork, rigid indoctrination, and stultifying bureaucracy have bred cynicism about diplomacy as a career. Anyone who remembers the American campus scene of 1960 and has troubled to talk with students and professors of 1970 knows that a great change of attitude toward the Foreign Service has taken place over the last ten years. Students are well aware of the limited possibilities for advancement and the many personal constraints in today's professional diplomacy, and they have heard a growing number of teachers and former public officials recommend *against* a Foreign Service career. They point out that the way to be "effective" in foreign policy is to pursue a career in academic life, or the law, or some other agency of government where chances for advancement are greater and the organizational framework is looser and less inhibiting. After rising rapidly in another field, a young man may become qualified for lateral entry into the State Department at a higher and more responsible level more quickly than following the "career route."

In December of 1969, when the Foreign Service exam was given for the first time since 1967, there was a drop of nearly 50 percent in the number of total applications. An average of 7,000 persons applied to take the test annually in 1960–1967, but only 3,875 applicants were heard from in the last year of the decade. More ominously, the "raw scores" of those who pass the test declined notably during the 1960s, indicating progressively lower academic preparation among those who took the test. If the trend is not just temporary or accidental, one might predict a "stupidization" of American public service in the 1970s, a vicious cycle of fewer and fewer people of progressively lower abilities joining the government. A career official who worries about these things said to me, only half in jest, in April 1970, "We're taking the best second-raters we can get."

History as well as common sense suggests that a declining curve of ability in recruitment into the most prestigious sectors of government is something to worry about. The example of Imperial Russia in the late nineteenth century may be an extreme case of this phenomenon, but it is one worth pondering. An unpopular government, trying fitfully to reform itself, lost touch with the ablest of its university students and logical future leaders. Recruitment into the bureaucracy was designed to meet high educational standards, but with each passing year fewer and fewer of the brightest students were motivated to apply. As "stupider" newcomers entered the administration each year, the regime became increasingly less responsive to the needs of the society and ever more heavy-handed. Growing incompetence in government bred growing cynicism and repression and a failure to address the serious problems of the nation, which made more and more of the intellectual elite go underground to fight the system. Revolution replaced reform as the only decent aspiration for the best of the nation's youth.

PART II

Toward a Better Structure

6

THE INTELLIGENCE AND PROPAGANDA COMPLEXES

There is something about the way the CIA has been functioning that is casting a shadow over our historical position, and I feel that we need to correct it.
—Harry S Truman

The "little" State Department established in 1947 to collect U.S. foreign intelligence is not so little any more. In the jargon of the trade, "a reliable source" has recently estimated the budget of the Central Intelligence Agency, which is classified and therefore not open to public scrutiny, at about $660 million today and between $500 and $750 million in each year from 1960 to 1967.[118] That would mean CIA annually spends at least 65 percent more money than the State Department. The same careful student puts CIA's personnel strength in Washington at 15,000, "with some several thousand additional agents overseas or elsewhere outside Washington."[119] That suggests that the CIA home staff is two to three times larger than State's. Separate military and cryptographic intelligence offices, controlled for the most part by the Secretary of Defense, are said to spend an additional $3 billion annually and to employ another 100,000 men and women.

The authority for these data is Harry Howe Ransom, a professor of political science at Vanderbilt University and for the past fifteen years a close and often sympathetic observer of American intelligence organizations. Former officials and Washington journalists have arrived at estimates only slightly less precise than those of Ransom. In 1968 Stewart Alsop of *Newsweek*, who has many acquaintances in CIA dating from his own World War II experience in cloak-and-dagger work, wrote in his book, *The Center:* "The whole 'intelligence community' spends on the order of $3 billion a year, and employs about 160,000 people. Of this, the CIA's share is around a half-billion, and less than 16,000 people (other than agents and other foreigners)."[120] Writing in 1965 and drawing on his White House staff experience of 1961–1963, Arthur Schlesinger reported that "the CIA's budget exceeded State's by more than 50 percent" and "It had almost as many people under official cover overseas as State; in a number of embassies CIA officers outnumbered those from State in the political section." Schlesinger added, "Often the CIA station chief . . . had more money at his disposal and exerted more influence [than the American Ambassador]."[121] In 1964 State's ex-intelligence chief, Roger Hilsman, wrote that when President Kennedy took office "CIA had almost as many officers abroad engaged in intelligence work as the State Department had for the whole range of its activities." The President, Hilsman said, "ordered a 'drastic and urgent' reduction in the number of CIA men overseas in the most visible of the 'official cover' positions, the term for intelligence men occupying a position in an embassy abroad ostensibly as an official of the State Department or some other government agency." The result? "A painful review was conducted and some reductions were made over the next year," Hilsman alleges, "but they were more than offset by increases in other places."[122] Expressing the unhappiness of U.S. diplomats about this state of affairs, the American Foreign Service Association noted in a public report of November 1968 that CIA's station chief in Saigon had "direct access on his own initiative to the senior officials of the South Vietnamese Government," quite independently of the U.S. ambassador.[123]

Ten years ago these revelations would have surprised most Americans. Today they are accepted as commonplace. Disclosed intelligence failures have come so fast and furious in the 1960s that many people are now prepared to expect almost anything from CIA, and little of it good. The ten-year change in attitude affects not just the general public, but most professional students of intelligence as well. Ransom is a case in point. In 1958 he published *Central Intelligence and National Security*, the first thorough, scholarly study of the evolution of U.S. intelligence organizations since World War II. While suggesting the need for some minor readjustments in the system, the 1958 Ransom analysis concluded on a note of high satisfaction: "If, as the Director of Central Intelligence has asserted, the intelligence estimate has a more influential place in contemporary American government than it enjoys in any other government of the world, this is cause for rejoicing."[124] The experience of twelve more years made Ransom change his mind. In a new study published in 1970, revising and updating the earlier one, he spoke of "the threat of a gargantuan intelligence establishment" and recommended "surgery" to meet that threat: a reorganization of CIA into two separate and smaller agencies much more tightly controlled from outside.

There are, of course, two sides to the argument. Former CIA Director Allen Dulles, under fire for his agency's handling of the U-2 incident of 1960 and the Bay of Pigs invasion of 1961, tried to counter this criticism several years later in a memoir entitled *The Craft of Intelligence.* "The statement that there are American embassies where the CIA personnel outnumber the Foreign Service personnel," Dulles wrote, "is a rather typical trouble-making bit of malice, as is the one that the CIA personnel in embassies can do what they please."[125] He insisted that intelligence operations abroad were always cleared first in Washington, at least with the President if with no one else. Much of the public evidence, however, does not support his contention, and anyone who knows the complexities of the Washington bureaucratic process, or has heard American ambassadors call CIA their "number one problem" is bound to regard the Dulles defense as hair-splitting at best. In the same year that Dulles published his *apologia,* former President Truman declared, "There is something about the way the CIA has been functioning that is casting a shadow over our historical position, and I feel that we need to correct it." Truman added, "I never had any thought that when I set up the CIA it would be injected into peace-time cloak-and-dagger operations."[126]

Intelligence fiascoes of the 1960s have damaged the American reputation at home and abroad. On the evidence, although only a fraction of it is public, it seems safe to award the argument, on points, to Truman, Ransom, Schlesinger, Hilsman, and the American Foreign Service Association. In addition to a long history of bungles and miscalculations in Southeast Asia, there was the disclosure in February 1967 of a fifteen-year CIA program to subsidize secretly the foreign activities of American student, labor, religious, academic, and philanthropic groups. University research institutes such as the Center for International Studies of MIT were revealed to have been funded by CIA from the beginning, in violation of the agency's charter, without the permission of Congress, and with only the most casual kind of review by four presidents and their staffs. Occasionally other embarrassments have come to light, often by accident. In 1965 the prime minister of Singapore, a friendly state, announced that several years earlier he had been offered a bribe of $3 million to keep quiet about an attempted CIA penetration of his own security services. In 1969 former intelligence officer Miles Copeland revealed that most of U.S. policy toward Egypt's President Nasser in the 1950s, including our aid program, was decided and discussed with Nasser by CIA officials, with little prior participation or knowledge by the State Department. The USS *Liberty*, torpedoed during the Arab-Israeli war in June 1967 with the loss of thirty-four American lives, and the USS *Pueblo*, captured by the North Koreans less than a year later, were revealed to be espionage ships conducting electronic eavesdropping on behalf of the Defense Department's National Security Agency. A Navy EC-121 aircraft was shot down over North Korea with all hands on a similar mission two years ago. In the summer of 1969 it was intimated in the press that the CIA had ordered Green Beret detachments of the Army to conduct political assassinations in Vietnam.

The roots of these problems go back to World War II, when the shock of Pearl Harbor gave birth to America's first large foreign intelligence effort. An Office of Strategic Services (OSS), headed by Colonel William J. Donovan, was established on June 13, 1942. It was responsible to President Roosevelt but organizationally subordinate to another new body, the military joint chiefs of staff, which had been formed only four months earlier. By the end of the war the OSS had 13,000 employees, military and civilian, and had infiltrated 1,600 Americans behind enemy lines to gather information and conduct clandestine operations against the Germans and Japanese.

The OSS was disbanded in October of 1945, and most of its employees were demobilized, while a remnant of them were transferred to the War and State Departments. During the next eighteen months the future of peacetime foreign intelligence was debated within the executive branch. The armed services sought to control the intelligence function, but for a time in 1946 it was passed to State. General Donovan favored an independent body, and the FBI proposed that *it* should control foreign operations. Some congressmen opposed continuing any secret intelligence work at all, fearing that it might lead to "a potential Gestapo."

The final result was a compromise. The three armed services and the State Department would continue to have their own intelligence programs, but a new Central Intelligence Agency, under the newly created National Security Council, would coordinate the government effort while developing its own independent capability. The powers of the new agency were loosely defined in a way that left no one but the President himself clearly in control of it. In a sense, this has entrapped the chief executive in an intelligence system that he lacks the time or often the knowledge to manage. And as Ransom has written, with President Truman's apparent concurrence, "When Congress created the CIA in 1947, the statutory language delegated intelligence (information) functions and nothing more. No indication was given in the statute that the CIA would become a vehicle for foreign political action or clandestine political warfare."[127]

An impressive mystique of secrecy and the formidable power of a large and only partially audited budget have given the intelligence agency unique bureaucratic strength. The director of CIA and his officers in the field can spend money on their personal vouchers alone; only about half of their budget is routinely audited by the General Accounting Office. Formally, the agency may report to the President and the NSC, but in practice even those handful of men in the White House who know CIA's total expenditures would be hard put to explain the meaning of each separate part of the whole. On paper there are a number of coordinating and liaison devices between CIA and the Defense and State Departments. A Foreign Intelligence Advisory Board, established under a different name in 1956, disbanded in 1961 and then recreated after Bay of Pigs, holds occasional meetings to give the President "outside" advice about CIA. Its two most recent chairmen have been Clark Clifford and General Maxwell Taylor.

There is some monitoring of CIA activity by the State Department's Bureau of Intelligence and Research, by ambassadors in the field, and by a top-level review body referred to as the "Special Group," or "303 Committee," chaired in recent years by the number-three or number-four official of State. But these controls may be more apparent than real. To some Washington observers, the 303 Committee (and its new White House counterpart, the "40 Committee") has often seemed a kind of rubber-stamp body, giving *pro forma* approval to well-advanced CIA plans that it has not troubled deeply to inform itself about. Hilsman has explained why it is easy for this to occur, and how other forms of evasion and weakness may nullify the control mechanisms. At the start of the 1960s, Hilsman discovered, the internal organization of the State Department "was fragmented, on the grounds of secrecy, so that people approving a particular proposal did not always know of other activities that had a bearing on the possible repercussions." One logical result of this fragmented authority was that often "the CIA intelligence officer sponsoring a particular proposal gave way to the human temptation, when confronted with alternative channels for approval, of choosing the channel through which approval was most likely to be forthcoming." All too frequently, Hilsman continues, "the channel that was most likely to approve was the channel that was least informed about that particular problem." One result of such CIA manipulation: "the right hand of the State Department did not always know what the left hand had approved, and neither in consequence had the knowledge to judge proposals fully and soundly."[128] What Hilsman confirms is what anyone familiar with the inside mechanics of secrecy knows: that it does not require a high degree of unscrupulousness or even talent to maneuver around normal controls in the name of "national security."

The CIA can and does bypass the "normal" mechanisms by going directly to the President or individual members of his staff. An intelligence officer is uniquely equipped—in the present system—to play one part of State or the White House against the other, citing mysterious "security" inhibitions, withholding full disclosure of the facts upon which a decision must be based. Even if the substance of secret operations is fully discussed among top policy makers, the administration of CIA—its important size and shape and interacting effect on other parts of the government—is not monitored except in the wake of exceptional "failures" that become public. When such failures are widely known, a

President will feel under special pressure to reassure the public that he is firmly in command, there is no cause for alarm, and major changes are not needed. This was the public reaction of President Kennedy in 1961 to the Bay of Pigs and President Johnson in 1967 to the National Student Association scandal, while at the same time both presidents ordered secret investigations to determine what had gone wrong. In both cases the chief officers of CIA itself participated in the investigations, which, along with their director's de facto membership on the NSC, meant that the results of the studies were mainly self-determined. As Ransom puts it, "CIA surveillance has come largely from internal self-studies . . . [and] at best has been sporadic. During its first twenty years of existence, no one was given the fulltime responsibility of intelligence surveillance for the President. He, of course, could not possibly give constant attention to the intelligence system."[129]

A mystique of secrecy-for-the-sake-of-secrecy, curiously compelling to many high officials of our government, contributes to the organizational confusion. Senator Alben Barkley showed how impressed even a former Vice-President could be with the ceremonial trappings of intelligence briefings. In 1956, during one of the Senate's few debates on the subject, Barkley declared, "Some of the information gathered by the Central Intelligence Agency and laid before the National Security Council itself was so confidential and secret that the very portfolios in which it was contained were under lock and key. I would lose my right arm," he added, "before I would divulge it to anyone, even to members of my own family."[130] In such a setting, the *secrecy* of secret information and operations comes to take precedence over the purposes they serve; intelligence becomes very nearly an end in itself.

One reason for this, Ransom believes, is intellectual confusion that comes from putting two distinct activities—research and analysis on the one hand and secret, political operations on the other—under the same organizational roof. This blurs distinctions and causes foreign policy to "be formulated in the midst of conceptual and semantic confusion." Thus "intelligence activities sometimes are undertaken for no other reason . . . than that an intelligence apparatus stands by awaiting an assignment," and "in some instances purpose and mission are not even discussed in high government councils because of 'security.' "[131]

Whatever the reasons, the size of CIA and its inestimable advantages of secrecy and independence inevitably cause pressures that distort foreign policy, situations where the intelligence tail wags the diplomatic dog. Intelligence staffs inflate the size of U.S. missions abroad, and the methods by which information is obtained as well as the broad, indefinite criteria applied in deciding what "intelligence" *is* are bound to create problems. There have been many cases, we now know, where the main point of a particular U.S. economic-aid program or of awarding a government scholarship or of cultivating a prominent public man is conceived to be the "intelligence value" of these activities. If the CIA staff in a given foreign country is particularly strong, the "intelligence value" of most U.S. activities in that country may take precedence over public foreign policy.

The causes and the cures of the problem are basically administrative. We employ too many intelligence analysts and operatives in foreign countries, and State Department officials are not in a position to monitor and control what they are doing and how they are doing it. Formal controls lend themselves to evasion or may not be exercised with vigor because of the mysterious aura of "national security" inhibition that surrounds intelligence work, and since CIA's secrecy and flexible budgetary resources give it unique status and power vis-à-vis the agencies that in theory should be controlling it.

Since 1961, an ambassador has in theory been the "boss" of his CIA station chief, but the very nature of the inter-agency relationship can turn this around. The station chief's access to unvouchered secret funds and other "exceptional" tools gave him a big advantage over this theoretical chief. An ambassador's interviews with intelligence personnel are apt to consist of "briefings" in which the boss is the passive and privileged recipient of information that he is expected, sometimes under oath, not to share with his own diplomatic staffs. The same kind of thing can happen in the upper reaches of government in Washington. In something akin to Masonic ritual, top policy makers passively participate in the daily intelligence briefing, delivered with an aura of mystery and importance by little men with locked black bags, or in more relaxed fashion by horn-rimmed senior officers with impressive maps, charts, and photos. The romance of secrecy has a seductive intellectual appeal, perhaps even a narcotic effect, on the minds of many otherwise level-headed statesmen.

CIA has the added bureaucratic advantage (as does the Defense Department) of its own confidential, high-speed global communications system, its "own channel" between the field and Washington. Indeed it even has a greater advantage over State, for most embassy communications equipment, serving State's own channel to Washington, is owned and operated by CIA. With diplomatic understatement, one American ambassador describes the effect of this as follows: "Because the CIA operates State communications systems throughout most of the world, the Ambassador at the least cannot always count on priority of communication with Washington."[132] It is an organizational accident of sorts that CIA has come to control diplomatic communications facilities, but the reasons why this has happened are fairly obvious: with a large, secret budget and strong support from Congress, the intelligence agency is not nearly so strapped for funds as is the State Department. As new embassies have opened and new technology has been developed in the postwar years, State has invariably had to turn to CIA to cover costs of "shared" equipment and code clerks that it could never afford by itself without requesting more money from Congress, money that might not be appropriated. Another obvious conclusion flows from these facts. The ambassador, although he will invariably see many of the reports his station chief submits to Washington, can never be sure that he is seeing all of the outgoing intelligence cables. Usually he doesn't, and in any case he must rely on the good will of his CIA subordinate to *volunteer* whatever intelligence information is available. The relationship favors the subordinate more than the superior.

Another diplomatic complaint is that intelligence officers on embassy staffs compete with Foreign Service officers for "contacts" in the government and the political and economic hierarchy of the countries to which both are accredited. Having more money at their disposal, it is not difficult for intelligence officers to "outspend" and outbid diplomats on their own ground. Inevitably but irresponsibly, CIA has been drawn into performing traditional functions of political reporting and diplomatic representation, essentially duplicating the work of diplomats. This practice goes far beyond the intent of the National Security Act of 1947. Over the years, almost unnoticed, CIA has so broadened its definition of intelligence functions—the concept of its "mission" in the government—that those functions and that mission have become vague, open-ended, and all-inclusive.

During a period of expanding U.S. commitments overseas, intelligence requirements have been defined in absolute terms. If Washington has a "need to know" *everything* in order to forewarn itself about impending "surprises" in the world, then intelligence inevitably takes a high bureaucratic precedence. One collects, with few inhibitions about the means of collection, all of the information one *can* collect on Zambian trade unions, Norwegian student organizations, and the independence movement of the Canary Islands. It might come in handy some day. *Anything* might come in handy some day.

The zealousness of collection methods and the massiveness of the effort have a distorting impact on foreign policy. If the United States has come at last to a pause in the expansion of its overseas interests and foreign involvements, it is surely time for a more limited conception of political intelligence. We don't have a "fact gap" about foreign countries. If anything, Washington is deluged with facts that carry divergent interpretations. The commodity that is always in shorter supply is political insight.

Most of the foreign countries with which Washington deals today were virtually unknown to Americans twenty years ago. It is hardly surprising that we lack experience and depth of insight into their changing cultures and political processes. Perhaps our overemphasis on ephemeral "fact" collection is a figleaf for this deeper ignorance. Overreliance on intelligence—and the immense volume of secret reporting that this produces—can even get in the way of good judgment by overwhelming busy officials with a pervasive present tense that has little coherent relevance to past or future tenses. Information preempts reflection in a bureaucratic setting that is overwhelmed with trivial detail and inundated with the flow of current events, as reported separately by diplomatic and intelligence officers.

The argument that the President and his NSC "control" the Central Intelligence Agency is fine for public consumption but wears extremely thin to many officials who have had dealings with the agency. A fragmented bureaucracy makes it easy for CIA to satisfy the *forms* of clearance with the NSC and State, while in fact maintaining considerable freedom of action. In all administrative logic, as noted in the two Hoover Reports of 1949 and 1955, it is inconceivable that either the chief executive or a small deliberative body of cabinet-level officers and their staffs can stay fully on top of the agency's daily doings. Although a variety of interagency coordinating devices exist, there is no effective continuing review of CIA conduct from outside CIA, nor is there fixed, consistent administrative authority, clearly located, to enforce limitations on overseas intelligence staffs. To an important degree, the President and his staff have to trust in the "voluntary self-regulation" of their secret intelligence agency.

Meshing intelligence with foreign-policy goals should depend on much more than an act of faith. If there is to be any disengagement from present U.S. foreign commitments in the 1970s, someone in Washington must cut swollen CIA staffs and come up with more restrained and selective guidelines about their work. Access to the necessary information needed in order to make the cuts is extremely restricted within the executive branch, for it is not unnatural for

CIA to want to protect its secret budget advantage. But "voluntary self-regulation" is not enough.

Ultimate administrative control over CIA should be transferred from the NSC and the President to the Secretary of State. He should determine the number of CIA officials sent abroad, the money they have to spend, and the purposes for which they may spend it. At the intermediate level of State's assistant secretaries and country directors, CIA's full intelligence output should be made consistently available to the State Department.

If State were given continuing responsibility for review and control of CIA, and if the intelligence agency treated State as the main consumer of its research products, then much of the *raison d'être* for State's own 352-man "Bureau of Intelligence and Research" (INR) would disappear. Today CIA, State's INR, and Defense's DIA are daily competitors in the production and evaluation of foreign political intelligence. Each—along with State's Seventh Floor Operations Center and the Pentagon's National Military Command Center—produces daily, weekly, monthly, and, in times of crisis, hourly intelligence digests and summaries intended for use by the President and other high officials and covering substantially the same ground. Each of the summaries and papers attempts to draw upon diplomatic cables, CIA reports, and military reporting. Because of the doctrine that various types of clandestine intelligence must be carefully segregated from more "overt" types of information, an additional series of clandestine-source summaries and digests are separately prepared for the President and his advisers on an ascending scale of secrecy. Each step of the redundant process imposes a greater burden on the time of middle and top level officials, including the President and Secretary of State and their staffs.

Toward a Better Structure

Much of the working day of many members of Washington officialdom is devoted to giving and getting "briefings." A healthy chunk of that time is probably wasted and wasteful. While intelligence digests are being prepared, a great volume of "raw," nonsummarized information is flowing to the top and all other levels of government, making the redundancy of *competitive* intelligence condensations seem all the more striking.

Program for CIA Reform

Several conclusions about the foreign intelligence organization of the U.S. government should by now be inescapable. They may be summarized as follows:

1. We have spread the intelligence net too wide in the post-war world; intelligence as an "absolute" value lacks reasonable conceptual limits, undercuts policy, and gets us into unwanted trouble abroad.
2. The large *size* of the U.S. intelligence presence abroad creates political and intrabureaucratic problems of its own.
3. The CIA is not under effective administrative control from outside; its unique independence, mystique, secrecy, and budget advantages are *bound* to give it a distorting impact on policy unless it is made responsible to more regularized outside authority.
4. There is competitive redundance among State, CIA, and Defense intelligence staffs.
5. Intelligence officers abroad engage in much duplication of diplomatic reporting and representational functions.

To begin to solve these problems, a minimum program of reform would include the following measures:

1. Assignment of a State Department adviser to CIA, who would be responsible for monitoring the foreign policy ramifications of intelligence activities; since 1947 one of CIA's two top officers has always been a military man; it does not seem unreasonable that one other officer should be a representative of the Secretary of State.

2. Absolute administrative control by the Secretary of State over the numbers of intelligence officers of CIA and other agencies assigned to diplomatic missions abroad; the setting and enforcing of fixed personnel ceilings for each country.

3. Tighter control by ambassadors over their CIA station chiefs; a policy of *full* disclosure to ambassadors of *all* CIA activities in their countries, and ambassadorial control over all secret funds and communications facilities.

4. Systematic and regular review by State of the foreign intelligence budgets of other agencies.

5. Submission of all CIA intelligence analyses and field reports *as a routine matter* to the State geographic bureaus; elimination of State's own Bureau of Intelligence.

6. Development by State and CIA of more specific and limited guidelines regarding the functions of intelligence officers in the field; it should be the *presumption*—unless a specific exception is granted for a particular country—that Foreign Service embassy officers handle traditional diplomatic reporting on the internal politics and economics of the country to which they are assigned, while CIA staff cover specific security-related targets and do so, wherever possible, in overt, cooperative liaison with the host country security services.

7. Reformulation, in writing, in Washington of all U.S.

foreign intelligence "missions" and "requirements"; such redrafting to be subject to the wishes—and veto—of the President and Secretary of State, as normally communicated through a permanent official on the Secretary's staff; collection of the resulting documents in one place within State, which should also see to their enforcement;

8. Transfer from CIA to State of the chairmanship of the United States Intelligence Board and the Board of National Estimates, the main interdepartmental estimating body.

This minimum program of reform concentrates only on the most pressing, short-term aspects of the problem. A maximum, longer-range reform would go much further. As separate White House and State study groups in 1961 and Ransom in his 1970 study have proposed, surgery is needed to separate research from covert operations. Secret political operations, Ransom argues, "should only be undertaken to prevent a direct threat to national security and as an alternative to overt military action,"[133] which means that they should occur rarely if ever at all, and should be fully controlled by the President through the State Department. The valid requirement of the government for research and study of foreign questions should not continue to be tarnished, as it has been, by association with undercover work. CIA's research part, by far its largest component, could become either an independent and overt research institute or a subdivision of the Department of State. The Defense Department's military, cryptographic, and electronic intelligence organizations, without being structurally detached, nonetheless need a more complete outside review of their budgets and output. They are not receiving such review today, and they are unlikely to in the future unless the Secretary of State is given authority by the

President to build a staff in his department that will watch the entire spectrum of foreign intelligence work in the federal government. What is tragic is that it may take another *Pueblo* incident and another Bay of Pigs for this to happen.

U.S. Information Agency (USIA)

Compared to the magnitude and the risks of the intelligence problem, our foreign propaganda and cultural activities seem small and benign. Yet here, also, is a case of bureaucracy overwhelming purpose.

The U.S. Information Agency employs 10,000 people and spends about $175 million annually. Its director, unlike the director of CIA, is theoretically responsible to the Secretary of State, although his agency functions separately in its own Washington headquarters. Abroad, a USIA staff is attached to every American embassy, subordinate to the ambassador. Separately, the State Department has its own Bureau of Educational and Cultural Affairs, with 339 employees and a $35 million annual budget, as well as a 130-man Bureau of Public Affairs for press and public relations. Some two dozen other federal agencies are listed in a government-wide directory* as having responsibilities that impinge on foreign cultural and exchange activities;[134] and the Defense Department, wherever U.S. troops are stationed abroad, conducts its own information programs and an extensive Armed Forces Radio and Television Service (AFRTS).

The USIA's Voice of America broadcasts 930 hours weekly

* The directory, *A Guide to U.S. Government Agencies Involved in International Educational and Cultural Activities*, is 188 pages long.

in nearly forty languages, using 104 worldwide transmitters. The agency also produces 66 magazines in 27 languages, and has subsidized foreign and American book publishers in producing and distributing more than 120 million copies of over 14,000 editions since 1950. It operates as well more than 200 overseas libraries in 83 nations, which are visited by 20 million persons annually,[135] and it radio-teletypes to U.S. embassies daily a 10,000 word file of government announcements and self-generated stories to be used in influencing the foreign press. In addition, USIA has its own small "intelligence" office, which in the 1950s sent leaflet-filled balloons behind the Iron Curtain and more recently, in Vietnam, has conducted "psychological warfare" operations. In the Congo when Moise Tshombe was premier, and in Laos and Thailand, American propaganda programs are said to have helped sell a foreign government to its own people. USIA performs these varied tasks with a staff of 3,300 home employees and another 1,300 Americans and 5,500 foreigners abroad. The main purpose of their effort is perhaps best suggested by the title of a series of congressional hearings into USIA operations, the last of them held in 1969: "WINNING THE COLD WAR: THE U. S. IDEOLOGICAL OFFENSIVE."

The agency's original sense of mission may be discerned in the statement to another congressional committee made in 1953 by Robert L. Johnson, the head of its bureaucratic predecessor, the International Information Administration:

"I think there are bonds that can be developed that are strong, and may prevent a third world war, and I think unless we win the cold war in the next two years we are apt to have a third world war. So I am anxious to use all the tools that honorable people can use to win the hearts and minds of the people of this world."[136]

In a reorganization and reinitialling, "USIA" replaced

"IIA" later in the same year. Both institutions were an outgrowth of the Office of War Information (OWI), formed during World War II to combat Nazi propaganda. The Voice of America's first broadcasts were in German. OWI was disbanded after the war, but many of its personnel were temporarily assigned to the State Department. Under William Benton, a former advertising executive and later senator, State developed a propaganda effort designed to compete with the Soviets in the early cold war period. The Smith-Mundt Act of 1948 gave legislative sanction and funds to this effort, and the semiautonomous new agency was finally moved out of State in the first year of the Eisenhower administration.

The cold war had seemed to settle the question of whether to engage in U.S. government-run propaganda efforts in peacetime. Broadcasts in foreign languages around the world were (and still are) designed to counter communism. Libraries and cultural centers were established first in occupied Germany and Japan, and later in other countries. Government scholarship and exchange programs began to bring key foreigners to the United States for study and "exposure." Books and films about America were produced and distributed, while attempts were made to influence foreign news media to favor U.S. foreign-policy objectives.

Necessity for Propaganda?

A question that has not been asked since World War II is whether it is really necessary that the U.S. government have any foreign propaganda program at all. Originally the invention of totalitarian states, massive public propaganda was adopted by free societies only under perceived "emergency" conditions. Emphasizing the exceptional nature of the effort, and the qualms of Congress, USIA's legislative charter makes clear that the agency is to operate *only* abroad, and not propagandize the American people. The added complication in a free-enterprise economy is that privately owned and operated U.S. news media operate overseas and are in a sense daily competitors with USIA. Many other, though not all, democratic countries today run foreign information and culture programs by means of subsidized quasipublic corporations, independent of government policy guidance and parliamentary pressures.

During the 1970s the national emergencies that spawned OWI and USIA are long since past, and we have had at least twenty years of experience in which to test the theory that official propaganda has a significant impact on world events. That theory has been found wanting. There is the dawning knowledge that the earlier wartime assumptions of the program are not in accord with the realities of a peacetime world; there is gnawing suspicion that money spent on propaganda may be money wasted; there are philosophic and aesthetic objections to the very idea of the government of a free society trying anxiously to "sell" itself to the inhabitants of other sovereign states. It is attractive to some to believe that if only the right message and technique could be devised, U.S. foreign policy would instantly become more effective and popular abroad. That is to pursue a chimera. As the 1969 congressional study on "Winning the Cold War" concluded, the main reasons why "the U.S. reputation has become tarnished in recent years" are "(1) The Vietnam War; (2) our race problem; and (3) crime and lawlessness."[137] This unsurprising conclusion accords with common sense: it is acts more than words that are decisive. In any case respect, not popularity, is the proper and the most prudent and realistic object of a great power living in a complicated world.

The idea of conducting foreign policy by competitive propaganda coup has few partisans any longer. The ups and downs of public opinion polls abroad which try to measure American popularity, and which for so many years have fascinated so many congressmen, no longer impress the rest of us as meaningful, except in presidential election years. The notion of a global American mission to propagate a particular brand of democracy is wearing thin, as is the idea that salesmanship is a substitute for performance. Although a handful of enthusiasts may still think in terms of winning important foreign gains by a big exercise in mass persuasion, Congress will be less than willing to vote funds for expanding a program whose purpose is being questioned and whose priority in the over-all budget is low.

Bruce Oudes, a journalist and former USIA officer, has carried this analysis a step further. "It is, indeed, hard to avoid suspicion," Oudes writes, "that without the USIA the course of recent history would have been the same, except a bit less noisy."[138] Like many other Americans who have lived abroad, Oudes notes that European broadcasting efforts such as Britain's BBC are more accurate, believable, and useful than the emanations of the Voice of America. Describing the "dreary, hackneyed" messages cabled abroad by USIA to influence foreign audiences, he cites a "story" on the Agency's wireless file reporting that 24,000 treaties had been drafted in the past 20 years. According to the USIA dispatch, "this represents 80 percent of all treaties drafted throughout history and indicates a heartening trend toward the avoidance of disputes between nations through resort to treaties."[139]

The example is all too typical, but the poor quality of its effort is not a sufficient reason to challenge USIA's right to exist. The main objections should be: (1) that it is neither right nor necessary for the government of a free society to propagandize itself; (2) that, in any case, it will not be able to "win the hearts and minds" of the world's people by this means; (3) that, even if it could do so, that would not have a significant influence on foreign policies, which tend to be based on national interest much more than popular emotion; (4) the facts upon which foreign peoples form their opinions of America are already amply reported in thousands of words and pictures daily by private U.S. news media and the representatives of foreign news agencies in our midst. A recent directory of foreign correspondents lists more than 500 of them in Washington and New York alone.

USIA has staffs in three cities in Canada: Ottawa, Montreal, and Toronto, where, Canadian journalist Raymond Heard has written, "there is little real need for it to function" since "Canada is already saturated with news and views from across that longest of undefended borders."[140] Many Western European journalists have a similar feeling about the redundance of USIA work in their countries. A final objection to U.S. government propaganda is one of style. As Oudes remarks, USIA gives the "impression of a country that is trying too hard. The image is not that of a nation that is mature, relaxed, confident, capable of taking care of itself and inspiring confidence in others—but rather of one that is young, nervous, uncertain, defensive"[141]

A separate question is that of government cultural and exchange programs, which are now jointly administered by

USIA and the State Department. Libraries and scholarships and visits by symphony orchestras are not "propagandistic" in the same sense as carefully tailored foreign broadcasts, leaflets, and press releases. But even such low-pressure cultural programs, when administered by the Washington bureaucracy, tend to inject national chauvinism into artistic, scientific, and humanistic fields where it has always been the boast of free societies that such considerations are irrelevant. Where culture bears the government label, subtle forms of corruption inescapably enter in. The Fulbright-Hays Fellowship program eliminates this by using private, independent, mixed, binational commissions to pick the exchange candidates on merit, but many USIA and State Department programs are less meritorious. CIA, armed with its considerable secret funds, has, as the 1967 disclosures showed, entered the cultural field by the back door, providing *ad hoc* subsidies that undercut the reputation of the entire government effort. It may be essential to an ambassador's flexibility that he have limited and strictly accountable contingency funds at his disposal for a variety of "targets of opportunity" under the USIA exchange visitors' program. Most ambassadors do have some minimal resources of this kind, but if the U.S. government is to operate effectively, an ambassador's subordinates from other agencies should not independently have such exceptional funds at *their* disposal. Exchange programs can be discredited if they are administered as political tools of the new diplomacy.

On the domestic front, government control over foreign propaganda and cultural programs makes them a congressional football. There is continuing debate over how much "truth" is appropriate to Voice of America broadcasts, whether the government can legitimately spend money to criticize itself abroad. Congressmen in budget hearings have questioned why an American ballet troupe in Europe performed "erotic" dances, why plays and books criticizing United States social problems should be sent abroad, and why four-letter "obscenities" are heard in a poetry reading at a U.S. cultural center.

These questions are as unsettling and chauvinistic in the domestic political arena as they are abroad. It seems increasingly a mistake to try to legislate or administer or propagate a particular view of American culture overseas, or even to try by governmental means to show off an alleged "selective diversity" about our society. Massive government-controlled projections of information and culture undercut American political beliefs in the virtue of free expression and the dignity of the individual, and contain harmful inconsistencies and hypocrisies. Measures adopted to meet the "emergency" of World War II and the first shocks of the cold war should not become permanently institutionalized features of a peacetime America.

This is not to say that the State Department or our embassies abroad have to function without public information programs or without trying to stay abreast of American opinion and to influence foreign opinion—traditional requirements of diplomacy everywhere. Press attachés have long been assigned to our embassies abroad, some of them Foreign Service officers and some of them USIA officials. U.S. ambassadors and diplomats have routine dealings with the foreign press and media, and have to address foreign public audiences as a part of their job. Effective public relations is implicit in the traditional diplomatic role, for the diplomat exists to represent his country's policies and influence others in a direction favorable to them. But it departs from this tradition to broadcast hypothetically "objective" news under the government label, and to organize large-scale programs of exchange and education designed mainly to further government policies.

Apart from these philosophic and practical difficulties, USIA may preempt some of the ingenuity and vigor of private programs. Government cultural ventures generally have a lower effectiveness and credibility than do private efforts. USIA libraries may be attacked and burned as a symbol of the unpopularity of United States policies, while privately controlled (though highly subsidized) institutions such as the American Universities in Cairo, Beirut, and Istanbul are spared violence. The latter kinds of institutions are rooted in the communities they serve, where they are seen as performing a useful role on their own merits. They are instruments of cooperation and education, not tools of the policy of the U.S. government. While the USIA effort is quite consciously an American attempt to "interfere" with foreign perceptions, U.S. nongovernmental programs function without this official handicap, more consistently reflecting the values that Americans profess.

The best answer to the cultural half of the USIA problem is embodied, curiously enough, in a report of the 1967 Katzenbach Committee on CIA subsidies. What the report said of secretly financed CIA cultural and philanthropic activities is equally true of the Information Agency's work. The Committee proposed that a "public-private body," a privately controlled but publicly subsidized corporation like the existing Smithsonian Institution, undertake "overseas activities . . . which are adjudged deserving, in the national interest, of public support." It noted that most democratic countries—Sweden, India, and Britain, for example—handled foreign cultural programs in this fashion. Thus the British Council, established in 1934, "operates in 80 countries, administering approximately $30 million annually for reference libraries, exhibitions, scholarships, international conferences, and cultural exchanges. Because 21 of its 30 members are drawn from private life, the Council has maintained a reputation for independence, even though 90 percent of its funds are governmental."[142] A later study by the Duncan Commission of 1969 concluded of Britain's cultural program that it should not "be regarded in any way as a mouthpiece for Government policy. To attempt to use it in this way would undoubtedly detract from its status as a cultural organization, whose activities are independent of the control of the Government of the day."[143] The French *Alliance Française* cultural program operates with much the same independence, although its employees are on government payrolls.

Libraries, schools, and exchange programs now controlled directly from Washington could plausibly be taken out of USIA and the State Department and reconstituted under the control of a mixed private-public corporation. Congress would have to legislate such a change, which might include an appeal to private businesses, media, universities, foundations, and citizens generally to participate in a national effort to devise better overseas cultural cooperation, with private as well as public funding. A nonprofit corporation of this type would be able to receive tax-deductible private gifts. Such an effort to summon the skill and financial resources of the private sector of the American economy might measurably improve the voluntary coordination of all U.S. forms of cultural action abroad, while removing the specter of "government control." Over time, the support now given to foreign educational institutions under AID and Peace Corps programs might well be absorbed by the new, independent American

Cultural Institute, which could possibly be an overseas branch of the Smithsonian Institution. Board members, appointed to fixed terms by the President, Congress, and representative private bodies, could insure high standards and independence from political influence. Foreign participation should be sought in staffing and coadministering programs. To be rooted in the foreign communities they serve, American-sponsored cultural institutions require a degree of binational cooperation in determining the most desirable programs to pursue. Instead of deciding unilaterally what American cultural "exports" to send abroad, we should solicit the advice and cooperation of governments and interested private foreign groups who are willing to give it.

But what of the other half of USIA's present tasks: the attempt to influence world opinion through mass communications? There is a case to be made for government support of foreign broadcasting and telecasting, but not in the present propaganda pattern. Once again, the United States has much to learn from other democratic nations. To return again to the Duncan Report, commenting this time on the semi-independent External Broadcasting Service of the British Broadcasting Corporation: "Because of its independence from Government control, which indeed is its main asset in maintaining overseas listeners' belief in the credibility of its news reporting and comment, the BBC, in our view, should continue to be regarded as one of the most effective means of projecting British news and views, and should certainly have a high priority compared with official printed publicity and hand-outs."[144]

A private-public United States Radio and Television Network, comparable in structure to the external service of the BBC, has been proposed on several occasions, most recently by Oudes, who points out that there may be as many as 3 million Americans now living abroad—2 million military and civilian government officials and their families, and 1 million private citizens—all of whom "deserve an intelligent external U.S. broadcast service." Since the present Voice of America and U.S. Armed Forces networks often broadcast on the same band, but give widely divergent news coverage, the impression is that we have two different government-run news systems, one for American and one for foreign consumption. The quality is poor and the censorship in both systems is enormous. The best way to "lower our voices" and improve the quality, honesty, and independence of our foreign broadcasting is to move toward a BBC-type system. This would require legislation by Congress establishing a U.S. broadcasting corporation having an independent board of governors and staff, appointed in much the same way as the proposed Cultural Institute. Oudes has noted that Congress, "in accepting the principle of publicly funded domestic television, has paved the way for the new Voice to be the external service of the Corporation for Public Broadcasting."[145] This is the right direction for a mature democracy to follow. Indeed, it is surprising that in time of peace we still engage in narrow broadcasting propaganda of the kind employed during World War II.

These proposals require the abolition of USIA and the State Department's Bureau of Educational and Cultural Affairs, but they do not diminish the need for American diplomacy to stay informed of home politics and to conduct the informational and public relations jobs that are a normal part of embassy work abroad. These requirements—largely a matter of cabling public statements and press digests to foreign posts—are already sometimes duplicated between

USIA and State's own public affairs offices. With or without USIA, embassy officers will continue to deal with the foreign press, stay on top of the news, and distribute American newspapers, magazines, and books wherever it is useful to our diplomacy.

To remove culture and broadcasting from tight governmental controls will be to show faith in the vitality of our principles. It is none too soon to expect Congress to act on such a program. As Oudes observes, "We are too mature a people to allow ourselves to be demeaned by the silly huckstering of propaganda."[146]

7

THE FOREIGN POLICY OF AID AND DEFENSE

. . . far too many decisions go unmade, critical issues are not addressed and the principle of personal accountability is lost in the diffused maze of "staff co-ordination."
—The Fitzhugh Report (1970)

Senator Kenneth Wherry of Nebraska told an election audience in 1940, "With God's help, we will lift Shanghai up and up, ever up, until it is just like Kansas City."[147] Most Americans share something of Senator Wherry's view when they think about foreign aid. National pride and cultural arrogance have mixed with humanitarianism, faith in progress, and fear of communism to produce our multibillion-dollar foreign assistance effort in fourscore countries around the globe. To some, American aid workers are what President Truman called them, "technical missionaries" spreading the gospel of efficiency and modernity; to others, they are a first bulwark in the nation's defense system. This confusion of motive has hampered the effort from the beginning. When a program is sold on conflicting ideological, military, and humanitarian grounds it becomes hard to conceive, let alone administer, on national interest grounds. The confusions have been institutionalized, and are one reason why our foreign aid dispensing agency has been reorganized and renamed six times in the last twenty years and is about to be reorganized again.

Although 46 percent of the American public, according to a 1970 poll by the University of Michigan, support the concept of foreign aid, a large minority—32 percent—oppose it.[148] In America the biggest complaint about foreign aid is its cost. Abroad the biggest objection is its size—the unsettling involvement of *so many* American officials in the divisive development problems of so many countries. Like it or not, the donor-recipient relationship looks suspiciously like a new form of colonialism to many of the receiving countries. It involves the United States deeply in their internal political and economic processes, and it often requires conscientious American officials to contradict what we claim as a national credo: that *self*-government is fundamentally more important than good government.

In 1970, American government assistance to developing countries was running less than 20 percent of our annual aid to Europe at the height of the Marshall Plan in 1948–1951. President Nixon asked for $2.6 billion in economic aid, and, after a bitter fight, Congress gave him $1.8 billion. This is a drop of nearly 50 percent compared to the amount we were spending a decade ago during the Kennedy administration. Although more than seventy countries are being aided, the bulk of the money—84 percent of it in 1968— went to fifteen nations, six of them in Latin America and nine elsewhere, mainly in South Asia: India, Indonesia, Korea, Laos, Nigeria, Pakistan, Thailand, Turkey, and Vietnam. Development loans, more than 90 percent of which go toward the purchase of American equipment, accounted for about half of the aid budget, with welfare and emergency relief and technical assistance grants in the form of advice from U.S. technicians accounting for the other half. In addition, food commodities valued by the Agriculture Department at $920 million, were provided under its Food for Freedom program, and $480 million was donated to international organizations such as the World Bank.

The drop in military assistance has been just as spectacular as the reduction in economic aid. U.S. military-aid programs reached their zenith in 1952—$5.74 billion, most of it to rearm NATO allies in Europe. In the past decade, the figure fell from $1.9 billion in 1963 to $350 million in 1970. This latest figure, however, excludes aid to Vietnam, which comes directly from the Defense Department budget and amounted to about $2.5 billion in 1969. Most of the $350 million goes to Korea, China, Turkey, and Greece, but small amounts are provided to 44 other countries, while 16 more countries receive credits for the purchase of U.S. weapons under the Foreign Military Sales Act. In almost every case where American economic or military aid is provided, a large staff of U.S. advisers, loosely attached to the American embassy, is sent to administer the program. Even in twelve countries where economic assistance has long since been terminated, a total of fifty-five personnel of the Agency for International Development remained active in 1970, presumably closing out the books on the completed programs.[149]

During the 1970 budget hearings Congressman Passman and Senator Ellender both remarked that they had been hearing the same executive branch arguments in favor of foreign aid for the last seventeen years, and remained unconvinced. They doubted the "national security" rationale that a given level of aid was necessary to protect the United States against communism, and they did not see that the humanitarian argument that the United States had a moral requirement as a wealthy society to help poorer nations had much practical significance in deciding how much we spend and where we spend it. Their conservative puzzlement was shared by many liberal legislators, who see aid programs as the vanguard of military intervention.

Both groups of congressmen are coming to realize that neither the old anticommunist approach nor a diffuse sense of American "responsibility" for raising the living standards of poorer states answers the questions, "How much?" and "For whom?" By 1970 it seemed clearer than in 1960 that aid was not going to create lots of "little Americas" around the world and, Senator Wherry to the contrary, that that should not be its goal in any case. Differential wealth is now recognized increasingly as a world problem that cannot be attacked by one nation acting alone with a short-term program. Despite the exaggerations of enthusiasts, the net economic effect of aid programs to date has not been great. Foreign aid has probably not reduced political tensions in developing countries, but has, instead, tended to stimulate instability and the dictatorial forms of rule, popular or oligarchic, which accompany any savage break with tradition. It is not at all clear that American voters and leaders favor these results. Hence, additional confusion about our purposes.

Some of the strongest Washington partisans of aid in the 1960s were men accurately described by James Thomson, Jr., as "technocracy's own Maoists," academics and politicians who, Thomson says, "have given a new life to the missionary impulse," in American foreign policy. Inside and outside government, these ideologues have argued that U.S. military might, technological supremacy, and benevolent intention give our nation, in Thomson's words, "the opportunity and the obligation to ease the nations of the earth toward modernization and stability: toward a full-fledged Pax Americana Technocratica."[150] Their doctrine, really only a latter-day elaboration of Senator Wherry's simple faith, has appealed to the traditional prejudices of the American people. It contains and caters to an enormous self-satisfaction about American society and the presumed uniqueness of our mission in the world. It is as denigrating to foreign countries and flattering to our own self-esteem as Thomas Jefferson's observation in 1801 that "before the establishment of the American states, nothing was known to history but the man of the Old World, crowded within limits either small or overcharged, and steeped in the vices which that situation generates."[151] It is as delusive as Wherry's vision of Shanghai emulating Kansas City.

These patriotic sentiments are the litany of an American political speech, but they do not help us to understand the complex and varied problems of economic growth and social change in other lands. They partake of what Walter Lippmann has called a fatal "universalism" in American thought, fueled by ignorance and a long experience of world isolation. During the 1960s our universal pattern for the developing nations took a particularly rigid shape. With American help, they were to "modernize" quickly through a process of "peaceful change" that assured "stability" in a noncommunist direction. Social scientists of MIT would call this a program of "conflict-avoidance," for it has been implicit in their thinking, and Washington's, that violent changes in government anywhere are undesirable. Although wars, attempted revolutions, and coups d'état are facts of life, especially in the Third

World (there were 164 significant outbreaks of violence between 1958 and 1966 according to Robert McNamara), the theorists of "world order" find these things unsettling and unnatural.

To preach a doctrine of minimum conflict and constant political stability on the one hand and fast economic growth and social change on the other is to insist on the most jumbled self-contradiction. Unrealistic as it is, the doctrine would be a good deal less damaging if it were not assumed that *American* effort is the key to Latino-Afro-Asian progress, and that failure of such progress or "political instability" in achieving it constitutes a grave rebuff and even a security threat to the United States. That so very unconvincing a doctrine could have gained widespread credence in Washington in the 1960s reveals, at the very least, a weakness of insight. Universalism has damaged our powers of discrimination. In the 1970s it is time to cast away false hopes as well as false fears. Our aid program, whose recent history reveals in microcosm many of the intellectual inconsistencies of American foreign policy, must be reformulated.

History of Economic Assistance

As in the case of foreign intelligence and propaganda, the economic assistance effort is a child of World War II. The beginnings were Lend-Lease, developed during the war years to help the Allies fight Hitler, and UNRRA, developed to assist postwar recovery. These were followed by the Marshall Plan for Europe in 1948 and by President Truman's "Point Four" program of technical assistance to developing countries.

Toward a Better Structure

Tied loosely to the State Department, we continually renamed and reshuffled the stumbling assistance program in the 1950s. An "Economic Cooperation Administration" and a "Foreign Operations Administration" preceded a "Mutual Security Administration" and were followed by an "International Cooperation Administration" that finally in 1961 became the "Agency for International Development" (AID).

In an upsurge of interest in development in the early 1960s, U.S. aid resources were spread rather thinly and widely around the world, raising expectations that every new nation was a potential recipient of U.S. assistance. AID staffs proliferated, and today most United States diplomatic missions to developing countries still have many more AID employees than State Department personnel. A declining budget has forced some cutbacks and greater selectivity, but in personnel and administrative terms the organizational strategy persists of putting large resident staffs of American AID officials in foreign countries to "run" AID programs.

The massiveness of the American AID presence abroad is politically disturbing to many recipient countries, as is the unilateral approach American officials tend to take in "running" the programs. Zealous U.S. administrative methods look very visibly like a form of deep interference in the internal decisions of sovereign foreign governments. Anxious to make a short-term "success" of their efforts, AID missions generally draw up development projects; fight for their approval, funding, and "clearance" by Washington; and *then* at the last stage present them unilaterally as a *fait accompli* to the foreign government to be aided, requesting the ratification of American plans. The aid-donor relationship is reversed, the donor AID director "lobbying" with the recipient government to win its acceptance of an American plan to give it aid, after he has engaged in an even more extensive lobbying process within the U.S. government. In the process, a cooperative relationship between the two governments based on mutual respect for sovereignty is apt to get lost, depleting an ambassador's always limited supply of political capital with his hosts.

The effect of a large American presence and a large flow of American resources on a developing country varies from place to place, but may easily be perverse and even undercut the development goal. Authoritarian government by small, educated, and modernized elites is the rule rather than the exception in the developing world. Only five out of twenty-one developing countries in Latin America have the beginnings of a "democratic" tradition as most Western political scientists would define the term. Of the South Asian countries, India and Ceylon stand virtually alone in this regard, and few of Africa's three dozen states have a parliamentary opposition. The task of "building democracy," if the words make any sense at all in a diverse international environment, will not be simple, easy, or quick. Political and social evolution, like economic growth itself, will only be marginally affected by American aid policies, if, indeed, it is affected at all. In most societies, a sudden inflow of foreign resources and influence is bound for a time to be disruptive and unsettling. It may well create acute social and political unrest while only scratching the surface of modern economic development—a complex task that requires many decades in most countries, and perhaps a century of concerted effort in the lowest income parts of the world.

The presence of many obviously prosperous and free-wheeling Americans in the major cities of very poor societies is not especially conducive to winning affection for the United States. Even the Peace Corps, for all the good will behind it, does not always look especially attractive to foreign peoples and elites who are unhappy with outside pressures that affect their accustomed ways of life. It is not only American diplomatic and aid officials, but also experienced educators, businessmen, journalists, and travelers who lack all but superficial understanding of the social and political, as distinct from the economic problems of the developing world. This ignorance should come as no surprise, for U.S. experience with most of the developing countries (outside Latin America) is extremely brief. The concept of a "Developing World" is less than fifteen years old, and neither trade nor politics required a major U.S. interest in these areas before World War II. Harvard University offered its first course in African politics in 1960. An American AID official who has served in Vietnam continuously since 1961 recently remarked that "there are no American experts on Vietnam." After twenty-seven months' service, in 1967–1969, in an African country with 3,000 years of recorded history, which the U.S. aid program "discovered" less than twenty years ago, I think I can add that "there are no American experts on Ethiopia." These facts in themselves should stimulate a kind of modesty and restraint that Americans have rarely shown to date in their approach to the Third World.

If we want to reduce provocative American "presences" in developing countries, then the very concept of the U.S. AID mission needs rethinking. Most other aid donors administer their bilateral programs directly through their embassies. This simpler approach is feasible for U.S. programs as well. An "economic section" is a normal part of each American embassy, and there is no reason why most functions now performed by elaborate AID missions could not be taken on within the smaller framework of embassy economic sections.

This would require abolishing AID missions and turning their responsibilities over to embassy economic staffs. Wherever possible, we should at the same time seek cooperative arrangements whereby U.S. technicians serve as temporary advisers *within* host-country economic institutions, rather than as U.S. officials in the direct employ of the embassy or AID mission. This, again, is what most other AID-giving nations do in most parts of the world.

These changes, which accord with the recommendations of a recent Presidential Task Force on Aid, accomplish at least three useful things:

1. They establish the principle of cooperation rather than unilateralism as the cornerstone of aid, building greater host-country confidence not only in the U.S. purpose but also in its own competence to run its own institutions, while reducing the size and visibility of U.S. staffs and the political hostility to the large U.S. presence;
2. They end ambiguity within the U.S. government over where to look for policy direction in the field as between the AID mission director and the ambassador; the ambassador's authority is strengthened, and host countries cannot play him off against a separate AID director whom they often tend to regard as "the man with the money";
3. While tightening control and administration within the U.S. mission, they put technical skill in proper perspective as the servant rather than the master of policy; substituting advice and negotiation for what today is all too often U.S. dictation.

Beyond structural problems, the size of AID staffing is a problem in itself. For the past eight years the Agency for

International Development has employed between 15,000 and 18,000 personnel per year, from 20 to 30 percent of them in Vietnam. About half are Americans and half alien employees. At the beginning of 1970, American personnel of AID who served abroad—5,234 of them—outnumbered the total overseas staff of the State Department, although State had representatives in 116 countries and AID in less than 90. About 3,500 AID officials man the home office in Washington, 700 of whom spend their full time auditing the program to meet statutory requirements. Most of them sit in the main building of the State Department, but operate independently from State employees, except for the single "integrated" bureau for Latin America, which is jointly staffed by State and AID personnel.

Hag-ridden by Congress, which has never looked with wholehearted favor on its program, AID has never been able to develop an effective career service. Like State's Foreign Service, it has a personnel bulge at the top levels, with many more senior than junior employees. It has had great difficulty in recruiting young development economists and all of the technicians that it needs—agronomists, hydrologists, and mechanics. The bulk of its technicians are hired on short-term contracts, loaned by private institutions. A large percentage of AID jobs in Washington and overseas, but one that has never been precisely determined, are controlled by congressional patronage. Although AID's Washington staff is only about half the size of State's, it is compartmentalized into nearly twice as many distinct offices. Operating under considerable restrictions set by Congress, it is perhaps not surprising that AID is known as one of Washington's slowest-moving bureaucracies. The office titles themselves are more than a mouthful. Consider the shorthand acronym AA/A/AID, which in fullest English stands for "Assistant Administrator for Administration of the Agency for International Development."

The Peterson Report

All of this will be changed by a drastic reorganization plan that was recommended to President Nixon on March 4, 1970. Sixteen economists, businessmen, and other interested citizens, headed by Rudolph A. Peterson of the Bank of America, submitted the report of a public task force that had been appointed by the President to study international development in the 1970s. The Peterson plan would bring home all but a small fraction of our overseas aid workers. It would also abolish the Agency for International Development, replacing it with several separate government corporations having much more modest staffs. Although it would substitute a somewhat more complex structure—giving State ultimate responsibility for military and security and emergency assistance, and administering development aid through a U.S. Development Bank and technical assistance via a U.S. research institute—the Peterson recommendations are a good step forward out of the present morass. They rightly stress the need to move away from a national, bilateral aid program and concentrate instead on giving economic assistance through international organizations. In 1970, for the first time, the total development outlay of the World Bank ($2.3 billion) was larger than that of the U. S. government, and the trend will undoubtedly continue. Welcoming this trend, President Nixon has accepted the Peterson recommendations and urged Congress to permit a restructuring of the entire American aid effort.

The Peterson Study criticized military as well as economic

aid practices of the past and present. "Large military assistance advisory groups and missions," it concluded, "are no longer necessary in many developing countries. . . . The United States can reduce its supervision and advice to a minimum, thus encouraging progress toward self-reliance. U.S. military missions and advisory groups should be consolidated with other elements in our overseas missions as soon as possible."[152]

The "ambitious" American development role adopted in the 1960s, the Peterson Report noted, "required a prominent U.S. presence in some countries; and friction with some governments resulted from attempts to influence sensitive areas of their national policy related to development."[153] It went on to warn that "a predominantly bilateral U.S. program is no longer politically tenable in our relations with many developing countries" and "the current practice of employing large numbers of technicians and advisory personnel in many fields and in many countries should be changed. It has required high overhead and large field missions."[154] A better program would channel most aid through international organizations and "operate with a minimum of field representatives." Such bilateral American efforts as remain should, Peterson argued, be under the over-all direction of American ambassadors, aided by "foreign service officers trained in development problems" and other outside specialists. A complicated—probably much too complicated—"Development Council" located in the White House would coordinate the entire aid program, but would do so under the broad policy guidance of the Secretary of State. The essence of the Peterson recommendation is for greater emphasis on cooperative multilateral lending and for replacement of the massive, interventionist methods of the new-diplomacy period with more relaxed and confident approaches to development that respect national sovereignty.

Whether these proposals are adopted by Congress this year or a few years hence, they surely make sense. The Agency for International Development, founded a decade ago, has played out its institutional life span. It is time to demobilize our large AID field missions and to create new institutions based on the Peterson model, staffed with new personnel. Aid can and ought to be taken out of the old, irrelevant cold-war context of political expediency, which perversely has been so unrealistic a measure of the American national interest, and put where it belongs as a world problem to be addressed by the world community at large. The sooner Washington travels that road the quicker will its relations with the developing countries return to orthodox diplomatic channels that respect sovereignty. At the same time many of the confusions of motive that rightly bother Congress and the public will cease to be annual subjects of disputation in our national politics. They will be mainly replaced, in time, with an appeal to the more generous impulses of our political life and with genuine pride in the efficiency and disinterestedness of a fitter organization.

The Foreign Policy of the Pentagon

A problem of the 1970s that may be more difficult, although certainly no less complicated than the aid dilemma, is what to do about the impact of our military establishment on our foreign policy. Size alone makes that impact substantial. The Pentagon employs 60 percent *more* personnel within U.S. diplomatic missions abroad than does the State Department. At the start of the 1970 fiscal year, there were 8,264 U.S. citizen

Defense Department personnel serving on embassy staffs, or 3100 more than the State total.

These figures represent but a tiny fraction of total Defense Department employment overseas. Excluding troops in Southeast Asia, South Korea, Berlin, and NATO commands in Europe, in 1970 there were 144,889 U.S. citizen Defense personnel serving in other parts of the world, 39,281 of them civilians. In addition, the Pentagon employed 324,682 foreign citizens.

We are told to expect all of these figures to decline during the next several years. The withdrawal from Vietnam, nearly halfway completed by April 1971, is only the largest of many U.S. military "de-commitments." President Nixon has promised to begin a pullout from our large Okinawa base by 1972. There is talk about withdrawing at least one-third, if not more, of our 300,000 NATO forces in Europe (with a like number of military wives and children), and unquestionably many will depart in the coming decade. In June 1970, the 4,600 U.S. Air Force personnel at Wheelus Field in Libya closed their base and departed. Some, if not all, of the 50,000 American troops in Korea are scheduled to leave before the mid-1970s, and they may be joined by servicemen now in the Philippines, Taiwan, Thailand, and Japan. In 1978, the agreement that keeps some 2,000 American personnel at a communications base in Ethiopia will terminate. Some of the defense pacts that we have with four dozen countries that were concluded in the 1940s and 1950s are coming to an end, and it is not clear that all of them will be renewed. Only the threat of a major war is likely to alter this downward trend.

Apart from the larger question of foreign troop deployments, however, the figure that more narrowly concerns this study is the 8,264 American personnel of the Defense Department attached to embassies and consulates. They are the single largest element in U.S. diplomatic missions. When military personnel outnumber diplomatic personnel at an embassy, which is invariably the case today, foreign officials are almost bound to receive a distorted impression of American priorities. The imbalance also imposes a unique administrative burden on the U.S. mission. The care and housing of military personnel and their dependents abroad tend to take precedence over other "housekeeping" chores and to produce the "PX Culture" referred to in Chapter 5—a living system that parochially throws American officials and their families together at the expense of wider contacts with their foreign hosts. The end result is large U.S. housing compounds, privileged American shopping centers and grocery stores and schools and women's clubs on the military model of "base living." Since the military, which expect these prepackaged arrangements, numerically predominate at so many diplomatic posts, the housekeeping system for *all* the embassy staff is often fixed by military administrative requirements. Here is a case where our foreign policy needs are distorted by the shape of organization and the sheer size of staffs.

Why are the military staffs at our embassies so large? There are, of course, good reasons for having personnel of the armed services attached to diplomatic missions. For the past eighty years the embassies of most major powers have included military attachés, who collect intelligence, give professional advice, and serve as liaison to the armies, navies, and air forces of foreign countries. The United States also has military aid and training missions in forty-eight countries, and credit weapons sales agreements with sixteen more; it needs to coordinate military staff work with NATO and other allies. It is useful to have military expertise in an embassy as a technical aid to the diplomats who negotiate for American base rights, landing and overflight privileges for U.S. military aircraft, port calls for the U.S. Navy, and for the many daily dealings between governments occasioned by our 1.1 million troops stationed overseas.

There is a need for *some* military expertise at a U.S. mission, but that does not explain the disproportionate size of our military staffs today, or their tendency, like that of CIA, to assert for themselves a role in policy making as distinct from giving technical advice and assistance to the ambassador and his diplomatic staff. The following are probably the main reasons why our military staffs have become so large:

1. The State Department does not control the number of military people sent to a diplomatic mission; the numbers are set by the Pentagon, as a "purely technical matter"; since practically no outside restraint is imposed, there is no administrative restriction on the number of people involved and no analysis relating the size of staff to the mission to be accomplished or to the over-all and over-riding needs of foreign policy. When ambassadors complain (as they frequently do) of excessively large military staffs, and recommend cuts, there is no single place in Washington with authority to act on their recommendations, short of the President himself.

2. The Defense budget is more accounted for and more widely and carefully scrutinized than that of CIA; however, it is such a large budget, and the part of it relating to diplomatic missions is such a small fraction of the total, that there is no particular pressure applied to this "tiny" fragment of an immense worldwide program; Pentagon wags in Washington remark to their State Department colleagues, "We 'spill' (i.e., 'waste') in one week more than you spend in a year," which points up the immense budgetary disparity between Defense's

$70 billion and State's $400 million annual resources; in effect, Defense budget planners think in terms of hundreds of millions of dollars whereas State thinks in terms of hundreds of thousands of dollars.

3. Uncomfortable with the political strictures and viewpoints of State, successive secretaries of defense and their military chiefs have sought to build their own independent channels of information and foreign policy assessment; to have large field staffs with an independent communications network strengthens the Pentagon in Washington debates, giving it a chance to challenge the "foreign policy experts" on their own ground; the confidence and prestige that a Washington agency head derives from having "his own man" in Havana or Paris or Prague, or wherever, is not limited to Defense or CIA but is a centrifugal fact of life throughout Washington, which makes most cabinet officials, if only for reasons of patronage and prestige, cherish the wish of having "their own men" in attaché jobs at embassies around the world.

4. The "missions" and "requirements" of military intelligence, like those of CIA, are defined by the parent organizations in Washington, without outside review, and tend to become inflated over time; some of these missions are of comic-opera proportion—for example, in the late 1950s the U.S. Army attaché's office at our embassy in Athens, then one of the largest attaché staffs in the world, had most of its staff travel throughout Greece measuring every culvert under every road, the object being to see whether they were wide enough to accommodate U.S. tanks.

To be aware of these habits is not to excuse them. The Secretary of State could and should slash Defense staffs at the embassies. Any poll of ambassadors would show that they regard attachés and military assistance and training staffs and liaison staffs to be far in excess of U.S. foreign-policy requirements, to the point where their size is a positive detriment to the over-all job of U.S. diplomatic missions. The 1970 Peterson Report on foreign aid reached the same conclusion. If State, working with Defense, were to draw up and enforce new ceilings on these staffs, it may not be unrealistic to expect a worldwide cut of as much as 80 percent. Because the military bureaucracy often, perversely, obtains a vested interest in the programs of foreign clients, reducing its size should be one way to reduce pressures on Washington to increase military aid and other forms of intervention. The Peterson Report, while recommending that military aid be terminated in the 1970s, was right to criticize the large and unilateral character of the present effort. Under existing procedures, it noted, "The United States now makes the basic determination of the amount and kind of military equipment the receiving countries need, and U.S. military missions do most of the detailed logistical planning and costing for them."[155] In other words, the initial decisions are made entirely by Americans, and are then "sold" to foreign governments, a thoroughly backward approach that has much in common with the reverse logic of many of our AID development programs as well.

The Fitzhugh Report

Larger problems of organization exist in Washington within the Pentagon itself. Many were identified by a blue-ribbon citizens' commission appointed by President Nixon in 1969 to study the Defense Department and recommend reforms. Headed by Gilbert W. Fitzhugh, board chairman of the Metropolitan Life Insurance Company, the panel issued its report on July 1, 1970. The Fitzhugh Report was scathingly critical of the Joint Chiefs of Staff (JCS) and the Defense Intelligence Agency (DIA), two central parts of the Pentagon's foreign-affairs apparatus, which moved the *New York Times* to comment, in an editorial, that "disturbing questions" had been raised "about the quality of top Pentagon advice and the way crucial military decisions are made." The findings, said the *Times*, are "startling" and suggest the need for a "radical overhaul."[156] As was also widely noted by the press at the time, the Fitzhugh panel confirmed that Defense Secretary Laird had been bypassed by the Joint Chiefs in advising the White House on preparations to intervene in Cambodia in April and May 1970.

Many State Department officials will find this information less than "startling," for the preponderance of military influence in foreign policy is a long-standing problem. At least six separate staffs within the Pentagon, their total size and cost much greater than that of the State Department, deal primarily with foreign-policy issues. These include the Organization of the Joint Chiefs, more than 2,000 strong, the international affairs and intelligence staffs of the three armed services and the three service secretaries, the 7,000-man Defense Intelligence Agency (DIA), and finally the 3,500 personnel of the Office of the Secretary of Defense (OSD), which includes an Office of the Assistant Secretary of Defense for International Security Affairs (ISA). The most influential of these are the Joint Chiefs Organization, which the Fitzhugh Report would partly abolish and partly reduce, and the ISA. The intelligence body, DIA, has not been a serious contender for influence in Washington since its founding in 1961, because much of its work has been regarded by other members of the intelligence community as sloppy and frequently inaccurate. But on occasion, once again in the case of the 1970 Cambodian intervention, there is reason to believe that DIA provided independent analyses for the White House, some of them containing factual errors or distortions that may have had some effect on President Nixon's decision, and particularly on the way he presented it to the public.

In his televised address to the nation on April 30, 1970, the President declared, "Tonight, American and South Vietnamese units will attack the headquarters for the entire Communist military operation in South Vietnam. This key control center has been occupied by the North Vietnamese and Viet Cong for five years in blatant violation of Cambodia's neutrality." The statement later proved embarrassing, for no such Communist headquarters was found by the attacking forces. The error was one that would have been corrected by almost any State Department officer having Southeast Asian experience, but apparently no official of State was consulted by the White House to cross-check the faulty DIA intelligence. The layman might plausibly think that military intelligence officers should also be expected to catch such errors, but most Washington insiders know better.

Evidence of the inaccuracy and inefficiency of Pentagon intelligence systems was beginning to emerge in public discussion even before the Fitzhugh Report. A former DIA officer, Patrick McGarvey, has written at length about "DIA's policy of compromise and of blandness, of pleasing everybody and therefore of informing or edifying nobody." DIA has made numerous misjudgments on Vietnam, McGarvey concludes, and "will doubtless continue to supply the nation's decision makers with evaluations that do them little good and potentially much harm."[157]

Military intelligence is a legitimate interest of the armed forces, but when it becomes a duplicated and inferior version of political intelligence, there is cause for concern. The Fitzhugh Report revealed further inefficiencies: "While the DIA was established primarily to consolidate the intelligence activities at the Washington level, each Military Department currently has a larger intelligence staff than it had before the creation of DIA."[158] On grounds of ten years of poor performance there may be a case for abolishing the DIA altogether. However the Pentagon and the three armed services choose to organize this aspect of their work, a stronger State Department, with presidential backing, should monitor and control the government-wide foreign intelligence effort more closely.

Other conclusions about the Pentagon reached by the Fitzhugh blue-ribbon panel are similar to those reached six years earlier by McCamy in his study of the entire foreign-affairs machine. Fitzhugh concluded, for example, that "excessive size" had become a major problem, and that it causes "an astonishing lack of organizational focus and a highly excessive degree of 'coordination,' a substantial portion of which entails the writing of memoranda back and forth between lower echelons of parallel organizational elements and which serves no apparent useful or productive purpose."[159] It found command channels cluttered—"awkward and unresponsive . . . even in crisis situations."[160] Since 1956, it reported, the staffs of the Joint Chiefs and the office of Secretary of Defense had more than doubled in size, in violation of statutory restrictions. A part of this growth was a result of program-budgeting reforms, which produced "a profusion of management information systems and reporting requirements" causing "a sheer mass of informational detail" that only "obscured" the most "relevant and important facts." As a result, ". . . far too many decisions go unmade, critical issues are not addressed, problems are deferred and the principle of personal accountability is lost in the diffused maze of 'staff coordination.' "[161] Among the changes recommended by the Fitzhugh panel, the most thorough public review of Defense organization in the past two decades, were the following:

1. A cutback in 1,500 personnel in the size of the office of the Secretary of Defense, down from 3,500 to a new ceiling of 2,000;
2. Reduction of the personnel now serving the Joint Chiefs of Staff, who number 2,145 (900 of them military officers), down to a new total of no more than 250 officers;
3. Cuts of "at least 30 per cent" in the headquarters staffs of the Army, Navy, and Air Force Departments.

The Fitzhugh panel was not authorized to consider questions of foreign policy, but a strong Secretary of State, having read their report, would be bound to question the Pentagon's need for keeping its own mini-foreign offices. The 321 personnel of ISA, for example, divide their tasks, in imitation of State, into geographic desks that cover the world, including those few parts of the globe that have yet to see an American military program. Over a period of years, ISA has established itself as the Pentagon's main channel of communication and coordination with State, the "co-drafter" of most cables and instructions going out to embassies that relate to military matters. (The Joint Chiefs Organization, however, which frequently feels that ISA does not represent *it*, also insists on separately clearing a substantial volume of State-military business.)

Instead of challenging this system or suggesting a better one, State in 1961 established a special staff for liaison with Defense, elevating it (in June 1969) to the new "Bureau of Politico-Military Affairs" ("PMA"), with ninety personnel under a director having assistant secretary rank. Thus, two essentially duplicative liaison bodies have emerged, each of which exists mainly to negotiate and give clearance to the work of the other. The proper solution is for the Secretary of State to insist that if the Defense Secretary needs foreign policy advice within easy reach he be assigned a senior State Department adviser with a few assistants instead of forming and recruiting his own foreign-policy staff. In asserting his senior role, the Secretary of State could assure that coordination occurs at the top rather than at the bottom of the chain of command, and could end the spreading confusion and duplication of effort that now exist in both departments. Above all, he could re-right a balance of authority that has shifted ominously in the past twenty years toward military technologists and away from foreign-policy planners.

Trying to decide and administer military assistance levels, foreign base agreements, arms sales, and crisis contingency plans are legitimate questions for State-Defense discussion. These questions, which often require high-level policy decisions involving the Secretaries of State and Defense and the President, need inputs of technical and political *expertise* in their preparation of a kind available in the two departments. Essentially, Defense's ISA and State's PMA complicate the matter by adding two extra, low- and middle-level negotiating layers above the already responsible regional and technical offices.

Congress, on its own initiative, has clamped down on another long-term abuse, the Pentagon's foreign affairs research program. In 1967 Washington agencies spent $41 million on grants and contracts to scholars, universities, and research institutes for international studies. More than 50 percent of the research was subsidized by the Pentagon; only six-tenths of 1 percent was paid for by State (which still spends only $150,000 annually on foreign affairs research),* [162] The Defense program first gained notoriety in 1965, when "Operation Camelot," a social-science project to predict the possibilities of revolution in Chile and Brazil, briefly strained U.S. relations with those two countries. Congress began to ask why the Defense Department needed to hire scholars to study foreign problems while the State Department did not. Finally, in the Military Procurement Authorization Act for Fiscal Year 1970, Congress insisted that no Pentagon funds "may be used to carry out any research project or study, unless the project or study has a direct and apparent relationship to a specific military function or operation." Even under these tighter restrictions, Defense continues to outspend State in its own field. Interpreting "national security" broadly enough to encompass any and every subject, in the same way that CIA has often construed "intelligence," the Defense Department has thus staked out a position as the major government contractor for academic work wholly unrelated to its function. Many scholars and private research organizations, who depend for their incomes on Pentagon contracts, are perfectly happy with this arrangement, an example of what some have called "The Military-Social Sci-

* An 83-page State Department publication, *Foreign Affairs Research: A Directory of Governmental Resources,* in 1967 listed 29 separate U.S. government agencies and 94 subdivisions within the agencies as being involved in foreign affairs research.

ence Complex" in action. But it is not a healthy relationship either for government or for scholarship. If the present congressional restrictions (applied for the first time in 1970) do not work, tougher ones are needed.

The research issue is a small but symbolic evidence of how military influence has come to dominate the budgetary and organizational structure of American foreign policy. The Fitzhugh reforms offer a much-needed backlash against the trend of the past twenty-five years. If they are taken seriously by the Nixon administration, we should soon see steps to curb the Pentagon's foreign policy functions and redefine the role of the Joint Chiefs of Staff. The defense establishment, Fitzhugh notes, has lost "the confidence of a significant segment of the American public" and suffers from even more overorganization than does the State Department. The fact that two or three Defense representatives—one from the Joint Chiefs, one from ISA, and sometimes one from the Secretary's personal staff—all sit on the main interagency committees is bound to give at least a numerical preponderance to the views of the Pentagon. The history and structure of the National Security Council also promote the military viewpoint in decision making. A program that cuts military staffs in the foreign policy field can go far toward restoring balance and proportion to the entire executive branch of government. Most important of all, perhaps, it will help presidents and their advisers begin to frame the main questions of our foreign policy in political rather than military terms.

8

THE ECONOMIC BUREAUCRACIES

> The American embassy in Rio de Janeiro needs a science attaché the way a cigar-store Indian needs a brassiere.
> —Ambassador Ellis O. Briggs

Washington keeps no central list of all government agencies involved in foreign affairs work. Figures released to Congress at the start of the 1970 fiscal year revealed that 65 percent of all personnel stationed at American diplomatic missions abroad worked for the Defense Department, AID, and USIA. Data for CIA were not given, but another 2,800 personnel, or 13 percent of the total, were said to represent "other" agencies. These "others" work for an estimated forty to fifty separate units of the executive branch. The American embassy in London, for example, in 1961 "housed representatives of forty-four agencies of the United States government" according to Arthur Schlesinger.[163] James McCamy earlier had discovered "forty-six agencies outside the Department of State that were concerned in part . . . with continuous economic functions in the field of foreign relations."[164]

The "others" obviously send fewer people abroad than do

the Big Four agencies and State, and their functions vary from the important to the trivial. Some, like the Peace Corps (whose 10,000 volunteer workers overseas are not included in the above totals), are treated as only quasi-governmental entities. Most, however, are engaged in economic or administrative work. The Coast Guard sends staffs to embassies to monitor maritime problems, and minerals attachés collect rocks and statistics for the Department of the Interior's Bureau of Mines. Foreign-based officials study dams for the Bureau of Reclamation and others follow fisheries problems for the Fish and Wildlife Service. FBI and narcotics agents at embassies coordinate law enforcement, members of the American Battle Monuments Commission look after overseas war cemeteries, Federal Aviation Agency staffs investigate air disasters, and Social Security officers process pension payments. In a jet age, a number of these functions could be performed just as readily, and at lower cost, by Washington staffs able to make occasional trips from the home base, rather than by resident officials overseas. Britain's Duncan Report, after conducting cost-benefit studies in 1969, reached this conclusion with respect to many nondiplomatic specialist jobs in the United Kingdom's overseas representation. No comparable studies have been made in Washington, but similar conclusions are not hard to imagine.

In its annual report of June 30, 1969, the U.S. Civil Service Commission lists thirty-four separate government agencies that employ personnel abroad. This report includes 150 countries or geographic areas, where 36,682 U.S. citizen government civilian employees are said to work, aided by 170,166 aliens, for a total payroll of 206,848.* Agency figures vary from

* On June 30, 1964, five years earlier, the same Civil Service survey showed 122,808 U.S. government civilian employees abroad—30,560 of them Americans and 92,248 aliens.

the Defense Department's 144,396, about 70 percent of the total, to, at the bottom of the totem pole, the Farm Credit Administration, which has one employee in Senegal, while the Tennessee Valley Authority keeps one man busy in the Netherlands. About two-thirds of the Americans and a smaller proportion of the aliens are attached to embassies. Leaving aside the Defense Department, State, CIA, AID, and USIA, the ten main U.S. domestic agencies represented overseas had, in mid-1969, the personnel strengths shown in Table 7. It should be cautioned that the Civil Service Commission data are incomplete and not entirely accurate, as is explained in a footnote.

The testiest critics of the proliferation of other-agency jobs at embassies tend to be former ambassadors who have suffered through the agony of trying to "coordinate" large staffs. Ellis Briggs, who, one gathers from his two volumes of memoirs, fought unavailingly through seven ambassadorships to cut excess staffs, has written, "Much of what we are doing abroad is blowing expensive soap bubbles, the principal admirers of which are the bureaucrats who are doing the blowing."[165] Edward O'Neill, a younger critic who left diplomacy for journalism, wrote in 1970 that "there is a great deal of promotion of American trade in countries with no foreign exchange to spare, gathering of esoteric statistics, encouragement of labor movements, poking into local mores and peculiarities. . . ." At a large embassy in Asia in which he had served, the writer alleged, "So many people were doing so many impinging things that about a third of people's time was taken up with 'coordination.' "[166]

Ambassador Briggs, while accredited to Brazil in 1958, was notified by Washington that a Ph.D. in physics was about to join his staff in the new job of "science attaché." He

Table 7
Overseas Employment of the Main U.S. Domestic Agencies, June 30, 1969

AGENCY	U.S. CITIZENS	ALIEN EMPLOYEES	TOTAL
Department of Agriculture	360	359	719
Department of Interior	408	19	427
American Battle Monuments Commission	38	363	401
Department of Health, Education, and Welfare	269	93	362
Department of Transportation	314	31	345
Veterans' Administration	26	282	308
Department of Commerce	175	120	295
Department of the Treasury	237	38	275
Department of Justice	184	27	211
National Science Foundation	209	—	209

SOURCE: U.S. Civil Service Commission, Annual Survey, June 1969.

NOTE: These figures are believed by most government statisticians to contain inaccuracies; for example, the table from which the above figures were extracted overestimates State Department employment overseas by about 20 percent, and underestimates AID employment by about the same margin, as compared with the more exact data furnished Congress for the same period (see Table 1, Chapter 1). Part of the difficulty may be caused by the need to "bury" CIA employment in other categories and the Civil Service Commission's method of assigning employment by the agency that pays personnel rather than by the agency that supervises them in the field. For the Defense Department, the Civil Service Commission figures list 21,355 overseas American employees and 123,041 alien employees. Nearly half of the aliens, but a much smaller percentage of the Americans, are concentrated in Vietnam; where, according to the Civil Service Commission data, 4,034 Americans of all agencies worked in mid-1969 alongside 60,580 aliens. Military forces, Peace Corps volunteers, and, presumably, some intelligence officers are excluded from all of these totals. A spot check of selected data by the author has revealed other inconsistencies that cannot be explained. For example, the Civil Service figures show twenty-two U.S. military personnel in Colombia, but the State Department lists a total of sixty-four military personnel attached to the embassy in Bogota. In Ethiopia, the Civil Service figures show 29 American-citizen Defense Department employees, whereas State Department tabulations show 109. Figures collected by the U.S. embassy in Paris show a larger number of American employees in France on June 30, 1969 and different agency breakdowns than the Civil Service data. The only safe conclusion to be drawn is that there is no accurate, central tabulation in Washington regarding overseas staffs. A number of State Department officials, in discussions with the author, have confirmed this conclusion.

replied in a famous cable, "The American embassy in Rio de Janeiro needs a science attaché the way a cigar-store Indian needs a brassiere."[167] Ten years later, the Rio embassy had *two* science attachés. A later ambassador to the same country, John Tuthill, received a mysterious cable in 1967 drafted in the bowels of the Washington bureaucracy that requested a survey on "bats and noxious birds" in Brazil and promised to send a team of specialists to conduct such a study. Tuthill, unlike Briggs, was somehow able to stop the unnecessary invasion, and even use it to convince Washington to cut his overblown staff. Such embassy staff reductions occur so rarely that they are long remembered. One of the most-repeated stories concerns, once again, Ellis Briggs when he was ambassador to Czechoslovakia shortly after the communist coup d'état of 1948. Briggs had been pestering Washington, without success, to cut his staff of eighty personnel (a large embassy by 1948 standards, but a small one today) by half, down to forty. One day the Czech government, unaware of this background, declared sixty-six of the American embassy's personnel *persona non grata* and gave them forty-eight hours to leave the country. The Prague regime had hoped to embarrass the United States by thus suddenly expelling five-sixths of its embassy staff, but to Briggs it was a blessing in disguise. "The American embassy in Prague then consisted of thirteen people," Briggs remarked. "It was probably the most efficient embassy I ever headed."[168]

Each separate agency that sends representatives to foreign missions argues that it has a job to do that relates in some way, however indirectly, to the interests and welfare of the American people. It is hard to challenge the sincerity of this claim, for even the survey of bats and noxious birds presumably had some defensible purpose. And it is understandable that each Washington department head is anxious for the additional patronage, prestige, and independence that come from having his own representatives in foreign capitals. But the extra jobs thus created, and the free-wheeling mandate that accompanies them, swell embassy staffs, confuse foreign governments, and tend to undercut ambassadors, who cannot possibly control all the extra specialists. Congress, responsive to domestic pressures, is often happy to vote funds for sending domestic agency representatives overseas, and the State Department has been too weak to resist the incursions. To the President, these are minor matters hardly worth his attention and certain to stir up a congressional hornet's nest should he interfere. As a result the United States is the world's only nation that includes as many as forty to fifty separate agency representations on its embassy rolls.

Four Main Domestic Agencies

The four most important of these many domestic agencies are the Commerce, Agriculture, Labor, and Treasury departments. Each has embassy attaché programs going back at least thirty years. Each also has Washington bureaus and divisions concerned with international affairs, and brings a degree of needed expertise to embassies that must report and negotiate on tangled commercial, financial, and agrarian problems. Their case for having large staffs abroad has much more surface logic than does the case of many of the other domestic agencies, for other major countries also send specialists in these fields overseas, though in nothing like the American number.

Treasury puts a corps of "financial attachés" in ten embassies. The program is paid for, without recourse to annual congressional appropriation, by interest payments received from an Exchange Stabilization Fund that was established upon the devaluation of the dollar in 1933.* Staffs have been kept reasonably small. They have a direct communication channel to the Secretary of the Treasury in Washington, supplied by the U.S. Navy, for matters that are thought too sensitive to be shared with ambassadors and the State Department.

Commerce and Agriculture have larger embassy staffs and programs, which appeal to U.S. farm and business groups. A commercial attaché service is run as one of several fields of specialization within the Foreign Service, with about 250 State employees supplemented by 300 Department of Commerce personnel. Routine commercial work at embassies consists mainly in making credit ratings of foreign companies and facilitating small business transactions between American and foreign firms designed to expand U.S. exports. In addition, a number of U.S. trade centers, attached to embassies, were opened in the 1960s to provide permanent, public displays of American products. These functions, which are really an aid to marketing, are tasks that large American corporations and major exporters are fully able to perform for themselves. The embassy effort is a form of service to domestic commerce dating from the nineteenth century, when foreign consuls were often important "middlemen" in international trade, and exporting firms lacked foreign branch offices, representatives, and fast communications media. Today, the thrust of the embassy commercial effort benefits small businesses that have minimum expertise in foreign marketing, and hence turn to the government for help. No one

* The law establishing the fund allowed proceeds from it to be used "for any purpose in connection with carrying out the provisions of this section," which Secretary Morgenthau and his successors interpreted broadly as the legislative mandate of their overseas attaché program.

knows whether the $20 to $30 million spent annually over the past 10 years for the Commerce program pays for itself. The suspicion is that it does not stimulate very much in the way of new American exports, certainly not enough to generate $20 to $30 million in government revenue. Congress, however, is importuned each year by Secretaries of Commerce and business lobbies to raise the budget and staffing of overseas commercial programs and to create independent "trade commissioners" of ministerial, or even ambassadorial, rank in U.S. embassies.

Having performed commercial work myself, I suspect that the present massive effort should be reduced rather than expanded. The largest commercial transaction I was able to stimulate was a $300,000 sale of American raw cotton to an African textile plant. New exports of even that modest size, however, are rarely the product of embassy commercial work. The kind of embassy economic work most useful to U.S. business is that of Foreign Service economic officers who follow foreign government policies and report them to Washington, rather than the product-oriented salesmanship and credit investigations performed by commercial attachés. An embassy sales job, which is in effect a public-relations effort on behalf of U.S. exporters, will have little result if U.S. industry or commodity prices are not competitive in the world market.

A distinction should be made between trade-development programs in the industrial countries of the north and the capital-starved nations of the south. In most of Western Europe, Canada, and Japan, where U.S. business contacts are good and industrial and trade information are readily available, there is no strong case for a large, redundant embassy commercial effort. In the relatively more closed societies of Eastern Europe and the developing world there is more of an "information gap" to be filled by embassy reports, but in many cases in these countries there is no foreign exchange available for payment for U.S. products. Indeed, in countries such as India the representatives of Commerce, trying to sell American goods, work at cross purposes with the representatives of AID, trying to conserve foreign exchange for development. Some information services and the facilitation of commercial contacts are a traditional and proper embassy function, but salesmanship should be left in the main to representatives of U.S. business and agriculture.

Congress gave the Department of Agriculture its own Foreign Agricultural Service (FAS) in 1954, to report on marketing opportunities abroad for U.S. farm surpluses and to study foreign competition. The FAS sends attachés to most American embassies, who communicate directly with the Secretary of Agriculture. In 1962 the total strength of the program was 693 American employees in Washington and abroad, and the FAS had plans to expand its staff to 856 in 1916, 956 in 1965, 1,044 in 1966, and 1,132 in 1967.[169] Growth of the FAS has not come as quickly as Agriculture has wished, but these figures suggest an inherent organizational dynamic, which becomes difficult to check when a program has its own independent legislative charter.

A similar trend is apparent in the Labor Department's embassy attaché program, which began with one man in 1939, jumped to 18 in 1946, 30 in 1950, 36 in 1956, 49 in 1960, and 66 in 1964, with a planned increase to 120 by the early 1970s.[170] Most of the officials in the program are former Labor Department officials and private trade-unionists hired by the State Department. They are supplemented by diplomats designated "labor reporting officers" at most overseas missions.

Labor attachés perform a political rather than an economic function. They are expected to keep tabs on foreign labor movements as a political force of significance for American foreign policy, and to promote U.S. policy to foreign labor leaders. In much the same pattern, USIA officials watch foreign educational, cultural, and journalistic leaders, other embassy officers follow student movements, and CIA separately duplicates most of these tasks. The specialist system of overseas representation, as exemplified by the labor attaché program, has several weaknesses. It tends, at least to a degree, to debase the currency of foreign relations and its foundations in international law. Diplomats, after all, subsume in the definition of their vocation a need to stay informed and in touch with the main trends in politics and economics of the countries to which they are accredited. By custom and international law, most countries recognize that one of the functions of foreign diplomats, living in their midst, is to have a wide variety of quite open contacts with a broad spectrum of the representative forces in the country, whether they be engaged in politics or business or education or labor. The specialist approach, on the other hand, involving special representatives from a wide number of Washington bureaucracies, suggests to foreigners a special attempt at influence, interference, and penetration. The effort may actually backfire and do more harm than good. The spate of kidnappings and assassinations of diplomats that has occurred in Latin America and elsewhere in recent years may in one sense underline this fact—for in the societies where these tragedies have occurred, diplomats have all too often behaved not as unobtrusive intermediates between governments, but rather as active "manipulators" of the domestic security situation.

The Labor, Commerce, and Agriculture overseas programs also raise the thorny question of how far it is in the national interest to give a special place and a special voice in foreign-policy making to particular domestic interest groups. Congress, the President, and the separate executive departments reflect the play of conflicting domestic interests in their daily work and decisions, but is it really necessary to duplicate the process in every overseas embassy as well? The labor program illustrates the difficulty of answering this question. Historically, its main impetus for expansion came in the tense cold-war period of the late 1940s, when there was a concerted effort by American trade unions and the CIA to prevent communist takeovers of a number of foreign unions. Since that time, labor movements have seemed to decline as a major political force in the world, but the U.S. labor attaché program has grown. The main supporter of the effort has been the AFL-CIO, which in large measure can be said to control the embassy labor attaché program. The Secretary of State's "special assistant for international labor affairs" for a number of years has functioned as a kind of liaison officer from America's largest union confederation, even though he sits in a government office. Non-AFL-CIO unions, such as the United Auto Workers, the Longshoremen, and the Teamsters, sometimes complain that *they* are not represented in this private-public arrangement. Each of these unions, and the AFL-CIO itself, has its own active international programs. In addition, the United States contributes heavily to the United Nations' International Labor Organization, which has headquarters in Geneva and programs throughout the world.

These facts make the embassy labor attaché programs seem redundant as well as of questionable legitimacy or usefulness. If Americans believe in trade unions as democratic associations, even though in many countries they are government-controlled, then to be true to our own principles we should leave specialized contacts on the private union-to-union level. While retaining "labor reporting officers," the specialized embassy labor attachés could be terminated with little pain. The Commerce and Agriculture programs need to be judged coldly on their economic merits. It has yet to be determined, on a cost-benefit basis, whether these activities even begin to pay for themselves. The result of any study would probably show that both programs should be reduced in size, with the bulk of their work done by visitors from Washington rather than by residents in the field. All remaining embassy economists, whether from Treasury, Agriculture, or Commerce, should be "seconded" into the State Department for the duration of their foreign tours, welded into a single, small economic section.

Although cutting staffs and abolishing functions can reduce the overseas problem, there is probably no simple answer to the built-in difficulties of making foreign economic policy in Washington. President Nixon, on January 19, 1971, appointed a new, White House-run Council on International Economic Policy, designed to coordinate the advice he receives. At the same time, Mr. Nixon noted that "of course, the State Department has the primary responsibilities." Earlier, two more sweeping changes had been proposed. One, advanced by business advisers to the Nixon administration at the beginning of 1969, would establish a separate cabinet department of foreign trade. The proponents of this plan argued that several other nations have such ministries, that an attack on our fluctuating balance-of-payments problem should be concentrated within one, strong agency, and that the State Department is not the place to put this power, since it is not sufficiently "friendly" to U.S. business interests. The second proposal, made by James McCamy in 1964, was to transfer the twelve main foreign economic and administrative policy units of Washington into the State Department proper. These separate entities were listed by McCamy as follows:[171]

1. Office of International Finance, Department of the Treasury
2. Office of Alien Property, Department of Justice
3. Immigration and Naturalization Service, Department of Justice
4. Foreign Agricultural Service, Department of Agriculture
5. Bureau of International Programs, Department of Commerce
6. Bureau of International Business Operations, Department of Commerce
7. Bureau of International Labor Affairs, Department of Labor
8. Office of International Affairs, Atomic Energy Commission
9. Office of International Programs, National Aeronautics and Space Administration
10. Export-Import Bank
11. U.S. Tariff Commission
12. Foreign Claims Settlement Commission

Today several newer units would have to be added to McCamy's list, for example, the Department of Health, Education, and Welfare's offices of international health and international education, and the foreign staffs of the Transportation Department and the Department of Housing and Urban Development.

A mammoth amalgamation of so many disparate units would cause more problems than it would solve. The more sensible course would be to strengthen the coordinating bodies that already exist in Washington while assuring State Department control of all overseas personnel. Interagency groups such as the National Advisory Council on International and Financial problems, chaired by Treasury, and the Trade Policy Committee, chaired by Commerce, may not always agree, but they ought to be capable of advising the President and his staff of the range of their disagreements. It might additionally assist liaison to place resident State Department advisers on the staffs of the Secretaries of Commerce, Agriculture, and Treasury.

Essential differences exist between the "national security" agencies on the one hand and the domestic economic departments on the other. In the economic sphere of foreign relations, unlike the fields of intelligence and defense, it is quite impossible to think secretly and unilaterally, to plot strategy in Washington without discussion in the marketplaces of domestic life and the wider world. Interdependence of business and government policies, at least among the industrialized nations, is a fact of life, and there is continual interplay between domestic and foreign economic issues. While the benefits of security and a successful foreign policy accrue equally to all American citizens, changes in economic policy affect us all unevenly. These economic questions are traditionally the main stuff of American domestic politics, indeed of the domestic politics of any nation. The life of Congress and of separate interest groups in the society revolves around them.

Complexity, ambiguity, impinging pressures, and demands for special advantage are at the heart of our economic debates, and should be reflected in their study and resolution. Inflation and regional unemployment at home have an effect on the balance of payments and demands from American industry for quota limitations on imports. Policy makers must weigh together the totality of foreign economic problems in relation to foreign policy, the claims of domestic interest groups, and some sense of the general welfare. Gold speculation, foreign famine, and trade discrimination by the Common Market each have different and special meaning as pocketbook issues for Wall Street bankers, Kansas farmers, and Detroit auto makers. Differential interest rates, competing patterns of fuel supply, a sudden French monetary devaluation spread profit and loss unequally through the society and among the membership of the International Monetary Fund and the General Agreement on Tariffs and Trade.

Economic expertise and the differential play of conflicting interests are scattered throughout the executive branch. The Secretary of State, backed by his number-four man, the deputy under secretary for economic affairs, State's Bureau of Economic Affairs (headed by an assistant secretary), and the geographic bureaus is only one among many participants in deciding U.S. foreign economic policy. More than is widely understood, the crucial decisions are made in the last analysis by the President himself, advised by his White House staff and other consultants at the end of a lengthy interagency adversary process. This was true during the Johnson administration on an issue so mundane as determining how much domestic copper to stockpile and how much—at what prices—to import from Chile and Zambia. It was just as true when the Nixon administration grappled with the question of how to reallocate our oil import quotas among Venezuela, Iran, the Arab producers, and Canada, and how changed import patterns would affect the domestic petroleum industry and the consumer prices. That battle, begun in 1969, is not yet over. State recommended freer imports, which would lower consumer fuel prices, and won approval of the White House for a time, over the objections of several others represented on an interagency committee, including the Commerce and Interior Departments. Then U.S. oil producers, who favor tight quotas to protect their markets, weighed in, and the White House reversed itself.

In 1962, while authorizing tariff-cutting negotiations with the Common Market, Congress insisted on creating a special office in the White House to carry out the cuts under a "Special Trade Representative." Congress believed that it would retain more control over the outcome of the trade talks—and get better cooperation from the executive branch—if it created a new office rather than relying on State or Commerce or Treasury or Agriculture. Congress may have been right, and in any case it was exercising its clear legislative prerogative. It has consistently opposed concentrating too much economic power in any one department or agency, and has tended to look askance at the economic policy units of State, which from the congressional point of view are not sufficiently responsive to domestic interests. In another current issue, a trade war over textiles with Japan, the key decision makers have been the President himself, the Secretary of Commerce, and congressmen from textile areas where jobs and income are affected by foreign competition. State Department officials, arguing for better relations with Japan and more attention to the wider interests of American consumers, have thus far played a relatively minor role in the textile debate. In effect, they have been asked by the President and Congress to "lie low on this one," since it is to be treated primarily as a domestic political issue affecting U.S. textile mills and only secondarily as a question of our relations with Japan.

By virtue of its constituency and tradition, the Commerce

Department tends to reflect the views of U.S. industrialists on a given issue, while the Agriculture Department looks out for the American farmer. The Treasury Department represents the financial community and the State Department is concerned with our foreign political relationships and with giving U.S. economic policies a global consistency that tends, in practical effect, to favor the American consumer. State speaks to a broad but weak national constituency, whereas the domestic economic departments represent narrower but more vocal special interest groups. These inherent conflicts of point of view are expressed in a complex series of interagency committees in which State is one voice among many, and generally a minor voice in the debate. The reasons for this are twofold. Business, farm, and labor lobbies bring considerable pressure to bear on the other departments of government, which by custom respond to those interests more passionately than does the Foreign Affairs Department. Second, economic policy is but one of many foreign policy concerns of State, whereas it is the central issue with the other departments concerned in the process. Treasury, not State, is the "expert" on monetary matters; Agriculture is the "expert" on U.S. farm surpluses; Commerce is the "expert" on American industry; while State speaks for a foreign policy that may seem quite remote if not abstract in comparison to these immediate home issues. State's logical domestic ally in these debates would often be the American consumer, who is unfortunately the least organized of the actors in our interest group domestic politics.

A given economic question is likely to receive more high-level attention from Commerce, for example, than from State. Seven of our ten Secretaries of State over the past forty years have been lawyers (one was a professional soldier, one a businessman, and the other a foundation executive). For a Secretary of State to possess special knowledge of economics is therefore accidental; it is not considered a prerequisite to the job. Few Secretaries of State (Dean Acheson and Cordell Hull are the recent exceptions) have been inclined or equipped to spend much time on foreign economic policy. The entire esoteric subject is generally delegated to subordinates. This in itself has made State "unequal" with Treasury and Commerce, whose Secretaries in the nature of things have had to take a direct, daily interest in the subject. Hence the position of State in interagency economic conflicts is often defensive. Since Secretary Hull took office in 1933 and made freer trade his personal hobbyhorse, State has been the main exponent of internationalist conceptions of economic welfare. Special interests almost always pull in the opposite direction—toward economic nationalism, protectionist measures, and autarkic trends—which tends to make State a minority of one in interagency debates.

The real world of Washington is, of course, a good deal more ambiguous than this general sketch would suggest. The framework of decision making, requiring as it does much cross-agency discussion, can seem both subtle and complex. Organizationally, however, it seems fair enough to say that State is not now prepared to wage an equal fight for policies it favors. It depends upon the accident of a single-minded Secretary such as Hull or economically competent Under Secretaries such as Will Clayton, Douglas Dillon, or George Ball for State to "take on" the domestic agencies and vested interests, making the strongest possible case for consistent foreign economic policies.

At the lower working level State frequently has a strong assistant secretary for economic affairs with a competent staff of economists, though it cannot hope to compete in *expertise* with the more economically oriented domestic departments of government. But its economic staff is weakened by the nature of the Foreign Service personnel process, the fact that most officers serve tours of no longer than four years in Washington and then go abroad again. Treasury and Commerce, on the other hand, have resident staffs who spend their entire careers in Washington. Thus they have an effective institutional memory—ten years of expertise per job, let us say, compared to a State Department officer's two years of learning-on-the-job, followed by rotation abroad. Economic policy issues, like foreign policy questions, are persistent and even historically repetitious, and it goes without saying that the more experienced staff one has to handle them, the better.

The press and play of special domestic interests are already well represented in Congress but the process essentially repeats itself within the executive branch as well. It would not be possible to change the pattern without a thorough reorganization of nearly every executive branch agency, which seems most unrealistic. In the short run, a stronger State Department might nonetheless tilt the balance of influence that now so often favors powerful domestic lobbies, by means of a few small structural reforms. By reviewing the budgets of all foreign programs of domestic agencies and controlling their personnel sent to embassies, State could at least exert a centralizing authority that does not now exist abroad. The other agencies, and their congressional interest group spokesmen, would resist these changes with vigor, and it would require nothing less than presidential action to bring them about. In Washington itself, however, State should be nothing more than an equal contender with the domestic agencies, expressing its position forcefully on interagency committees and, when necessary, to the White House. To do this, at least one of its top three officials must spend most of his time on economic policy questions, pulling coordination up to a reasonably high level of government. Since most of the decisions are made in the White House anyway, it is perhaps most important of all that the President hear out the arguments and have a full-time foreign economic policy staff man who can make the issues explicable to him.

In the long run, administrative logic might point toward the creation of a single Foreign Trade bureaucracy as a subdepartment or division of State, which several past studies have proposed. Neither Congress nor the business and farm lobbies would tolerate this at present, and perhaps they are right. Keeping foreign components in the largest domestic departments reflects, after all, the reality of constant interplay between home and international aspects of economic problems. The challenge is to introduce enough orderly procedure into the system to prevent chaos—and special interests—from dictating policy. A strengthened State Department cannot solve the problem, but can add balance to the system, and assure the President that he is getting the best advice.

The Peace Corps

Two noneconomic small bureaucracies, which exist in semi-independence of the State Department, are the 286-man Arms Control and Disarmament Agency (ACDA) and the Peace Corps. ACDA has its offices within the State Department Building and acts as an operating part of the department, although in theory it is quasi-independent. Over time, it will undoubtedly be joined with the International Organizations bureau of State, where a specialist staff in negotiating arms control most logically belongs.

The Peace Corps remains, ten years after its birth, an experimental contradiction in terms, a bureaucracy that claims not to be a bureaucracy. With a budget of $100 million per year, a Washington staff of about 1,000 and 473 administrators attached to embassies in the field, the corps supports about 10,000 American volunteer workers in 57 countries. A former associate director of the program believes that it has already achieved a place in the American mind "somewhere between the Boy Scouts and motherhood."[172] For the Peace Corps insists that it is essentially an apolitical, "people-to-people" volunteer service agency that is not primarily a tool of foreign policy. Most of the volunteers, largely young Americans in their early twenties, are English teachers in the secondary school systems of developing nations; a minority are social workers, nurses, legal advisers, and rural technicians.

The motive behind the program is basically domestic rather than foreign. When candidate John F. Kennedy proposed the creation of a Peace Corps in a campaign speech in San Francisco's Cow Palace on November 2, 1960, his purpose was to discredit the Republican opposition. Drawing on the popularity of the best-selling novel, *The Ugly American,* Kennedy alleged that teachers, doctors, and other experts were "pouring forth from Moscow to advance the cause of world communism," and that "they can only be countered by Americans equally skilled and equally dedicated."[173]

The Peace Corps, unlike the Marshall Plan, was not a

response to the requests of foreign countries for assistance, but rather a unilateral American proposal first put forward mainly for domestic political consumption. Even after it was established, it was necessary for its first director to travel around the world to "sell" the idea to potential recipient governments. In effect, the normal donor-recipient relationship was reversed, the great power soliciting permission from smaller states to assist them (a pattern also common in AID programs). Whatever the good intentions, the impression created was one of a pressing American desire to intervene, both for humanitarian and anticommunist reasons.

The fearsome prediction of *The Ugly American* of a communist takeover of Africa, Asia, and Latin America through zealous missionary work did not materialize, but for a time had great impact on American opinion. It may not be fair to call the Peace Corps, as one critical professor has charged, the "colonial civil service of imperial America."[174] Still, the corps is really a domestic program sent abroad, more popular in the United States than in most of the countries in which it serves. By 1970 the Peace Corps had been asked to leave nine nations and to reduce its presence in a number of others. After nearly a decade of existence, the program has been judged something less than a total success.

It is probably difficult for the American public to understand why this should be so, for the Peace Corps appeals to many who believe in the value of an "above politics" approach to foreign peoples, rather like the wide appeal of the American Christian missionary effort in China forty years ago. It satisfies the common American view that conflict is fundamentally irrational, that somehow if "people" could only get to know each other a little bit better, if there were improved communications among them, it would logically follow that everyone would like and appreciate his fellows, and there would be fewer unnatural tensions and disagreements among states.

But, strange though it may seem, to know an American is not always to like him, even if he is trying terribly hard to be liked. Foreign leaders and peoples, while welcoming outside help with their shortage of trained teachers and technicians, inevitably begin to have mixed emotions about an influx of young Americans who seem to "interfere" with their cherished traditions and local political and social habits. That these Americans are paid by the government makes them seem, in the eyes of most foreign authorities, to be "U.S. officials" who are sometimes even suspected of conducting secret intelligence work. The truth—that this massive, peaceful form of intervention is apolitical, that the 10,000 volunteers are sheep in wolves' clothing—is too unlikely to inspire wide belief.

Experience has shown that frictions grow when the *number* of volunteers sent to any one country passes a reasonably low limit—1,000 in some countries, 100 or 200 in others. In several African states the number of U.S. volunteers has increased to the point where Americans constitute more than one-quarter of the total high school teaching force. When that point is reached, failures of the educational system suddenly tend to become "the fault of the Americans" in local eyes and virulent anti-Peace Corps demonstrations ensue. The heavy presence and often the very youth of the American guests are seen as an implicit reproach to foreign peoples for being unable to do the whole job themselves.

The way to take the sting out of the program is to keep it modest and eventually to remove it from government. It would also ease the political embarrassment of the receiving countries if, wherever possible, exchange volunteer workers from those countries could return the favor by doing similar work in the United States. In the 1970s, the Peace Corps might very well become part of the quasi-public American Cultural corporation proposed in Chapter 5.

9

WHAT IS TO BE DONE?

> The staffs on which modern executives come to depend develop a momentum of their own.
> —Henry A. Kissinger

In the spring of 1970, a key official of the Nixon administration, addressing a private audience of former ambassadors, declared, "State is being run on all over town."[175] He was merely repeating what many others have known for the past decade. Former Ambassador William Attwood has described the Washington foreign affairs bureaucracies as a "labyrinth"; former Under Secretary Nicholas Katzenbach compares the policy-making process to a "taffy pull"; and a distinguished former colleague of both men says the State Department reminds him of "an unusually well-staffed hospital."[176]

There are many reasons for State's decline in effectiveness and authority, as the preceding pages have tried to suggest. There is also a large body of analysis that can cut through present confusions and help to build a better system: the Hoover Task Force Report of 1949, the Duncan Report of 1969 in Great Britain, the current reform proposals of William

Macomber's task forces, the Fitzhugh and Peterson Reports of 1970, the lessons of the Kennedy and Johnson administrations, the Jackson Subcommittee hearings of the early 1960s, and the critical memoirs of a host of former officials; all or most of this information is readily available to the inquiring layman. A study of past efforts offers no single, simple program for change, but rather a background of historic fact on which to base a new attack on old problems.

It should be clear by now that excessive size and fragmented authority are what make the system so unmanageable. At the same time, divided and proliferating functions have made American foreign policy more interventionist than it need be. In ways that presidents, secretaries of state, and even bureaucrats themselves may only dimly perceive, the machine has indeed come out of control. Its momentum will not be redirected without the most serious, even radical innovation.

Ways to reform the military, intelligence, aid, propaganda, and domestic departments have been outlined in the preceding chapters, but the key to the over-all puzzle, and to the success of the other-agency changes, lies in the State Department itself. Can it, at last, "take charge" of the administration of American foreign policy? The obvious answer is no, it cannot, unless the President wants it to; and no postwar President, with the possible exception of Harry Truman, has shown that intention. Ample experience demonstrates that the President, even when he is aided by a large personal staff, cannot make the machine work by himself. Organizational chaos, and the unwise policy it breeds, will continue until the White House is able to confer real confidence and considerable operating power on its institutional foreign office. This would not be an abdication of responsibility or a simple deferral to "expert advice." It would involve the centralization of a responsibility that is now absent from Washington, since it is divided to the point of practical disappearance; the creation of orderly procedure that should make the decisions of the President and the deliberations of Congress as well more truly responsible, more able to sift wheat from chaff in policy debates.

A President, in other words, will not get better advice simply by asking for it. He needs to make changes in the very structure of advice giving and decision making, and he can make those changes only if he understands what is the matter with the bureaucracies he has inherited. Few men can help him "learn on-the-job," for his closest political advisers, and most of the bureaucrats beneath them, change jobs so constantly and rapidly that they have had little time to comprehend and reflect upon the immense system in which they work and act.

Let us assume that a president sincerely desires to restructure the system. How would he proceed? What must he do, first of all, to build a better State Department?

Building a Better State Department

Size is the first problem to attack, and bureaucratic surgery is the answer. State might adopt a Five-Year Plan of abolishing functions and reducing personnel, designed to trim the 7,000-man Department of today by 50 percent or more, to a new ceiling in the low 3,000s. Naturally this or any other genuine reform program would benefit from wide public discussion and support, for to be lasting it must be more than the solution of only one President or one administration. Between 1,000 and 1,500 of the necessary cuts would involve an abolition of function; the balance, elimination of redundancy and overstaffing in Washington offices. These reductions are not as severe as they will sound to some bureaucrats. In the mid-1960s, State's Washington staff reached a high point of above 8,000 employees, and over the past four years more than 1,200 employees contained in that inflated total have been painlessly dropped from the rolls without noticeable effect.

The methods used to attain a "phased withdrawal" of State personnel need not simulate those of an unsettling purge. Normal attrition (now running about 10 percent a year, but subtract 5 percent for new recruitment) takes a certain rhythmic toll.* Further position abolitions could follow a study that sets ceilings on the numbers of officers and clerical workers in each bureau, and the administrative support supplied from Washington to oversees missions. Incentives for early retirement should be continued to ease overpopulation in the senior ranks, along with a more serious application of selection-out to low performing Foreign Service officers. At least the lower 5 percent, or 160 officers per year, could be eliminated, rather than the 70 per year who have been let go since 1967 and the much lower annual total of the early 1960s. Cutbacks can also come in the Foreign Service "reserve officer" category. Of the 750 "FSRs" now serving in Washington as temporary specialists, an estimated 250 or one-third of the total are congressional patronage jobs.

Cutting functions should also include reducing the number of chains of command in State. Nine of the present sixteen bureaus headed by assistant secretaries (or equivalents) could be usefully abolished, leaving a new total of seven. This, in essence, is the original Hoover Task Force plan of 1949 and

* One-third of this rate is forced retirement.

it is also the basic McCamy proposal of 1964. The five main geographic bureaus for Europe, Africa, East Asia, Latin America, and the Middle East, with 980 personnel in all, should remain as the basic core of the policy machine. They should be supplemented by a sixth Bureau of Multilateral Affairs, combining the staffs of the present Economic, Scientific, and International Organizations bureaus. A total of 483 employees now work in these three offices, a number that might be reduced as much as half during the process of amalgamation. Housing State's economic and scientific specialists and its United Nations and international conference staff, the new Multilateral Bureau's work should be mainly advisory to the rest of the department, with the exception of specific "action" tasks assigned from above and liaison chores with other executive branch agencies.

The six bureaus to be abolished now employ more than 1,000 workers in what is often duplicative work. The portion of their activity that is not redundant can be brought into the regional and multilateral system and up to the Secretary of State's office. The affected bureaus are those for Congressional Relations, Public Affairs, Educational and Cultural Affairs, Intelligence and Research, Politico-Military Affairs, and the office of the Legal Adviser. Their disappearance would permit the Secretary's own staff and each of the geographic bureaus to handle directly without superfluous and confusing intermediaries, which are often bypassed today, their relations with Congress, the Pentagon, and the CIA, as well as their work that concerns publicity, cultural exchange, and matters of law. A small press and information staff and a legal staff should be retained as integral parts of the Secretary of State's office.

Another 300 to 400 personnel in the large Bureau of Security and Consular Affairs might be transferred out of State to other agencies. Several prior studies, including the Hoover Task Force, have recommended that the visa office be included in the Immigration and Naturalization Service (INS) of the Justice Department, which now controls the entrance of aliens into the United States. This would permit embassies and consulates in the field, which issue visas, to communicate directly with the enforcing authority at home, and eliminate an extra layer of bureaucracy. With more than a million foreign visitors annually entering the United States, and past travel restrictions being progressively eliminated by Congress and the Supreme Court, it has become less and less necessary to retain visa procedures that smack of the nineteenth century. There is every prospect that Congress will waive visa requirements entirely for ninety-day foreign business visitors and tourist travelers in the early 1970s. Issuance of passports to American citizens is also becoming increasingly automated with the current travel boom, and much of the work could profitably be decentralized to post offices throughout the United States, operating under central guidance from State's passport office.

Reducing staffs and chains of command and abolishing functions should help to improve internal communications and the flow of decision making while more clearly fixing responsibility in departmental business. This would ease pressures of size and fragmentation that have sired the sluggish, compromise-making committee system of today, which was christened by Robert Lovett[177] "the foul-up factor" of foreign policy. As most serious students of government have recommended, State's long-established process of horizontal clearance of all work should be eliminated. Each matter requiring action should, in the language of the Hoover Report, be "assigned to a single officer" who must himself take responsibility for consulting (but not obtaining clearance from) other interested parties in the decision. Within the State Department the effective flow of policy making should be up and down, not sideways.

Substantial reductions can also come in the field of administration, where about half of State's employees work. If consular work is included with administration, more personnel, 3,307 in all, serve in personnel, security, communications, general services, and other management offices than in *all* of the other 15 policy divisions combined. In addition, as was noted in Chapter 5, the policy bureaus contain a "buried administrative factor" of 20 to 30 percent, since that many administrative liaison officers work in the executive directors' offices of nonadministrative bureaus. These latter offices could be eliminated with a saving of perhaps as many as 400 to 500 positions. The "housekeeping" side of administration could then be centralized under the assistant secretary for administration, responsible and responsive to the Secretary of State and the other six assistant secretaries.

Budget Reforms

Two new administrative tasks, currently not being performed by anyone in Washington, need to be taken on by a reformed State Department. It should prepare a single, unified foreign-affairs budget for the entire government, and it should control government personnel sent abroad on foreign missions by all agencies. Achievement of these objectives requires a bureaucratic revolution of sorts, but it is a revolution worth making, for it could give American foreign policy new coherence and discipline, as well as reduce costs. A single budget would also be a considerable service to Congress, the President, and the public, giving all Americans a much clearer conception of what purposes their money serves in international affairs. The revolution will not be accomplished overnight, nor will it occur without presidential action. But it is time to begin. State's present number-five official, the Deputy Under Secretary for administration, could be redesignated Deputy Under Secretary for the budget, responsible to the Secretary, with other-agency agreement, to prepare an integrated foreign affairs budget for the executive branch. The international division of the White House Office of Management and Budget (OMB), comprised of about fifty personnel in all, should be transferred into the new State budget office. Ultimately, American ambassadors in the field should be called upon to justify and control all annual government expenditures in their countries, and the five regional assistant secretaries of state should also review these expenditure plans. The Secretary of State should be directly accountable to the President for control over the entire spectrum of moneys and staffs employed abroad, with the exception of military troop costs.

An alternative would be to vest these same powers in the OMB, which is presently the President's final budgetary review body before he makes his annual submissions to Congress. But OMB has not been able to do anything like the job that is contemplated here, and it is difficult to imagine how it ever could. Its international staffers are financial management specialists, not planners of foreign policy. Few of them have lived or served abroad or have any but the most general notion of U.S. foreign policy objectives and what it requires to attain them. Today they consider each agency's budget separately, and not as the related part of an over-all scheme. They are effective civil servants, but they are not the proper evaluators of where and how the United States should conduct its diplomacy and overseas programs. That decision is properly the province of the highest officers of government—in the last analysis, of the Secretary of State and the President. But the government is not now organized in a fashion that makes it possible for the President and the Secretary to receive information in a form suitable for such decision. They receive and consider parts and pieces of the whole in a relative vacuum—a military-aid program to Country "X," a trade dispute with Country "Y," a harassing annual round of budget debates with fourscore agency heads, but no consistent framework for broader, longer range priority setting and decision making.

Unlike the White House Budget office, State at present has few financial managers but many foreign affairs specialists. Training in financial management, and a commitment by State to build its own home staff of budgeters, should help narrow the gap. In the meantime, the transfer of some if not all of OMB's international budget analysts into State would meet the problem.

This is not "program budgeting" in the Johnson administration sense of the word. The Johnson-McNamara approach was wrong in its emphasis on "programs" rather than policies, in its tacit assumption that "all programs are equal" and that the most important aspects of foreign relations are those things that can be quantified. As such, it was a tool of activism if not interventionism. It also seemed likely to bury an already supine bureaucracy in new reams of paperwork: "country plans" and country budgets written and rewritten, cleared and cleared again in a vast haggling process throughout government. It is time, instead, to think of "policy budgeting," an attempt by senior officials to establish priorities and a few working hypotheses about American foreign policy without recourse to endless, elaborate, and ultimately useless piles of "country papers." Washington, in other words, at the level of the President, the Secretary of State, his budget chief, and assistant secretaries must let the overseas missions have an approximate idea of the resources deemed desirable to expend, request more detailed budget plans within such a framework, then review, change, or approve an annual budget divided into four or five geographic segments. Such interagency haggling as must occur, best expressed perhaps in the form of "dissents" from other department heads, should be handled near the top rather than the bottom levels of government, by the Secretary of State's budget staff and the President's staff. Too much "country" and "program" planning promotes bureaucratization of the worst kind and can have a momentum all its own. Attention at the top, vested in a senior budget staff, can keep this tendency under control. Lack of central authority today is one powerful stimulant to the mindless compartmentalization of foreign policy and parochial competition among separate agencies.

It will be argued that Congress is not yet ready to accept a single foreign-affairs budget. Its antique committee structure jealously parcels out separate sums to distinct departments, and no committee chairman would gladly relinquish his power to some more inclusive body. That is true, but it is no excuse for the executive branch to avoid experiments in central budgeting. One day Congress will have to reform itself, and meanwhile a single budget could be drawn up annually as an internal executive branch planning document, and then be subdivided into the more traditional categories required for presentation to the legislative branch.

Organizational Reforms

At the top of the ladder there is no simple way to ease the burdens of a modern Secretary of State. Recent Secretaries have spent about half of their time testifying before Congress, traveling to international conferences, and advising the President, with only a remainder of the schedule free for superintending the day-to-day business of their department. They can no more delegate leadership to their deputies than presidents are inclined to delegate work to vice-presidents, but there *are* ways of helping a secretary make better use of his time and exert clearer control over the sprawling bureaucracy beneath him. At present 336 staff aides and advisers and office helpers comprise the personnel of the State Department's seventh floor, where the Secretary's office is located. These men and women are not organized in a coherent way, but perform overlapping tasks with confused mandates. A large executive secretariat (120 strong) competes with a smaller policy and coordination staff and with miscellaneous personal consultants and assistants to serve the needs of the Secretary, the Under Secretary who is his deputy and alter ego, another Under Secretary whose duties are ill-defined, and a number-four man called the Deputy Under Secretary, whose job is also that of a vague extra helper. These latter two officers should be given specific tasks, and they should not clutter the chain of command between the assistant secretaries on the one hand and the Secretary and his deputy on the other. One of them might be denominated as a Deputy Under Secretary for foreign economic policy, acting as the chief economic adviser to the State Department and as its main point of contact with the

Treasury, Commerce, and other economic departments. The other officer could be styled as a Deputy Under Secretary for Coordination, acting as the Secretary's monitor and watchdog of the CIA, the Defense Department, and the military establishment, with his own representatives on the staffs of the military and intelligence agencies.

In a smaller State Department, a single secretariat of modest size should continue to organize the meetings, appointments, and papers of the Secretary and Under Secretary. It should also be able to give them independent advice on pending business, formulate their decisions in writing, and communicate on their behalf with the President's staff. The Secretary needs a small policy-planning staff as well, detached from day-to-day responsibilities and empowered to conduct such studies as he may require.

By the end of the decade, a State Department restructured along these lines might resemble Table 8, which appears on the next page.

As reorganization and reduction proceed, the department ought to move its main offices back into the Executive Office Building next to the White House, its pre-1948 home. Closer proximity to the President should, of itself, eliminate the need for a major buffer in the form of a large White House foreign office with its separate committee structure between the President and his Secretary of State. Even at State's present size, the total number of personnel in the geographic bureaus (980), the "heart" of the policy machine, is barely larger than the entire department of prewar vintage (963). If a president wants his secretary close at hand (as Eisenhower once proposed to Dulles), then the logical solution is to move the Secretary's office back to Pennsylvania Avenue.

As should be clear from a glance at Table 9, the White House staff system of decision making today is incredibly

Table 8
The Department of State in 1980:
A Scheme for Future Organization

	APPROXIMATE NUMBER OF PERSONNEL
Policy Level	
Secretary and Under Secretary, with attached legal and public affairs advisers, secretariat, and planning staff	75
Advisory and Liaison Offices	
Deputy Under Secretary for budget	75
Deputy Under Secretary for foreign economic policy	25
Deputy Under Secretary for coordination (CIA, Defense)	25
Assistant secretary for multilateral affairs	300
Expert Level—Action Offices	
Five assistant secretaries and bureaus for Europe, Africa, Latin America, the Middle East, and Far East	800
Supporting Services	
Assistant secretary for administration	1,000
Passport and consular services	300
TOTAL WASHINGTON STAFF	2,600

cumbersome. Military and intelligence representation on all of the complex White House committees, including the NSC itself, is overwhelming. The Council has, as the Hoover Task Force predicted it would in 1940, strayed into "matters of foreign affairs which are strictly not its business." Official descriptions of a few of the major "national security" staffs are given below.

To list these committees and their theoretical duties is to suggest how bureaucratized the Nixon White House has become. Power is increasingly being centered in staffs and committees which have no clear political responsibility or accountability to Congress and the American public, no continuity from one administration to the next, and, in many cases, no expertise in the specific foreign affairs problems they deliberate. Military and intelligence officials are heavily represented on nearly every committee, symbolizing an important shift that has gradually occurred in American perceptions of the outside world: "national security," a conception of permanent crisis, his displaced "foreign policy," a more generalized notion of the peaceful and only occasionally violent ebbs and flows of international politics and national interests.

Each postwar president has wanted to experiment with his own staff arrangements, as will each future president. One would think that the ideal presidential staff on the foreign policy side, whatever its nature, would have a few common features: it would be small, not duplicating work done elsewhere, and it would be flexible, giving the President inde-

Table 9
Presidential Foreign Policy Staffs, 1970

The National Security Council (NSC)
Formal Members: The president, vice-president, secretaries of state and defense, and the director of the office of emergency planning.
De-Facto Members: Assistant to the president for national security affairs, director of the CIA, chairman of the Joint Chiefs of Staff.
Staff: Approximately 120 personnel supervised by the assistant to the president for national security affairs.

NSC Interdepartmental Groups (IG's)
Chairmen: Assistant secretaries of state for each of five regional areas.
Members: Representatives of Defense, CIA, the Joint Chiefs of Staff, the assistant to the president for national security affairs, and "other agencies . . . depending on the issue under consideration."
Duties: Discuss and decide interdepartmental issues that can be settled at the assistant secretary level, including issues arising out of the implementation of NSC decisions. Prepare policy papers for consideration by the NSC. Prepare contingency papers on potential crisis areas for NSC review.

NSC Review Group
Chairman: Assistant to the president for national security affairs.
Members: Representatives of State, Defense, CIA, the Joint Chiefs of Staff

Table 9 (Continued)

and "other agencies . . . depending on the issue under consideration."

Duties: "To examine papers such as those coming out of the Interdepartmental Groups . . . or departments prior to their submission to the NSC" in order to assure that "the issue under consideration is worthy of NSC attention; all realistic alternatives are presented; and the facts, including cost implications, and all departments' and agencies' views are fairly and adequately set forth."

NSC Under Secretaries Committee

Chairman: Under secretary of state.

Alternate: Under secretary of state for political affairs.

Members: Deputy secretary of defense, assistant to the president for national security affairs, director of CIA, chairman of Joint Chiefs of Staff, and "ranking officers of other agencies at the discretion of the chairman."

Duties: To consider "issues referred to it by the NSC review group; operational matters pertaining to interdepartmental activities of the U.S. Government overseas" (on which agreement has not been reached by NSC interdepartmental groups and that do not require presidential consideration); and "other operational matters referred to it by the under secretary of state and the assistant to the president for national security affairs."

Council on International Economic Policy

Chairman: The President

Vice Chairman: The Secretary of State

Members: Secretaries of Treasury, Agriculture, Commerce, Labor; Director of OMB; Chairman of the Council of Economic Advisers; assistants to the President for National Security Affairs and Domestic Affairs; special representative for trade negotiations; executive director.

Duties: To "achieve consistency between domestic and foreign economic policy."

Additional interagency committees (all chaired by Dr. Kissinger, the President's national security assistant) include the Vietnam Special Studies Group, the Defense Programs Review Committee, the Verification Panel (Strategic Arms Talks), The Washington Special Actions Group (Crises), and the 40 Committee (Covert Action).

SOURCE: *Foreign Affairs Manual Circular No. 521,* February 6, 1969; reprinted in *Department of State News Letter,* No. 94, February, 1969, pp. 6–7. See also, *New York Times,* January 19, 1971.

pendent advice and extra pairs of eyes and ears. It would see that the President's decisions were reduced to writing and communicated to those who must carry them out, and it would consist of at least an assistant for foreign and defense policy and a deputy assistant for foreign economic policy, with an additional "troubleshooter" or two and subordinate staff. This type of staff dissipates its energy, and the energy of the President and his chief advisers, in an elaborate structure of permanent committee meetings; indeed, after a while, the major policy makers have to put the committee structure on the back shelf if they are going to get their normal work done. Reforming the major bureaucracies and centering the main control job in the hands of the Secretary of State can, in effect, give a President much more control over the bureaucratic system than he now has, for his own large staff and committee structure isolate him from the main levers of power, diffuse responsibility to a degree that it becomes difficult to pinpoint, waste a great deal of time, and build Byzantine layers of work and authority between operators, experts, advisers, and deciders.

Personnel and Recruiting Reforms

Questions of the quality and ability of personnel remain. Who belongs in a leaner, fitter State Department? Do changes in organization really accomplish anything without changes in people?

The answer to the last question is Yes and No. Without changing staffs one can expect the existing people to do a better job in a better structure. The "people" who manned the State Department in 1970 fell into several distinct categories. About 1,300 of them were Foreign Service officers on home assignment, another 1,200 were specialist "reserve officers" and senior civil servants (of the GS-12 level and above), while most of the remaining 4,000 employees could be loosely classified as clerical workers. But that begs the question: how good is the staff of today's State Department? The answer is probably not good enough for leadership in foreign affairs until major changes are made in personnel policy. Twenty years of institutional decline and presidential neglect have taken their toll. The McCarthy attacks and the Wriston reforms of the 1950s weakened the spirit of the Foreign Service, and the heavy majority of senior career men in the State Department today are either the survivors or the beneficiaries of that unhappy period.

History cannot be repealed, but some of its effects are self-liquidating as older men retire. The saving grace of the Foreign Service remains its tough entrance standards, which are higher than those of any other government personnel system. Only about 5 percent of all applicants pass the diplomatic exams, and in the 1960s a small but steady stream of new recruits, about 150 a year, have been coming into the service. Operating within a merit system, the FSOs now in the 30-to-40 age group have had a professional experience that links them more closely to the Kennan-Bohlen generation of the 1920s than to the McCarthy-Wriston generation of the 1950s. Today's middle-rank FSOs missed the worst domestic traumas of the early cold-war years and the diplomatic purge that it engendered. They are, on the whole, better educated, more proficient in languages, and more flexible in outlook than their immediate superiors; and they are also less cautiously conformist in bureaucratic style. Impatient with slow promotions and a top-heavy rank structure, some of them have left diplomacy for better opportunities elsewhere, and have done so in unprecedented numbers; but many of them remain.

Other things being equal, by the middle of the 1970s members of this generation of FSOs would begin to reach the senior ranks of our career diplomacy. But other things are not equal, and there is no absolute assurance that this will occur. Other things that are not equal include Vietnam and its effect on the outlook of young Americans, a skewed rank structure in a profession that is "overage" by most contemporary standards, some corruptions of the merit system, and, the result of all these things, a growing cynicism among the Foreign Service and its friends about the possibilities of doing useful work in the context of a long government career. A straw in the wind, perhaps only a temporary one, is that by 1970 the universities and graduate schools of public service seemed to be advising their graduates to avoid a Foreign Service career, and the graduates seemed to be taking this advice. Princeton's Woodrow Wilson School of Public and International Affairs, founded a decade ago as a private training ground for future public servants, has sent none of its forty annual master's degree graduates into the Foreign Service since the class of 1967. Many leading educators and even former ambassadors are today urging young men to avoid government career commitments and instead plan "in-and-out" mixtures of private and public life, which seem a better path to maximum influence and usefulness.

To remain vital, any career service constantly needs to recruit able newcomers. At the start of the 1970s the level and quality of recruitment into the Foreign Service seemed to be dropping off, and no one could say how long this trend would continue. Efforts to lower admission standards into the Service, by substituting simple aptitude tests for difficult academic examinations covering history, English composition, the social sciences, and foreign languages, may be in harmony with this downward trend. Already candidates having no knowledge of any foreign language may enter the American Foreign Service if they pass all other tests, but must remain on probation and not receive more than one promotion until they prove their competence in at least one language. Most of the world's other diplomatic services—the Russian, the French, and the German, among others—require candidates to master at least *two* foreign tongues before they enter the profession. Some State Department reform groups today are considering eliminating the language requirement altogether. Their reasoning is that high academic standards are "screening out" people with business management skills, discriminating against minority groups, and building a Foreign Service that is too much of an intellectual elite.

The ablest, most ambitious college graduates will naturally stay away from a profession that announces a wish to lower its standards of excellence. It is just as damaging at the present time, however, that the reputation of government among young people is low. More than unpopular policies and unpopular leaders have caused this change in attitude. The bureaucratization of government has also been a heavy contributor to cynicism in the academic community about the possibilities of public service. Today's youth are taught, and seem to see examples of the teaching every day, that careers in government reduce men to mindless cogs in a Kafkaesque bureaucracy. This is another reason why structural reform in government is so urgently needed. The Foreign Service will regain its traditional drawing power with the next generation only if it seems to be a serious and attractive profession, capable of recapturing its élan and effectiveness.

The way to overcome present "tokenism" in minority-group hiring is not to lower entrance standards but to request money from Congress for special scholarship, training, and tutoring programs for blacks and Spanish-speaking Americans. In 1961 only seventeen Foreign Service officers were black out of a corps of 3,700, and by 1967 the total had risen to a mere nineteen.[178] Of 103 new FSOs in 1968, only four were black. By 1970, there were a total of 34 black FSOs. Instead of seeking federal funds for its equal opportunity program, the Foreign Service encouraged the Ford Foundation in 1963 to make a $600,000 grant to Howard University for a special Foreign Affairs Scholars program. Of the 154 participants in this four-year program from 1963–1967, more than half ultimately passed civil-service examinations but a mere seventeen passed the written Foreign Service exam. This is not an unusually low average, however, for only about 5 percent of all candidates normally pass this difficult examination. Another approach, adopted for the years 1968 through 1972, is an attempt to bring in a minimum of twenty new minority group officers each year as probationary interns, who will have a better chance of passing the examination after special training and experience.

These are modest programs not capable of making a significant dent in the natural suspicion, which seems to exist in much of the black community, that the State Department is an "Establishment" institution with neutral or negative relevance to U.S. domestic problems. An honest effort to make the Foreign Service more representative requires, above all, the courage to ask Congress for enough money for a long-term scholarship and training program. For fear of offending the legislative branch, State has never acted on a Wriston Committee proposal of 1954 that it promote a national scholarship program for college juniors and seniors and selected graduate students. Short of a determination to request and use adequate funds, "equal opportunity" in the Foreign Service seems bound to remain more a slogan than a reality.

Women face a separate and somewhat more subtle "discrimination problem" in State. They comprise 5 percent of the Foreign Service officer corps, and hold 2 out of 116 American ambassadorships. Most women FSOs tend to be shunted by the personnel system away from prestigious political jobs and toward less demanding consular and administrative chores. As women begin to take a more equal place alongside men in the main tasks of American society, it is not unrealistic to expect wider opportunities for them in diplomacy as well.

Personnel policy since 1950 has not been consistent, and it is only by consistency—by making sensible rules and then sticking to them—that a profession can develop and its talents can flower over a long period of time. There has been little manpower planning, looking ahead five and ten years to the future representational needs of the nation, and regulating assignments, training, recruitment, promotion, and attrition in terms of a central scheme. Personnel reform would encompass each of these elements. It might begin with a fifteen-year program for the Foreign Service designed, with the support of Congress, to attract a yearly limited number of the best candidates from American universities into career diplomacy. The skills they bring to the job, both in language and knowledge of particular geographic areas of the world, should be strengthened and developed by experience in those languages and areas. Ideally, for example, a diplomat might expect to spend half of his professional time in whatever region of the world his major area of *expertise* lies, a quarter of it in other regions, and a final quarter divided between training or experience outside of government and home assignment in Washington. Only the most rudimentary beginning of such planning exists today. A new recruit does not know how his career will be spent and to what degree his special skills and interests will be used.

To begin, an examination that is already known and respected for the high standard it sets should be retained. A knowledge of at least one foreign language should be made the prerequisite for entry into career diplomacy, as was true before 1956. Tutoring and scholarship grants can assure that this is no bar to low-income or minority candidates; indeed to some of them—Spanish-speaking Americans—it will be an advantage and an added incentive. The goal of the Service should be, in the words of the Wriston Report, a corps "fully representative, in its excellence and variety, of the best of American youth."[179] The recruitment, promotion, and retirement systems should be planned in a way that assures balance among ranks, ages, skills, and language abilities. Before that can be done, the Secretary of State and his advisers must decide what the right balance should be, based on their present needs and future projections. This is a policy decision of the first order, and not a technical administrative matter to be delegated to minor functionaries far down the line of command. It needs attention and frequent review by the Secretary himself, consistent with the policies of the President.

A proper balance would require, at the least, a radical revision of the age and rank structure of today's service. A task force informed President Kennedy in 1961 that if he had entered the Foreign Service instead of politics, he would barely be eligible at that point for promotion to Class 2 in the Service, and would have to wait for seven more years before he could even hope to become a career minister.[180] The age gap continued to grow throughout the 1960s, and today the average age of an American ambassador is well over 50, while the "Class 2" position that Kennedy could have hoped to attain at 43 now carries an average age of 49.7 years.

Had there been consistent planning from the top over the

past two decades, there would be no rank bulge today, with twice the number of officers in the upper half of the Foreign Service as in the bottom half. Diplomatic positions in Washington and overseas need to be reclassified an average of two grades downward. As John Kenneth Galbraith told the American Foreign Service Association:

"The Foreign Service should be a young man's service. . . . It is only by being young that a bureaucracy keeps itself abreast of change. . . . You should urge, I believe, that a successful man become an ambassador at forty or before, and, unless there are the most compelling reasons to the contrary, he should retire by fifty."[181]

One does not have to go as far as Galbraith to realize that ranks and ages are topsy-turvy in the present diplomatic system. The tools to correct this imbalance are available, if a Secretary of State would only use them. One of his basic charters, the Foreign Service Act of 1946,[182] gives him wide powers to police a merit system, which, through neglect, has become less meritorious with each passing year. Section 621 of the Act declares: "All promotions of Foreign Service officers shall be made by the President, in accordance with such regulations as he may prescribe. . . . Promotion shall be by selection on the basis of merit." Section 622 continues, "The Secretary shall, by regulation, determine the minimum period Foreign Service officers must serve in each class and a standard of performance for each class which they must meet in order to become eligible for promotion. . . . [if] a Foreign Service officer has rendered extraordinarily meritorious service . . . the Secretary may exempt such officer from such requirement." Section 625 of the Act adds that the Secretary is "authorized to grant to any officer additional increases in salary . . . based upon exceptionally meritorious service."

From 1946 to the present not a single early promotion has been made on the basis of "extraordinarily meritorious service," and the incentive of small salary increases in accordance with Section 625 has been rarely used for FSOs.

Reading further down the statute, one comes to Section 633, which empowers the Secretary to eliminate low-performing officers if they have not satisfied a minimum standard of performance or if they have remained in class without promotion for whatever maximum period he prescribes by regulation. The Secretary may also terminate the services of a probationary officer of the lowest two ranks "at any time," and may retire a chief of mission simply by failing to give him a new assignment within three months of his departure from his previous post.

In other words, the Secretary has wide authority to decide how many career officials to promote and to "select-out" or prematurely retire, and what standards to apply in making these decisions. It is an authority that has rarely been used. From 1946 until the middle of the 1960s, an average of no more than twenty FSOs per year were "selected-out" by the Foreign Service personnel system. Since 1966, when more rigid standards were applied at the personal prompting of the Under Secretary of State, about seventy per year—or 2 percent of all FSOs—have been prematurely retired. For most of the past decade the only restraining criteria applied to the question of how many annual promotions to make to different ranks have been budgetary. Many more officers have been promoted than have been fired or retired, further crowding the top ranks and depleting the bottom. A tacit seniority system has taken root; with each passing year the Service has aged in its personnel structure, which has resulted in more overcrowding and hence less room at the top for younger men, all this, quite apart from the McCarthyite ravages of the 1950s and the infusion of 2,500 middle-aged, middle-rank officials during the Wriston program.

For a Secretary of State willing to study the problem, its solution would seem almost childishly simple. He has only to prescribe a fixed number or percentage of promotions and forced retirements each year, in accordance with a long-range plan designed to achieve whatever balance among ranks and ages he thinks desirable. He might order the Foreign Service selection boards, for example, to eliminate the lowest-ranking 5 percent of all officers, about 160 per year. He might at the same time direct that the highest-rated 5 percent (or different percentages in each rank) be given accelerated promotions for merit; or, if this upsets rational rank projections for the future, that they at least receive substantial pay increases within their present grades. Even the much-abused military promotion systems for Army and Navy officers make annual provision for identifying a small number of "fliers," *i.e.* men capable of jumping ahead much more quickly than normal rules would allow. It is entirely consistent with the Secretary's existing powers, the career system, and the intent of Congress, that he push able younger men ahead of lower performing senior men, bringing, if he chooses, the average age of an ambassadorship down to forty rather than above fifty.* Several years of consistent effort may be necessary to accomplish these aims, but they are entirely and even easily possible. All that is required is a decisive commitment to the spirit and legislative intent of the Foreign Service Act of

* Other nations have periodically faced and dealt with the same problem. The Duncan Report of 1969 noted there was "overcrowding in the senior grades" of Britain's diplomatic service, and recommended a program "to eliminate 'bulges' in certain age groups by means drastic enough to ensure that the present structural imbalance is really cured." Subsequently, thirty British ambassadors were given premature retirements *en masse*.

1946. The alternative is for Congress to enact its own strict standards of personnel policy, going back to the principle of the Rogers Act of 1924, which insisted that no more than 6 percent of all FSOs at any one time could be "Class 1" officers, and no more than 30 percent could inhabit the four topmost ranks.

Retirement at age fifty, with pension, is the rule rather than the exception for American military officers. Only specialists in short supply and men capable of rising to the highest rank are kept beyond twenty years of service after the terminal age is reached. When the present age and rank distortions in the Foreign Service have been cured, that principle could apply as well to our career diplomacy. Legislation would be needed, giving FSOs retirement advantages comparable to those now enjoyed by their military counterparts.

A little common sense, and the practical application of existing rules, are all that are required to rebalance the personnel structure. Reducing the age and rank bulge should pose neither a complicated nor a very difficult task once the problem is recognized; it can be accomplished in the course of reducing functions and positions within State. The principle of the merit system—"promotion-up or selection-out"—simply requires serious enforcement.

Improved Use of State Department Personnel

The weaknesses of the State Department, however, are not entirely the weaknesses of the Foreign Service. In addition to officers skilled in foreign diplomacy, a strong Department requires a separate cadre of men and women to control and manage the Washington machine. Transient FSOs have careers that for the most part are pointed toward overseas service; their home tours of duty are generally only two to four years at a time. This makes it extremely difficult for FSOs to stay on top of their opposite numbers in the Defense Department, the Treasury, and other home agencies, who maintain a permanent Washington staff. Ever since the Wriston reforms of 1954, State has lacked a strong, resident civil-service staff of its own. To be sure, some senior civil-servant specialists remain in State, about 700 in all, but they are being encouraged to transfer into the Foreign Service and become available for "worldwide duty" along with FSOs. This final unification of personnel systems, if it takes place, will deprive State of the last vestiges of its once substantial permanent home staff. It will destroy whatever is left of that institutional memory that any organization requires if it is to be effective.

All foreign offices benefit by an ability to learn from their past mistakes. Foreign-policy problems are repetitious, and if all personnel are in constant rotation, continuity of error and lack of depth become built-in defects of the system. When in August 1965 an Asian prime minister announced that the CIA had attempted to bribe him four years earlier, the State Department immediately denied the charge. The prime minister then produced a letter written in 1961 and signed by Secretary Rusk, apologizing for the incident. State's explanation for this astonishing *gaffe* was that "the officers who knew of it had been rotated somewhere else and those currently in charge of . . . Southeast Asian affairs knew nothing about it."[183] Criticizing similar tendencies in parts of the Pentagon that suffer from the constant rotation of personnel on short tours of duty, the Fitzhugh report notes that there is no substitute for "corporate memory. . . . recall capability which would prevent or minimize recurrence of past mistakes." A deficiency in this area, the report concludes, "cannot be remedied by . . . data storage and retrieval capabilities made possible by computers. Some individual must recognize the familiar circumstances of earlier experience to indicate that the recorded data connected with earlier history can provide guidance on current problems."[184] The enterprise of diplomacy, more than most professions, requires a precise knowledge of history. Negotiations between states are a never-ending process, and consistent on-the-job training for a perpetually moving officialdom can never adequately replace the knowledge of a permanent staff.

There is compelling reason for State, in its home staffing, to return to the pre-Wriston system: a department composed mainly of resident civil-service officials willing and able to spend their careers entirely in Washington, assisted by a small number of rotating Foreign Service officers on home tours as well as the political appointees of the President then in power. Some men of ability will always prefer to remain in Washington, while others are happiest and most effective in a variety of changing overseas assignments. Neither group should be forced into a single mold in the name of a false uniformity, for each kind of official complements and badly needs the services of the other. If the Foreign Service needs a fifteen-year program of high standards, new recruitment, and manpower planning, so does the Home Service of the State Department.

As a corollary, the heavy majority of FSOs ought to be deployed *abroad* and should remain at their posts for longer periods of time than the present two-to-three-year average. Of the 89 American ambassadors at their posts in May 1969, the average time on the job was 22.9 months, just under two years. That in itself was an improvement over the 107 ambassadors on duty in May of 1963, who averaged only 18.9 months' experience apiece.[185] The Jackson Subcommittee hearings in the Senate, which revealed some of these data in 1963, may have helped bring about the modest improvement, for the Senators were sharply critical of the high rate of turnover in diplomatic posts. Still it is surprising that our chiefs of foreign missions have even a more rapid rate of turnover than their staffs. Eighteen months to two years is a short time to be effective at diplomacy; the ideal average would be closer to four or five years. A former career ambassador states it in this way: "The most important as well as the easiest way to improve the conduct of foreign affairs would be to leave each ambassador at his post long enough for him to become fully effective. This means five or six years at a post instead of one or two years as at present."

He adds that it takes "at least one year in a new country for even the most diligent and experienced professional to dominate the immensely complicated job of a modern ambassador. Performance results from confidence in the character, intentions, and ability of the new American envoy, and confidence cannot be achieved without developing personal re-

Table 10

Deployment of U.S. Foreign Service Officers

YEAR	AT HOME	ABROAD	PERCENT ABROAD
1948	185	1,147	86
1954 (pre-Wriston)	201	1,084	84
1962	1,252	2,435	66
1970 (est.)	1,274	1,810	58

SOURCES: For 1948, Hoover Commission, *Task Force Report on Foreign Affairs* [Appendix H], p. 123; For 1954, Wriston Committee, *Toward A Stronger Foreign Service*, p. 61; for 1962, Herter Committee, *Personnel for the New Diplomacy*, p. 148; for 1970, Department of State, *Summary of Employment, August 31, 1970*, p. 5.

lationships with the key foreign officials concerned: President, Prime Minister, industrialist, monarch, labor leader, prelate—whoever the leaders of the country may be."[186]

Today nearly as many FSOs are assigned to Washington as are stationed outside the country. This is a curious situation for a diplomatic service, for most other nations keep an approximate balance of at least two-thirds of their career diplomats overseas and no more than one-third located in the home capital at any one time. The American ratios, compared with those of the recent past, are particularly startling:

This distribution is largely an accident, the cumulative result of years of forgetfulness. It serves to demonstrate how unplanned State's personnel policies have become.

Overseas Reforms

Reforms in the Washington machine require a comparable set of changes overseas at our 252 diplomatic missions in 117 countries. Gigantic size and its confusions hamper the work of our embassies no less than that of the home department. Crammed with separate staffs, American embassies are ostentatiously larger than those of other nations. At least 78 percent of all Americans serving at diplomatic missions do not work for the State Department, and the actual figure is probably a bit higher, for it can be presumed that the CIA component at embassies, whose size is not a matter of public record, is at least partially hidden in the total figure given for State Department employees. Some State officials admit as much in explaining why, when they request funds from Congress, they are not always able to satisfy congressmen that embassy staffs need to be quite so large.

Comparison may help suggest the proportions of the problem. Our mission in Saigon, the largest embassy in modern history, in 1970 had a staff of more than 4,000, of whom 357 were State Department employees. The military headquarters staff in Saigon, of course, considerably overshadows the embassy; according to Richard Holbrooke, it is larger in number than the staffs that planned the Normandy invasion in 1944. Today more than 1,000 officials are stationed at our embassy in Thailand, 495 in Germany, 460 in Turkey, and 275 in Colombia. When alien clerical workers and diplomatic wives and children are included, the total size of each American presence swells to a number three or four times greater than that given.

In 1965 Henry Villard reported that our embassy in Rome, with 800 to 900 total personnel, was ten times larger than the French and British missions, while in the small African nation of Burundi American officials outnumbered the entire Belgian colonial administration that had run the country before independence. Reflecting on his own experience as chief of mission to a North African country, Villard reported:

> . . . I had on my staff in Libya a military attaché, an air attaché, and an agent of Central Intelligence, all of whom vied with the trained members of my political section in gathering intelligence. Since the sources of information in that country were necessarily limited, those who furnished the intelligence were often taken aback at being asked the same questions by representatives of different agencies; those who did the asking stumbled over each other in their efforts to garner the available scraps.[187]

What Ambassador Villard describes is no isolated case of diplomatic snafu. What occurred in Libya is endemic in the system; it occurs daily in countless capitals on every continent.

The fundamental answer to the problem is to cut functions and slash staffs. The total of 22,000 Americans who now serve at our embassies could be profitably reduced, over several years' time, by more than half, to about 10,000 personnel worldwide. This should be accomplished *without* closing consulates, the 126 diplomatic branch offices located away from capital cities, which are an important adjunct to our embassies and a training ground for younger diplomats. Indeed, some of the three dozen consulates closed for economy reasons during the past decade could be usefully reopened, for consulates keep American officials in touch with the regional and provincial bases of political and economic influence in ways that supplement an embassy's attention to problems in the national capital.

The heaviest cutbacks should come in military and intelligence staffs, which are the most swollen component of the embassies. Large aid and propaganda staffs, as well as some programs of the lesser economic bureaucracies can, as I have argued in earlier chapters, be significantly reorganized and reduced.

It has hardly ever occurred to Washington that sending large numbers of official Americans to small, poor countries can have negative side effects on our relations with those countries. Large U.S. missions create an impression of massive American interference. When those large missions are compartmentalized among separate government agencies, with each agency's staff competing for the time and attention of foreign officials, we convey the impression of a diffuse and unfocused policy that lacks seriousness. Although the Secretary of State does not now control (nor does anyone else) the numbers of personnel sent by other agencies to our embassies, he can be given that power by the President, along with control over their foreign budgets. In 1970, our largest diplomatic posts (with the exception of the superembassy in Saigon) employed 500 to 1,000 Americans from all agencies, and only the very smallest embassies had staffs of less than 50 to 100. In the future, fixed personnel ceilings should be set for each of the four categories of our missions, for example, a maximum of 150 personnel for Class I missions (London, Tokyo, Paris, Moscow), 75 for Class II (Hong Kong, Ottawa, Brussels, Warsaw), 35 for Class II (Teheran, Rabat, Copenhagen, Bucharest), and 15 for Class IV (Bamako, Katmandu.) Ideally, the size of our staff should bear some rough relationship to the importance of its mission and the priority accorded by the U.S. government to its relations with a given state. The non-State Department contingent generally ought not to exceed 50 percent of the total mission personnel.

All personnel of all agencies should serve "at the pleasure of the ambassador." To enhance an ambassador's authority, the ownership and operation of embassy coding and communications equipment should be transferred from the CIA to the State Department. All other-agency personnel serving at embassies, military and civilian alike, should be "seconded" to the State Department and made subject to its internal discipline for the duration of their tours. Finally, ambassadors should be accountable for *all* U.S. government funds expended by *all* U.S. agencies in their country.

As I mentioned in Chapter 5, the State Department currently receives $120 million each year in fund transfers from the budgets of other executive branch agencies, above and beyond its congressional appropriation. If other approaches cannot be found for financing American diplomacy, State will continue to be tied to a pattern of large embassy staffs and an overseas "PX Culture." The solution to the problem requires candor on the part of the Secretary of State and good will from Congress.

The Secretary should request from Congress the full sum required to finance overseas operations, rather than depend upon informal payments negotiated with other departments of the executive branch. As other-agency staffs at our embassies are drastically curtailed, the need for many of the present administrative services should diminish, permitting sizable cutbacks in the embassy administration sections. These are now the largest segment of the State Department portion of U.S. missions. The bulk of their work can be performed, more fully than today, by alien clerical workers under the supervision of a small American staff. A survey should be made to determine the cost of eliminating all special food and clothing stores, post exchanges, and housing compounds administered directly by U.S. embassies or their military members on a "nonappropriated fund" basis. Smaller staffs will not require such elaborate services, and will welcome greater independence to administer themselves in their own way in matters of personal food, clothing, housing, and education for their children. Only in the most compelling circumstances of physical danger is there a case to be made that our officials should live together in an "American ghetto," remote from the environment around them. George Kennan, who criticizes the continuance twenty-five years after the end of World War II of "all of the government housing compounds and military PXs selling American food and clothing to Embassy people," has also stressed the positive benefits of ending paternalistic administration. "We need to permit the individual to have more control over his own destiny," Kennan remarks, "and to lead his own life in his own way, for that expresses the genius of our country and it also makes for a better diplomatic representation."[188]

Unusual personal expenses, which are invariably a part of running a diplomatic household and representing one's country abroad, should be compensated for by generous cash allowances, as is the practice in every other major diplomatic establishment in today's world. Foreign officials living in Washington, for example, receive allowances that frequently are three to four times greater than their home salaries, to account for price differences and the higher standard of living they are expected to maintain as representatives of their governments abroad. Congress allows U.S. Foreign Service families modest allowances for foreign housing, the education of their children, medical or physical hardship and, in a few countries, cost of living differentials. Only in the most exceptional case do these payments amount to as much as one-quarter of an American official's salary; only a minority of officers in a minority of countries qualify for any allowance at all. Most FSOs find that the moving expenses they incur when transferred from one post to another are only partially covered by government funds. The military services and CIA fare far better at the hands of Congress, for both the Pentagon and intelligence agency have larger budgets than State, and their funds are not as closely scrutinized by legislators. Hence it is often a CIA man or a military attaché at an embassy who has extra leeway to entertain foreign officials when his Foreign Service colleagues are already out-of-pocket.

Congress is especially stingy with what it calls "representational" funds for State, which, in business parlance, would more accurately be described as expense-account entertainment of clients. Since 1965 State has received an annual appropriation of $993,000 to cover all costs of official entertaining done by all ambassadors and Foreign Service officers stationed abroad. No funds at all are available for FSOs to entertain foreign officials in Washington or at the United Nations in New York. By comparison, the French diplomatic service, much smaller than our own, receives an annual 11 million francs, or $2.2 million for overseas entertaining, an amount two and one-half times greater than the American total.[189] A former ambassador made these additional comparisons in 1965: ". . . the American embassy in Bonn received $19,325 for representation and personal expenses; West Germany . . . spent three times that much in Washington. In Rome, our ambassador was given $15,540; the Italian ambassador to the United States received some $45,000. . . . The 'personal expense and representational allowance' of the British ambassador in Washington is . . . more than double what the American ambassador in London gets in salary and expense allowance."[190] The Russians, he adds, are even more generous with their foreign representation.

Money can be saved by reducing the quantity of U.S. overseas employment, but Congress must realize that money must be spent to improve the quality of that representation. Instead of appropriating funds for multimillion dollar housing complexes and stinting on personal allowances, a more effective diplomacy could be encouraged by reversing these priorities.

In an age of rapid travel, some of the main administrative chores now performed at embassies should be done in Washington, supplemented by occasional trips to the field. Shipment of embassy supplies and personal household goods wherever possible should be handled by air, which is an increasingly less costly and more efficient means of transport than more traditional media. In the same way, many statistical collection jobs now performed at embassies by resident specialists could just as well be done from home by a few air trips abroad each year, at considerable savings. Travel within foreign countries, to consult with colleagues at embassies in neighboring countries and to Washington as well, should also be encouraged. Antique travel regulations, a small travel budget, and excessive red tape make each of these things a rarity in American diplomacy today. Administrators and congressmen should heed the words of Britain's Duncan Report in this regard: "Not to use the modern resources of rapid travel to the full is wasteful not only in terms of the high manpower cost of correspondence but even more in terms of the expensive misunderstandings which can arise in the absence of direct person-to-person contact at sufficiently short intervals. . . . Commercial organizations . . . would never hesitate to let their overseas representative report in person to headquarters where this seemed useful."[191]

On a cost basis, the authors of the Duncan Report were able to prove the efficiency of keeping specialist officials at home and letting them conduct most of their foreign business by frequent air travel rather than stationing them residentially abroad. They found, for example, that "the difference in cost between keeping a full-time resident Counsellor in Paris and having visits of one week's duration each by officers of the same grade would allow as many as 120 such visits per year. . . ."[192] In the case of Tokyo, the cost differential was fourteen weekly visits per year; for Nairobi, ten visits; for Teheran, nineteen; and for Kuala Lumpur, fourteen. Looking ahead to 1973, the study found this cost ratio improving with every year. The figures on air travel from Washington would differ from those for London, but the principle is the same. The evidence is conclusive that, on a cost basis, air travel permitting short business trips from headquarters to the field is considerably cheaper than stationing specialist residents in the field. It seems to follow that really major cutbacks in overseas staffs of administrators are possible and profitable alternatives to the present practice of maintaining large permanent staffs at our embassies.

Democratizing the Diplomatic Corps

Reform at our overseas missions would be incomplete if it did not also try to improve the style of diplomatic life. Because of ancient, often archaic, forms of deference, and more reasonably because an ambassador, like a ship's captain, heads a highly disciplined organization, it is possible for embassy life to develop undemocratic qualities of a kind repugnant to most Americans. Ambassador Attwood has written of the "dragon-ladies," who, in their roles as wives of ambassadors, occasionally terrorize the lives of their husbands' subordinates: "I have known of some who ordered the wives of staff members around like servants; one who put a hairdresser off limits to other wives because she didn't like him; one who insisted the staff speak to her in French; one who would whimsically appropriate a cook or piece of furniture from subordinates."[193]

The sins enumerated above are petty and amusing, but perhaps a more serious and universal cause for complaint in the Foreign Service today is the tendency of "first ladies" of our diplomatic missions to insist upon organizing the women beneath them in various forms of busy work and charitable endeavor. Few American embassies do not have an "American women's club" of one sort or another. Its president and guiding light, of course, is Mrs. Ambassador, and its compulsory membership includes, of course, the wives of her husband's subordinates who are pressed, willy-nilly, into pursuing the hobbies and running the errands of the head lady. At an embassy in the Far East recently, a senior diplomatic wife sent a "memo" to the wives of her husband's subordinates, asking them to "let me have regular reports on how you spend your time each day."

There is something very close to an abridgement of civil rights in these curious forms of social usage, which are all too common in our embassy communities today. Able men and spirited women will not put up with it. They are better representatives of their country as well as happier human beings when permitted to pursue their own individual styles of life outside the office.

Among embassy officers there is always the danger that proper discipline may become obedience, and obedience become obeisance. John Kenneth Galbraith called attention to this difficulty, which, he felt, was often a "grievous fault" of embassy life. An American ambassador, Galbraith declared, "if we have pride in our democratic faith, should never be more than the first among equals for all purposes unrelated to function. He is captain, not a monarch. He should be a leader on duty, a neighbor off. . . . For if the ambassador is an oriental figure in the embassy, it is inevitable that he will suppress ideas or insure that they are never offered."[194]

These are matters of style that will vary from person to person and place to place. They may also express, in part, a difference in the generational outlook between that group of senior diplomats who survived the McCarthy and Wriston changes of the 1950s and a bright, brash, less inhibited body of younger men and women who came later to the scene. No single "reform" can bring greater honesty and informality to the atmosphere of an American embassy, and an awareness of the problem is the first step toward its solution. As Galbraith remarks, "Let there be a clear distinction between a man who accepts discipline and the man who is a bootlicker."[195]

Another, final Galbraith proposal that makes eminent good sense is that the American Foreign Service Association publicly advise the President and the Senate of its professional opinion of all persons nominated for ambassadorships. In this way, AFSA would come to perform a function similar to that of the American Bar Association when it passes on the professional qualifications of candidates for federal judgeships. By this simple act, the association could encourage the appointment of qualified men, in most cases career professionals, to high diplomatic office. As the Hoover Commission recommended in 1949, the President should by tradition "explain his special reasons" whenever he appoints an ambassador from outside the ranks of the professional career service.

Conclusion and Final Recommendations

The President and the Secretary of State can, with some cooperation from Congress, accomplish most of the reforms that have been suggested. New legislation is needed to shake down the CIA, AID, and USIA, but major cuts in personnel the State and Defense Departments can occur by executive throughout the government and an internal reorganization of action alone. If such action is not taken early in the 1970s, Congress will be all the more tempted to propose its own solutions. The power of the purse gives it at least a negative means of forcing changes by cutting budgets.

As reforms in the major foreign affairs departments are carried through, it is time for the President and Congress as well to reconsider the role of the National Security Council and the presidential staff system as it has evolved since 1947. It should be clear that the present process of advising the President on foreign and military matters has serious faults, and that the NSC today is something considerably different from what many of its creators envisioned two decades ago. Instead of concentrating on national security questions—the defense budget and military strategic and tactical doctrine, for example—the NSC has become a foreign policy making body. Three of its seven statutory members or advisers—the Defense Secretary, the Chairman of the Joint Chiefs of Staff, and the director of the CIA—weight the body heavily toward military and intelligence perceptions, which in the nature of things are biased toward a fearful view of world affairs, toward a preoccupation with "threats" and "capabilities," real or imagined. Most Presidents and Vice-Presidents in the postwar period have been greatly, perhaps unduly, impressed with military and intelligence assessments. The very structure of decision making has made them conceive policy more often in military than in political terms. Unless, like Dwight Eisenhower, a President has had enough personal experience in the military bureaucracy to make him knowledgeable and skeptical of its workings, he is likely to be impressed and even overwhelmed by them.

Another statutory member of the NSC, the director of the Office of Emergency Preparedness, is a minor official of no stature in Washington, and should have long ago been eliminated from NSC membership. This leaves only the Secretary of State—one man out of seven—to speak for diplomacy in what has become a major foreign policy body.

Reforming the State Department should, over time, allow the NSC structure to be redirected toward narrower military security issues, as was originally intended, and away from foreign policy. This should also help pave the way for abolition of the complex interagency committee substructure that is once more in the Nixon administration, like in the Eisenhower years, growing up around the National Security Council. Again, as the Jackson Subcommittee observed in 1961 of the Eisenhower NSC, there is emerging "a highly formalized and complex 'policy paper production' system" that "is not a creative instrument for developing and bringing forward imaginative and sharply defined choices, particularly in uncharted areas of policy" but has instead "a built-in drive toward lowest-common-denominator solutions."[196] The committees also institutionalize at every level majority representation by military and intelligence officials, tending to make them foreign policy makers rather than specialized technical advisers.

Where does this leave the President's own staffing needs, the practice of appointing a foreign policy assistant to the White House such as Kennedy's McGeorge Bundy, Johnson's Walt W. Rostow, and Nixon's Henry Kissinger? The Jackson Subcommittee addressed this question sensibly a decade ago. "The President should at all times," it concluded, "have the help and protection of a *small** personal staff whose members work 'outside the system,' who are sensitive to the President's own information needs, and who can assist him in asking relevant questions of his departmental chiefs, in making suggestions for policy initiatives not emerging from the operating departments and agencies, and in spotting gaps in policy execution."[197] Clearly, any president will need a staff of

* Emphasis added.

helpers to organize his work and communicate on his behalf, but the operative word is "*small*" staff. For, as Richard Neustadt observed in 1963, "The personal assistant begins to bog down as a personal watchdog and intimate servant once he starts to preside over fifty, eighty, or one hundred subordinates," a numerical point that has been recently passed in the present White House foreign affairs staff and the NSC system. So large a staff, Neustadt perceptively argued, would tend to add "another echelon, another level for clearances, another level for negotiations, another set of . . . officials who have to relate every day with the Pentagon and the State Department. . . ."[198] Large presidential staffs, in other words, imitate the worst features of the rest of the large governmental bureaucracies, instead of helping a President master them. A small, compact, informal staff will be the proper White House parallel to a smaller, more proficient, and self-confident State Department, headed by a Secretary who is clearly regarded and used as the President's senior foreign policy adviser.

Experience—twenty-four years of it spanning five administrations—should dictate the wisdom and even the necessity of these structural changes. At this late date it would seem an evasion for Congress or the President to appoint yet another public commission to restudy the organization of our foreign departments. Many studies have already been made, from the two Hoover Commissions of 1947 and 1953 to the Herter Committee of 1962 to the recent Peterson and Macomber Task Forces and the Fitzhugh Study of 1970. By now the dimensions of the problem should be evident to all.

Unnecessary though it may sound, however, the appointment of a presidential or congressional commission to recommend reorganizations is probably in the cards, and it may not be such a bad idea after all. For in the psychology of American public life, the blue-ribbon public panel has a special symbolic significance. In a time of dissatisfaction and confusion, it is the one proposal to which men of differing opinions can agree. It focuses attention and public discussion on issues too serious for narrow partisanship. It mobilizes opinion and builds support for change of a kind that no single party or group of citizens can quite carry off by themselves. So, if we *must* have another public study, let it come.

But let it be a more honest, a more thorough, a more comprehensive study than so many of those that have gone before. And let those who make recommendations that the President approves be asked to stay on and see that the recommendations are carried out. Since the first Hoover Commission of twenty years ago, which had perhaps a unique prestige because of its chairmanship by a former president, there has been no single public survey of the organization of *all* the foreign-affairs departments of the executive branch. No subsequent study has been so competent, so complete, so insistent on considering together the jobs of diplomacy, intelligence, and military action in a single coherent scheme. It is because the first Hoover report was imperfectly heeded that we face many of our organizational problems today.

Lecturing to Harvard undergraduates ten years ago, Henry Kissinger liked to remark that a foreign policy is only as strong as its weakest link: the bureaucracy that implements it. In an essay published in 1966, Kissinger criticized Washington's "elaborate and fragmented" bureaucratic mechanisms and observed that "the staffs on which modern executives come to depend develop a momentum of their own." He added that as each administrative machine becomes "increasingly absorbed in its own internal problems, diplomacy loses its flexibility," and "serving the machine becomes a more absorbing occupation than defining its purpose." Hence,

Kissinger concluded, what begins as an aid to decision makers "often turns into a practically autonomous organization whose internal problems structure and sometimes compound the issues which it was originally designed to serve."[199]

The difficulties this bureaucratic welter pose for an effective foreign policy were well described nearly twenty years ago by Harold Nicolson, a wise foreign observer of American diplomacy. "The misfortune of the American system," Nicolson said, "is that no foreigner, and few Americans, can be quite positive at any given moment who it is who possesses the first word and who the last: and although the Americans in recent years have been in process of creating an admirable service of professional diplomatists, these experts do not yet possess the necessary influence with their own government and public." It is "regrettable," Nicolson remarked, "that the authority exercised by the United States is not more consistent, convincing, and reliable."[200]

Kissinger's analysis and Nicolson's comments are as accurate today as they were a few years ago. What has been lacking thus far is a plan of reform designed to correct the known deficiencies of the system. Although the postwar period of foreign policy has come to an end, the institutional forms that emerged in that earlier era are still very much with us. The continuance of those forms, devised in haste and accident more than twenty years ago, undercuts the announced purposes of American foreign policy in the 1970s. We are still organized more to engage in a clash of ideologies than to negotiate a balance of power, and the voice of diplomacy has become weak within the structure of our government. If an era of negotiation is ever to get off the ground, policy changes abroad must be accompanied by bureaucratic reform at home.

NOTES

1. The 1965 April Fool's Day summary has now been retired to the archives. A similar prank in 1966 had similar results. No April Fool's Day summary has appeared since.

2. My sources are several Washington officials, interviewed privately in the spring of 1970. Substantially the same account appears in Richard Holbrooke, "The Machine That Fails," *Foreign Policy* (Winter 1970–1971); and John Franklin Campbell, "Clearing Foggy Bottom," *Interplay* 3, no. 8 (April 1970): 33–36.

3. Holbrooke, *op. cit.*, gives the same account, which was repeated to me in an interview with an "elder statesman."

4. Quoted in Arthur M. Schlesinger, Jr., *A Thousand Days* (Boston: Houghton Mifflin, 1965), p. 406.

5. Joseph Kraft, "Washington Insight: Fudge Factory" (released May 20, 1966 by Publisher's Newspaper Syndicate for publication in *The Washington Post* and other newspapers).

6. Jack Anderson, "Nixon Ready to Reform State Dept.," *The Washington Post*, August 18, 1969, p. B–11.

7. Holbrooke, *op. cit.*

8. John F. Campbell, "An Interview with George F. Kennan," *Foreign Service Journal*, 47, No. 8 (August, 1970): 22.

9. Richard Nixon, *U.S. Foreign Policy for the 1970s, A New Strategy for Peace* (A Report to Congress, February 18, 1970, U.S. Government Printing Office, Washington), p. 2.

10. Bruce J. Oudes, "The Great Wind Machine," *The Washington Monthly*, 2, no. 4 (June, 1970): 30–39.

11. Richard M. Pfeffer, ed., *No More Vietnams?* (New York: Harper, 1968), p. 11.

12. Roger Hilsman, *To Move a Nation* (New York: Delta, 1968; © 1964), p. 564.

13. Harry Howe Ransom, *The Intelligence Establishment* (Cambridge: Harvard University Press, 1970), p. 249.

14. Anthony Hartley, "From World Policeman to Fortress America?" *Moderne Welt* 7 (Duesseldorf: 1969): 98–99.

15. *Time*-Harris poll, in *Time*, May 2, 1969.

16. Stanley Hoffmann, *Gulliver's Troubles, or The Setting of American Foreign Policy* (New York: McGraw-Hill [for the Council on Foreign Relations], 1968), p. 254. Hoffmann is partly paraphrasing George Kennan here.

17. John Kenneth Galbraith, *Ambassador's Journal* (Boston: Houghton Mifflin, 1969), p. 212.

18. Stewart Alsop, *The Center* (New York: Harper & Row, 1968), p. 114.

19. Holbrooke, *op. cit.*

20. Alexis de Tocqueville, *Democracy in America* (Henry Reeve Text), Vol. 1 (New York: Vintage, 1957), p. 243.

21. Harold Nicolson, *Diplomacy*, 3rd ed. (London: Oxford University Press, 1963), p. 93.

22. George F. Kennan, "The Future of Our Professional Diplomacy," *Foreign Affairs*, 33, No. 4 (July, 1955): 573.

23. Quoted in Nicolson, *op. cit.*, p. 57 and in Harold Nicolson, *The Evolution of Diplomacy* (New York: Collier, 1962), pp. 112–113. There is some variation in the translation from the French as between these two books.

24. Dean Acheson, *Present at the Creation* (New York: Norton, 1969), p. 733.

25. *Ibid.*, p. 214.

26. Campbell, "An Interview with George F. Kennan," p. 20.

27. Quoted in Hans J. Morgenthau, *A New Foreign Policy for the United States* (New York: Praeger [for the Council on Foreign Relations], 1969), p. 83.

28. "Excerpts from a report of Ferdinand Eberstadt for Secretary of the Navy James Forrestal, September 25, 1945," in *The National Security Council*, ed. Senator Henry M. Jackson (New York: Praeger, 1965), pp. 291–294.

29. General Maxwell D. Taylor, Speech to the American Foreign Service Association, March 31, 1966, reprinted in *Foreign Service Journal*, Vol. 43, No. 5 (May, 1966), and in *Toward a Modern Diplomacy*, a report to the American Foreign Service Association, Washington, 1968, p. 185.

30. The Committee on Foreign Affairs Personnel, "Herter Report" *Personnel for the New Diplomacy* (Washington: The Carnegie Endowment for International Peace, December, 1962), pp. 3–4.

31. *Ibid.*, pp. 2, 4.

32. George W. Ball, *The Discipline of Power* (Boston: Atlantic-Little, Brown, 1968), p. 222.

33. Morgenthau, *op. cit.*, p. 142.

34. Richard E. Neustadt, "White House and Whitehall," *The Public Interest*, No. 2 (Winter 1966), pp. 59, 68–69.

35. Richard E. Neustadt, *Alliance Politics* (New York: Columbia University Press, 1970), pp. 142–143.

36. Acheson, *op. cit.*, p. 734.

37. Harvey H. Bundy and James Grafton Rogers, *The Organization of the Government for the Conduct of Foreign Affairs*, Task Force Report on Foreign Affairs [Appendix H], prepared for the Commission on Organization of

the Executive Branch of the Government, Washington, GPO, 1949, p. 3.

38. *Ibid.*, p. 51.
39. *Ibid.*, pp. 15, 29.
40. *Ibid.*, p. 58.
41. *Ibid.*, pp. 67–68.
42. *Ibid.*, p. 2.
43. *Ibid.*, pp. 3–4.
44. *Ibid.*, pp. vii, viii.
45. Schlesinger, *op. cit.*, p. 431.
46. Quoted in Lynton K. Caldwell, *The Administrative Theories of Hamilton and Jefferson* (Chicago: University of Chicago Press, 1944), p. 223; see also p. 228.
47. *Ibid.*, p. 44; p. 239.
48. Holbrooke, *op. cit.*
49. Campbell, "An Interview with George F. Kennan," p. 20.
50. Schlesinger, *op. cit.*, pp. 407, 426.
51. *Ibid.*, p. 413.
52. *Ibid.*, pp. 414, 417.
53. *Ibid.*, pp. 408, 410.
54. James Thomson, Jr., "How Could Vietnam Happen?" *Atlantic* (April, 1968), p. 48.
55. John Paton Davies, Jr., *Foreign and Other Affairs* (New York: Norton, 1963), p. 198.
56. Hilsman, *op. cit.*, p. 30.
57. *Ibid.*, p. 31.
58. Quoted in Henry Raymont, "Kennedy Library Documents, Opened to Scholars, Illuminate Policies on Cuba and Berlin," *The New York Times*, August 17, 1970, p. 16.
59. Schlesinger, *op cit.*, pp. 248–252.
60. Thomson, *op. cit.*, p. 49.
61. Schlesinger, *op. cit.*, pp. 876, 878 and William N. Fraleigh, quoted in *The New York Times*, August 17, 1970, p. 16.
62. *Schlesinger*, op. cit., pp. 878, 880.
63. Quoted in *The New York Times*. August 17, 1970, p. 16; see also Mauro Lucentini, "Lunghi Colloqui al Quirinale—Kennedy e il Centro Sinistra," *Il Mondo* (Rome), September 6, 1970, pp. 4–5.
64. Robert F. Kennedy, *Thirteen Days* (New York: Signet, The New American Library, 1969), pp. 114–115.
65. A Report to the American Foreign Service Association, *Toward a Modern Diplomacy*, Washington, 1968, p. 155.
66. *The Federalist* No. 70 (March 18, 1788) in the Modern Library edition of *The Federalist* with introduction by Edward Mead Earle (New York: Random House, 1937), pp. 460–461.
67. *The Federalist*, No. 23 (December 18, 1787) in *ibid.*, p. 144.
68. Quoted in Caldwell, *op. cit.*, p. 45.

69. V. I. Lenin, *State and Revolution* (New York: International Publishers, 1932), pp. 38, 83–84.
70. *Newsweek* (International Edition), October 14, 1968, p. 4. Letter to Editor from W. G. Gilchrist, Jr.
71. Quoted in Eric F. Goldman, *The Crucial Decade—And After* (New York: Vintage, 1961), p. 126.
72. Quoted in Daniel J. Boorstin, *America and the Image of Europe* (New York: Meridian Books, 1960), p. 21.
73. George F. Kennan, "History and Diplomacy as Viewed by a Diplomatist," in *Diplomacy in a Changing World*, ed. Stephen D. Kertesz and M. A. Fitzsimons (Notre Dame: University of Notre Dame Press, 1959), pp. 106–108.
74. George F. Kennan, *Memoirs, 1925–1950* (Boston: Atlantic-Little, Brown, 1967), footnote, p. 405.
75. Acheson, *op. cit.*, p. 733.
76. Alsop, *op. cit.*, p. 61.
77. Testimony of Charles L. Schultze, August 23, 1967, at Hearings before the Subcommittee on National Security and International Operations of the Committee on Government Operations, U.S. Senate, in *Planning, Programming, Budgeting*, Washington, G.P.O. 1970, p. 181.
78. Thomas C. Schelling, "PPBS and Foreign Affairs," *The Public Interest*, no. 11 (Spring 1968), p. 35.
79. Aaron Wildavsky, "Rescuing Policy Analysis from PPBS," in *The Analysis and Evaluation of Public Expenditures: The PPB System*, Vol. 3, a compendium of papers submitted to the Subcommittee on Economy in Government of the Joint Economic Committee, 91st Congress, 1st sess. (Washington, D.C.: Government Printing Office, 1969), p. 842.
80. Frederick C. Mosher, "Program Budgeting in Foreign Affairs: Some Reflections," in U.S. Senate, *Planning, Programming, Budgeting*, Washington, G.P.O. 1970, p. 146. See also Frederick Mosher and John Harr, *Programming Systems and Foreign Affairs Leadership* (New York: Oxford University Press, 1970).
81. John Ensor Harr, *The Professional Diplomat* (Princeton: Princeton University Press, 1969), p. 83.
82. *Ibid.*, pp. 120–121.
83. Department of State, Foreign Affairs Manual Circular Number 385, March 4, 1966.
84. The quotations in the next five paragraphs are all from General Taylor's speech, reprinted in full in *Toward A Modern Diplomacy*, a report to the American Foreign Service Association, Washington, 1968, pp. 179–185.
85. Edward Weintal and Charles Bartlett, *Facing the Brink, An Intimate Study of Crisis Diplomacy* (New York: Scribners', 1967), pp. 178, 180.
86. Acheson, *op. cit.*, p. 733.
87. Keith C. Clark and Laurence J. Legere, eds., *The President and the*

Management of National Security, A Report by the Institute for Defense Analyses (New York: Praeger, 1969), Chapter VII.

88. Chris Argyris, *Some Causes of Organizational Ineffectiveness within the Department of State,* Occasional Paper No. 2 of the Center for International Systems Research, Department of State, Washington, 1966, p. 46.

89. Richard E. Neustadt, *Presidential Power* (New York, Mentor, copyright 1960, 1964), pp. 150–151.

90. *Ibid.*, pp. 149–150.

91. Acheson, *op. cit.*, p. 734.

92. Concluding Statement by Senator Henry M. Jackson, November 15, 1961, in *The National Security Council* (New York: Praeger, 1965), p. 67.

93. Quoted in Stephen Grover, "Diplomatic Dissent—Restive 'Young Turks' Lead Reform Movement at State Department," *The Wall Street Journal,* November 12, 1969, p. 1.

94. William B. Macomber, "Management Strategy: A Program for the '70s," Department of State Press Release No. 9, January 14, 1970.

95. John Kenneth Galbraith, "Advice to the Foreign Service" (speech before the American Foreign Service Association, October 24, 1969), *Foreign Service Journal,* 46, no. 13 (December, 1969), p. 21 ff.

96. Quoted in William W. Kaufmann, "Two American Ambassadors: Bullitt and Kennedy," in *The Diplomats, 1919–1939,* eds., Gordon A. Craig and Felix Gilbert (New York: Atheneum, 1963), p. 655.

97. Kennan, *Memoirs,* p. 362.

98. Richard H. Rovere, *Senator Joe McCarthy* (New York, Meridian Books 1960), p. 23. See also John F. Campbell, "McCarthy and the Anti-Libertarian Tradition in America," *Adams House Journal of the Social Sciences* (Spring 1961).

99. *Congressional Record,* February 20, 1950, p. 1954 (quoted in Seymour Martin Lipset, "The Sources of the 'Radical Right,'" in *The Radical Right,* ed. Daniel Bell (Garden City, New York: Anchor, 1964), p. 361; Goldman, *op. cit.*, p. 142; Joseph McCarthy, *America's Retreat From Victory: The Story of George Catlett Marshall* (New York: Devin-Adair, 1951), p. 171.

100. Rovere, *op. cit.*, p. 15.

101. Goldman, *op. cit.*, p 233; Rovere, *op. cit.*, p. 49.

102. Goldman, *op. cit.*, pp. 127–128.

103. *Ibid.*, p. 125.

104. Rovere, *op. cit.*, p. 18; Ross Y. Koen, *The China Lobby in American Politics* (New York: Macmillan, 1960), p. 240.

105. Rovere, *op. cit.*, pp. 32–33.

106. John Paton Davies, Jr., *Foreign and Other Affairs,* p. 198.

107. Thomson, *op. cit.*, p. 48.

108. Report of the Secretary of State's Public Committee on Personnel, ["Wriston Report"], *Toward a Stronger Foreign Service,* June 1954, pp. 1–2.

109. *Ibid.*, p. 8.

110. *Ibid.*, p. 11.

111. Harr, *op. cit.*, pp. 180–181. For 1969–1970 figures see *Department of State Newsletter*, August, 1970, p. 34.
112. Acheson, *op. cit.*, p. 246.
113. The "Herter Report" (see footnote 30), p. 52.
114. Hoffmann, *op. cit.*, p. 268; James L. McCamy, *Conduct of the New Diplomacy* (New York: Harper & Row, 1964), Chapter 6.
115. McCamy, *op. cit.*, pp. 54–56.
116. *Ibid.*, pp. 64–68, 96.
117. Campbell, "An Interview with George F. Kennan," p. 23.
118. Ransom, *op. cit.*, pp. 88, 182.
119. *Ibid.*, pp. 87–88.
120. Alsop, *op. cit.*, p. 240.
121. Schlesinger, *op. cit.*, p. 427.
122. Hilsman, *op. cit.*, pp. 77, 80.
123. *Toward A Modern Diplomacy*, p. 30.
124. Harry Howe Ransom, *Central Intelligence and National Security* (Cambridge: Harvard University Press, 1958), p. 216.
125. Allen Dulles, *The Craft of Intelligence* (New York, Signet, 1965), © 1963, p. 185.
126. Harry S Truman, in a syndicated article for the North American Newspaper Alliance, as published in *The Washington Post*, December 22, 1963; also quoted in Ransom, *The Intelligence Establishment*, pp. 159, 240, and Hilsman, *op. cit.*, pp. 61, 63.
127. Ransom, *The Intelligence Establishment*, p. 82.
128. *Ibid.*, pp. 89, 249; Hilsman, *op. cit.*, pp. 75–76.
129. Ransom, *The Intelligence Establishment*, pp. 232–233.
130. *Ibid.*, p. 169.
131. *Ibid.*, p. 236.
132. Letter to the author from an American ambassador, February 2, 1970.
133. Ransom, *Intelligence Establishment*, p. 253.
134. Policy Review and Coordination Staff, Bureau of Educational and Cultural Affairs, Department of State, A *Guide to U. S. Government Agencies Involved in International Educational and Cultural Activities*, Department of State Publication 8405, International Information and Cultural Series 97, (Washington, D.C., Government Printing Office, September, 1968).
135. John W. Henderson, "The Present Program of the United States Information Agency," in *The Case for Reappraisal of U.S. Overseas Information Policies and Programs*, eds. Edward L. Bernays and Burnet Hershey (New York: Praeger, 1970), pp. 27–28; also Oudes, *op. cit.*, p. 31,
136. Quoted in Adam Yarmolinsky, "The Military Establishment," *Foreign Policy*, No. 1 (Winter 1970–1971).
137. U.S. Senate, 91st Congress, 1st Session, House Report No. 91–130 on Winning the Cold War: The U.S. Ideological Offensive, by the Subcommittee on International Organizations and Movements of the Committee on Foreign Affairs, "The Future of United States Public Diplomacy," p. 1–R;

reprinted as George Gallup, Jr., "The Image of the United States Abroad in 1969: A Report," in *The Case for Reappraisal of the U.S. Overseas Information Policies and Programs*, eds., Edward L. Bernays and Burnet Hershey (New York: Praeger, 1970), p. 13.

138. Oudes, *op. cit.*, pp. 31–33.

139. *Ibid.*, p. 33.

140. Background Paper, One Day Conference on Reappraisal of U.S. Overseas Information Programs (The Overseas Press Club, New York, October 22, 1969), p. 8.

141. Oudes, *op. cit.*, p. 33.

142. Report of the Katzenbach-Helms-Gardner Committee to Review CIA Secret Subsidies, *Department of State Bulletin* (April 24, 1967), pp. 665–668; see also, The British Council, *Annual Report*, 1968/69, London, H. M. Stationery Office, 1969.

143. "Duncan Report," *Report of the Review Commission on Overseas Representation*, 1968/69, London, H. M. Stationery Office Cmnd. 4107 (July, 1969), p. 106.

144. *Ibid.*, p. 103.

145. Oudes, *op. cit.*, pp. 37–38.

146. *Ibid.*, p. 39.

147. Quoted in Goldman, *op. cit.*, p. 116.

148. Survey by Institute for Social Research, University of Michigan, quoted in Foreign Policy Association, *Foreign Policy Priorities for 1970–71* (New York: Collier, 1970), p. 75.

149. Edward A. O'Neill, "Foreign Aides Still in Surplus," *The Washington Post*, March 29, 1970, p. B-1

150. Thomson, *op. cit.*, p. 53.

151. Quoted in Boorstin, *op. cit.*, p. 19.

152. Report to the President from the Task Force on International Development ["Peterson Report"] *U.S. Foreign Assistance in the 1970s: A New Approach*, March 4, 1970, Washington, GPO, p. 14.

153. *Ibid.*, p. 9.

154. *Ibid.*, pp. 22, 29.

155. *Ibid.*, p. 14.

156. "Need for Pentagon Reform," *The New York Times*, August 16, 1970, editorial.

157. Patrick J. McGarvey, "CIA: Intelligence to Please," *The Washington Monthly*, 2, No. 5 (July, 1970) 69, 75.

158. "Fitzhugh Report," *Report to the President and the Secretary of Defense on the Department of Defense by the Blue Ribbon Defense Panel, 1 July* 1970, Washington, GPO, pp. 45–46.

159. *Ibid.*, pp. 37–38.

160. *Ibid.*, pp. 1, 27.

161. *Ibid.*, pp. 23, 25.

162. E. Raymond Platig, "Research and Analysis," *The Annals of the*

American Academy of Political and Social Science, Vol. 380 (November, 1968): 51–52; Harr, *op. cit.*, p. 105; Cyril E. Black, "Government-Sponsored Research in International Studies," *World Politics,* No. 4 (July, 1970): 582–596; Office of External Research, Bureau of Intelligence and Research, U. S. Department of State, *Foreign Affairs Research: A Directory of Governmental Resources,* Washington, 1967.

163. Schlesinger, *op. cit.*, p. 410.

164. James L. McCamy, *The Administration of American Foreign Affairs,* (New York: Knopf, 1950), p. 120.

165. Ellis Briggs, *Farewell to Foggy Bottom* (New York: McKay, 1964) p. 168.

166. O'Neill, *op. cit.*

167. Briggs, *op. cit.*, p. 163.

168. *Ibid.*, pp. 170–171.

169. Robert E. Elder, *Overseas Representation and Services for Federal Domestic Agencies* (Carnegie Endowment for International Peace, 1965), pp. 14, 18.

170. *Ibid.*, p. 34.

171. McCamy, *Conduct of the New Diplomacy,* p. 82.

172. Harris Wofford, quoted in Marshall Windmiller, *The Peace Corps and Pax Americana* (Washington, D.C.: Public Affairs Press, 1970), p. 1

173. John F. Kennedy, quoted in *ibid.*, pp. 40–41.

174. *Ibid.*, p. 169.

175. The author was present during this "off-the-record" speech, which was sponsored by a nongovernmental institution whose house rules preclude me here from naming the speaker or the institution.

176. William Attwood, "The Labyrinth in Foggy Bottom," *Atlantic* (February, 1967); Nicholas de B. Katzenbach, address to the American Foreign Service Association; November, 1966; John Kenneth Galbraith, *The Triumph* (New York: Signet, 1968), p. 12.

177. Robert A. Lovett, "Perspective on the Policy Process" (testimony delivered to the Subcommittee on National Policy Machinery, February 23, 1960) in *The National Security Council,* ed. Senator Henry M. Jackson (New York: Praeger, 1965), p. 78.

178. Idris Rossell, "Equal Employment Opportunity—Too Much or Not Enough?" *Foreign Service Journal* (January 1969); *Department of State Newsletter,* October 1970, p. 34.

179. "Wriston Report," p. iv.

180. Schlesinger, *op. cit.*, p. 409.

181. Galbraith, "Advice to the Foreign Service," p. 21.

182. *The Foreign Service Act of 1946, As Amended,* Public Law 79–724, Department of State, Washington, 1968.

183. Smith Simpson, *Anatomy of the State Department* (Boston: Houghton Mifflin, 1967), p. 220.

184. "Fitzhugh Report," p. 36.

185. U.S. Senate, 88th Congress, staff reports submitted to the Committee on Government Operations by its Subcommittee on National Security Staffing and Operations, *Administration of National Security*, Washington, GPO, 1965, pp. 183–196; the May, 1969 figure was computed by the author from data published in *The Foreign Service List*, May, 1969.

186. Ellis Briggs, in *Administration of National Security*, p. 158.

187. Henry Serrano Villard, *Affairs at State* (New York: Crowell, 1965), p. 28.

188. Campbell, "An Interview with George F. Kenman," p. 23.

189. This figure, which appears in the current administrative budget of the French Foreign Ministry, was first called to my attention by officials of the ministry during talks with them in Paris in July, 1969.

190. Villard, *op. cit.*, p. 110.

191. "Duncan Report," p. 39.

192. *Ibid.*, Annex H, pp. 178–181.

193. Quoted in Alsop, *op. cit.*, p. 104.

194. Galbraith, "Advice to the Foreign Service," p. 22.

195. *Ibid.*

196. "Analysis and Findings: The National Security Council," a staff report of the Subcommittee on National Policy Machinery, December 12, 1960, in *The National Security Council*, pp. 33, 35.

197. *Ibid.*, p. 41.

198. Richard E. Neustadt, "Staffing the Presidency" (comments by Professor Neustadt during the question period, Subcommittee on National Security Staffing and Operations, March 25, 1963) in *The National Security Council*, p. 282.

199. Henry A. Kissinger, "Domestic Structure and Foreign Policy," *Daedalus* (Spring 1966), reprinted in Kissinger, *American Foreign Policy: Three Essays* (New York: Norton, 1969), pp. 18, 20, 22, 24.

200. Nicolson, *The Evolution of Diplomacy*, p. 124.

INDEX